A GUIDE TO

KENYA
AND NORTHERN
TANZANIA

A GUIDE TO
KENYA AND NORTHERN TANZANIA

DAVID F. HORROBIN

Professor of Medical Physiology
University of Nairobi
Kenya

Photographs by
D. F. and F. W. Horrobin

EAST AFRICAN PUBLISHING HOUSE

Published in East Africa in 1971
by the

EAST AFRICAN PUBLISHING HOUSE
Uniafric House, Koinange Street
P.O. Box 30571, Nairobi

First published by MTP, Aylesbury, England

SBN 852 00030 8

Printed in England by Eyre & Spottiswoode Limited
at Grosvenor Press Portsmouth

Contents

List of Maps and Diagrams

Introduction

East Africa is rapidly becoming one of the most popular areas in the world among the increasing numbers of travellers who are prepared to venture outside their own continent. To those of us fortunate enough to live here, the reasons for this popularity are quite apparent. Much of the region enjoys an equable climate all the year round with no extremes of either heat or cold and with plenty of sunshine. Scenically the area is one of the most beautiful on earth with a marvellous variety of landscape. The beaches are vast and clean and unspoilt. But the outstanding attractions of East Africa, for most people, are its fascinating peoples and the unparalleled abundance of its wild life.

This guide is the first of three planned to cover the whole region of East Africa. It deals with Kenya and Northern Tanzania. The other guides will deal with Uganda and the rest of Tanzania.

Many books have been written about East Africa. They come into four main categories; the magnificent picture books, the geography books, the stories about animals and the detailed technical books on such special aspects as game conservation, bird life, prehistory, or butterflies. None of these is suitable as a practical guide for either the local resident or the average intelligent visitor, who is interested in everything but is not an enthusiastic specialist in any particular subject. This guide attempts to fill that gap. It is full of practical information about climate, health, hotels and travel. It describes briefly the history, geography and peoples of the area. It describes all the places which the local resident or visitor will want to see, some of which are internationally famous and many others of which deserve to be so famed but are at present known only to a few. It describes all the animals which are likely to be seen and gives an introduction to knowledge of other forms of wild-life, such as birds, snakes, insects and flowers. Finally a comprehensive further reading list guides the person with a special interest to those books where he can find the information he requires.

For visitors, the guide is meant to be read before the holiday in anticipation, to be carried around during the holiday as a practical handbook and to be treasured afterwards as a constant reminder of a never-to-be-forgotten experience. For residents of Kenya and Tanzania, the guide is meant to increase their appreciation of their own countries and to act as a constant and well-used companion.

About the book

The guide is in two major sections, the first and larger part being printed on white paper, the second on brown paper. In the first part, the countries, their peoples and their animals are described in full. The second part consists of practical information about travel, about hotels, about books to read and about Swahili phrases. It also contains many useful addresses of people and organisations concerned with tourism, sport, culture, and so on. I believe that all the information in both sections is accurate at the time of going to press but I should be most grateful if those who notice any possible errors could write to me in order that the next edition may be improved.

A word about the photographs may not be out of place. They were all taken by my father or by myself who might accurately be described as keen amateurs: neither of us is in any sense of the word a professional photographer. The equipment which we used was good but not fantastically expensive. Most of the photographs were taken with an Asahi Pentax camera with either a 55mm or a 200mm lens. Almost all were taken on Agfacolour film which was processed locally in Nairobi. In short, the pictures in this book are ones which could have been obtained by any reasonably competent amateur.

❧ 1 ❧

The Land and its Climate

Any landscape as seen by the human eye depends on two main things, the underlying structure of rock and soil and the vegetation which clothes them. In turn the types of vegetation depend mainly on the rainfall and temperature.

THE STRUCTURE OF THE LAND

The fundamental structure of East Africa is extremely complex in detail but relatively simple to understand in broad outline. About 25 million years ago East Africa seems to have been a vast plain, consisting of many different types of old rocks weathered down to give a relatively flat surface with numerous minor depressions filled by shallow lakes. But about that time there began an extraordinary series of earth movements which are responsible for most of the outstanding features of the landscape which can be seen today. The most dramatic of these movements was the upthrusting and splitting of the earth's crust along a length of over 4,000 miles to form the Great Rift Valley. The Rift as it is commonly known begins in the Jordan Valley, comes down through the Red Sea, crosses Ethiopia, Kenya and Tanzania and finally peters out in Southern Africa. The result of this rifting process was the formation of two sets of highland regions ('The rise to the Rift') separated by a valley varying roughly from twenty to sixty miles across and from a few hundred to several thousand feet deep.

Many lesser rift valleys were formed as branches of the Great Rift. In East Africa the most spectacular of these is the Western Rift whose west wall separates East Africa from the Congo. The Western Rift contains a series of the deepest lakes in the world (up to 4,700 feet deep) which are major suppliers of the waters of the Nile. Between the east wall of the Western Rift and the west wall of the Great Rift lies an immense shallow depression largely filled by Lake Victoria. This is relatively shallow (no more than 270 feet deep) and in area is the second largest body of fresh water in the world, only Lake Superior being bigger.

In Kenya, the earth's upward movement was greatest (and the valley is consequently deepest) in the hundred miles or so running north of Nairobi. The floor of most of the Great Rift has no outlet to the sea. The lakes in it tend to be shallow and to have a very high mineral content resulting from the evaporation of water leaving the solid salts behind. Lake Magadi, for example, is little more than a mass of solid soda. Lakes Nakuru, Elmentaita, Natron and Manyara are not quite so uniformly solid but they do have large soda flats and the water has an extremely high salt content. Lakes Rudolf and Baringo are fresh enough to enable a rich fish life to exist and Lake Naivasha, supplied by fresh springs welling up from deep in the earth supports fish, plants and birds in almost incredible super-abundance.

The formation of the Rift Valley has not yet been completed. The most recent studies suggest that it is still slowly widening and that perhaps ultimately, in many millions of years, the whole of Africa east of the Rift may split off to form a new sub-continent. As a result of this massive insult, the earth's crust in the area has, of course, been considerably weakened. Several million years ago this weakening was made apparent by the development, in the floor of the Rift itself and along the cracks of weakness radiating from the main valley, of the vast numbers of volcanic formations on which much of the beauty of the region now depends. The most spectacular of these volcanoes are of course the giants of Mount Kenya, Mount Elgon, Mount Meru and Kilimanjaro (Kilima is Swahili for mountain and Mount Kilimanjaro is therefore a misnomer), but the Aberdares, the Chyulu and Taita Hills near Tsavo Park, the Ngongs near Nairobi and Longonot and Suswa in the floor of the valley are all beautiful and readily approached by the traveller. The oral traditions of the local people confirm that many of these volcanoes were active within the past few hundred years and most of them now contain hot springs and steam jets. One mountain, Ol Doinyo Lengai (The Mountain of God) in Northern Tanzania has been frequently active within living memory and last erupted violently in 1966.

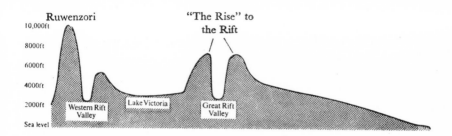

Cross section of East Africa showing the Rift Valleys (not to scale).

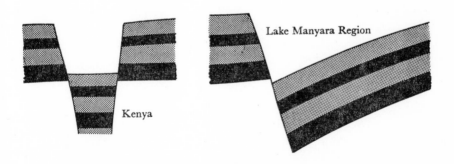

The structures of the Rift Valley in Kenya and in the Lake Manyara region.

Outstanding among the volcanic features of this part of the world are the structures known as calderas most typically seen in the vast craters of Ngorongoro near the Serengeti and at Menengai near Nakuru. A caldera is not a volcanic crater in the usual sense. It results from the inward collapse of whole mountains following the erosion of the interior of the cone by volcanic action.

In summary, therefore, East Africa consists of a narrow coastal strip formed from old coral and the silt carried down by rivers (of which in Kenya there are only two major systems, the Galana and the Tana). From this narrow strip, the land rises steadily towards the heart of central Africa. The evenness of the rise is dramatically interrupted by the much sharper rise and the precipitous fall of the Rift Valley and by the very numerous volcanoes. This is the structural basis of one of the most magnificent landscapes on earth.

THE CLIMATE

The pleasantness of a climate, the vegetation which covers the land and the wild life which lives there depend on three major factors; the temperature, the rainfall and the humidity. Over the greater part of East Africa all three factors are governed by the altitude. In general, the low areas are very hot and the temperature very obviously falls as one climbs higher. The low areas also tend to have a scanty rainfall and a dry atmosphere with very low humidity. The main exceptions to these rules in the region covered by this guide are the coastal strip and the area along the shore of Lake Victoria. Both are hot with a high rainfall and a high humidity. The main varieties of climate are described in more detail in the rest of this section.

1. Hot and wet. This describes the coast and the region around Lake Victoria. The term wet simply means that there is a high annual rainfall. It does not mean that it rains all day, every day, and on most days there are prolonged periods of bright sunshine. In the few places where there is little cultivation, this type of climate produces a very dense, tropical forest type of vegetation. But in these areas population density is usually high and cultivation is intense, the dominant features being coconut and banana trees and maize.

2. Very hot and very dry. In this type of area, the average annual rainfall is very low. Not only that but it is very irregular, not falling consistently

at any one time of the year and varying enormously from year to year
in amount. Storms are violent and the whole of the rain for one year
may come within a few minutes and flow quickly away without doing
any benefit. There are no trees and very few plants can survive. Most
of the ground for most of the year is not covered by any form of vegetation.
An astounding transformation may however take place after rain, when
myriads of flowers can spring up, produce drought-resistant seeds and
wither within a matter of days. This country supports only a very
sparse population of tough pastoral people with their camels and goats
and cattle. It covers large areas of northern and eastern Kenya and can
be seen at its most typical by those who visit the fishing resorts at Lake
Rudolf or who make the arduous journey to Marsabit. The Samburu-
Isiolo reserve is on the edge of this country and some fine stretches of it
can be seen near there. Game is on the whole very sparse but the few
oases and water holes attract animals and birds from vast distances.

3. Hot and dry. Rain falls fairly regularly every year but is very small
in quantity. The vegetation consists primarily of small bushes with
vicious thorns and occasional huge baobab trees with their grotesque

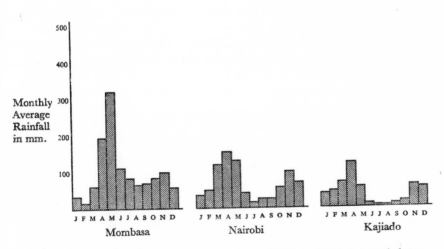

*The average monthly rainfalls in Nairobi, Mombasa and Kajiado. Kajiado has a typical open
plains climate.*

trunks and stubby branches. Except during the rainy season the trees and bushes are often leafless and appear dead. There is very little grass on the ground and again the population density is very low. Tsetse flies, rather like European or American horse flies, are often common and can carry sleeping sickness. The most typical animals are those which browse on trees, such as elephant, rhino and giraffe. Grazing animals and predators occur but they are not prolific. The smaller animals are often difficult to see because of the thick bush. The visitor may most easily see this type of country in Tsavo and Meru Parks, in parts of Amboseli and on the road from Nairobi to Magadi.

4. Hot, dry for much of the year, but with a reliable and fairly abundant seasonal rainfall. This climate typically produces the open type of country known as savannah with Acacia trees or small evergreen bushes interspersed with wide areas of grass. In some places the trees do not grow, possibly because of the frequent deliberate burning of the countryside by the cattle-owning pastoralists such as the Masai. The burning produces the vast wide open spaces of the Mara, the Serengeti and the Ngorongoro regions. The long coarse grass is burnt because the cattle will not eat the tough stems and leaves but they thrive on the new green shoots which spring up after the fire. Because of the grass this type of country supports vast herds of what are usually called 'plains game', gazelles, wildebeest, zebra, topi and the like. And of course these are followed by the predators. Because of the open nature of the country the animals can easily be seen and the savannah and grassland areas are perhaps the favourite areas with tourists. These areas are of course also excellent for cattle ranching and the potential conflict between cattle and game is an important one which has yet to be resolved completely satisfactorily.

5. Warm with moderate and reliable rainfall. This type of climate is found over much of the higher areas of Kenya including the region formerly known as the White Highlands whose climate and scenery reminded settlers from Britain of summer at home. When not subject to cultivation, this climate typically produces open woodland but there are now very few unfarmed areas. Most of the land is intensively culti-vated with maize, wheat, tea, coffee, pyrethrum and dairy cattle the most important lines. Tea grows particularly well in the wet areas around Kericho which receive rain virtually every day all the year round. Pyrethrum is the low greyish-green plant which when not flowering looks from a distance rather like a carnation plant. The small white flowers are the source of a powerful insecticide and they can be gathered profitably even from a tiny plot. A relatively new and very rapidly growing industry in the Highlands is horticulture and market gardening. Especially during the European winter fresh flowers, strawberries and vegetables flown to Europe by the new, fast and relatively cheap air freight services can command high prices.

6. *Cool and wet.* This describes the upper slopes of the Aberdares, Mount Kenya, Mount Meru, Mount Elgon and Kilimanjaro. There is dense forest with bamboo the dominant plant in many regions. The dominant animals are elephant, rhino, buffalo and monkeys. The famous Treetops Hotel is in this zone.

7. *Cold and wet.* This type of climate is found high above the forest zone on all the main mountain massifs. It is characterised by beautiful moorland with crystal clear streams, often stocked with trout. A Scot might have to look closely at the landscape to make sure that he was not in his native land. The main difference is that the plants, heathers, groundsel and lobelias, grow to vast proportions, often higher than a man.

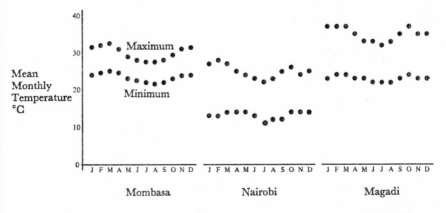

The average monthly minimum and maximum temperatures in Mombasa, Nairobi and Magadi. Magadi is on the floor of the Rift Valley.

They give the impression of species which should have become extinct millions of years ago.

SEASONS AND THE VISITOR

Because Kenya is right on the Equator, changes in temperature around the year are small compared with those in non-tropical countries. There is no real summer or winter and there is no season when it can be said that visitors should definitely not come. However some times of the year are undoubtedly better than others for particular activities and this section is meant to give a rough guide to these variations.

1. Game viewing. This is the main reason why most tourists come to East Africa. In most of the game areas the animals are undoubtedly easier to see in large numbers in the months which are almost always dry, from July to early October and from December to early March. This is because during the wet seasons both water and grazing may be found in many parts of the country and the animals are widely dispersed. In the dry season they are concentrated near water holes and rivers and are much more easy to locate. The main exception to this rule is the south-east corner of the Serengeti where the sweet short grass which springs up in May attracts plains game and predators in phenomenal numbers. Another reason for normally preferring the dry season for game watching is that travel on the dirt roads in the parks and reserves is much more reliable at this time and you are much less likely to be bogged down.

2. Scenery viewing. Many local residents feel that the country is at its most beautiful during and after the rainy periods from late March to early June and in October and November. At these periods the grass is green instead of brown, the flowers come out in large numbers and many of the birds are in their striking breeding plumage. The main drawback is undoubtedly the difficulty of travel but those with enough money to fly from place to place may decide that the rainy season is the best time to visit East Africa, for even during these months there is often sunshine for long periods every day. It is certainly the quietest period in the hotels and the time when you will most easily get individual attention.

3. Sunshine. Especially in the hotter, drier areas there is sunshine most of the time on most of the days all the year round. In the Highland areas the months when sunshine can be most certainly expected are September and early October and December to early March. July and August although usually very dry are also often cool and cloudy and at the coast a number of the hotels are closed during this period.

4. Climbing. Mount Kenya and Kilimanjaro can be climbed at any time but again good views are most likely in September and from December to mid-March.

5. Fishing. In Kenya there are four main types of sport fishing which may interest the visitor, black bass in Lake Naivasha, tiger fish and Nile perch in Lake Rudolf, trout in the mountain streams and big game fish in the Indian Ocean. Only trout fishing and big game fishing are markedly seasonal, the former being best during the dry seasons when the rivers are relatively clear and the latter best from October to March when the big fish come in towards the coast.

CLOTHES AND THE CLIMATE

If one had to summarise in a phrase clothing fashions in Kenya one would say that they were smart but informal. In the cities and big hotels the clothes are similar to those in any European city in summer. Whilst travelling around the country the most important thing is to be comfortable and anything that is comfortable and in which the wearer feels happy is right. The commonest error is a failure to bring one or two warm cardigans and sweaters. At any place, but especially in the Highlands, and at any time but especially in July and August, the evenings can be definitely chilly.

If you wish to buy clothes locally, perhaps the best things are the following:

1. Safari boots. These are soft suede shoes which fit snugly around the ankles. They are very comfortable, ideal for safari travel and surprisingly cheap (about 40 shillings or 5–6 dollars).

2. Safari shirts and slacks. Neutral in colour, loose fitting, comfortable and with large pockets, these too are ideal for travelling in the game areas.

3. Colourful printed shirts and dresses. These are worn by many local residents, both African and European, and can be had in a wide variety of styles and designs.

4. Headscarves. High quality silk scarves decorated with pictures of African birds or animals are favourites with lady visitors.

The Development of Man

In 1911, Professor Kattwinkel, an entomologist from Berlin, was chasing an unusual butterfly across the wide open grassland of the south-east Serengeti Plain. More intent on capturing the butterfly than on looking where he was going, he failed to notice an immense gorge suddenly opening up in front of him. He lost his butterfly and almost fell to his death on the rocks of Olduvai three hundred feet below. After recovering from the shock he decided to clamber down to explore his new discovery. Almost immediately he noticed an abundance of fossils in the exposed rock face. These fossils of Olduvai Gorge, amply supported by finds made in other parts of Africa, have radically changed our ideas about the early dawn of man's history. It used to be thought that man evolved from sub-human ancestors somewhere in the Middle East or in Asia. It is now clearly apparent that in fact Africa was the cradle of mankind and that the human race spread across the world from small beginnings in the part of the earth which we now call Kenya and Tanzania.

THE EARLY ANCESTORS

About twenty to twenty five million years ago there lived here a type of creature known as Proconsul with a relatively small skull which nevertheless has features in common with our own. Moreover Proconsul walked upright. No animals of the Proconsul type are alive today but it is probably from them or their relatives that both we and the modern apes come. Man has not descended from the apes. Both we and the apes are twigs on the vast family tree of mammalian life. We both spring from Proconsul or one of his relatives who was one of the main branches.

Proconsul would not be recognised by us as human and if we could see him alive today we should have no hesitation in saying that he was an animal. But gradually over the succeeding millenia he probably became transformed into the group known as the Australopithecines whose skulls were bigger and who walked even more uprightly. If we could meet an Australopithecine today we would probably be uncertain as to whether we should classify him as human or not. He would certainly appear to us much more human than any ape and we would have the uncomfortable feeling of gazing upon the face of our own past.

THE TOOL MAKER

Man used to be called the tool-user but this definition has now been abandoned. There is increasing evidence that apes, birds and perhaps even other animals can take natural articles such as stones and sticks and use them as tools. The definition of a human being has therefore been changed from one who uses tools to one who takes natural articles and then shapes them to make tools out of them before employing them. There can be little doubt that anyone who takes a rock and shapes it into a cutting tool has a mind which is very similar to that of modern man.

Until 1959 it was assumed that only individuals whose skulls were unmistakably similar to those of modern man were capable of making tools. It was also assumed that such tool makers had been on the earth for no more than about half a million years. But in that year, working in Olduvai Gorge, Dr and Mrs L. S. B. Leakey discovered the skull of an Australopithecine relative known as Zinjanthropus. Zinjanthropus had enormous back teeth and because of them he has since been nick-named Nutcracker Man. But perhaps the most important thing about him was that his bones were found lying in a stratum which contained numerous pebbles chipped on two sides to make a cutting edge. Lying with these were many fragments of bones of small animals and birds. It seems highly probable that it was Zinjanthropus himself who made these pebble cutters.

In 1961, the age of Zinjanthropus and the stratum in which he lay was determined by the very reliable potassium-argon method of dating. To the astonishment of the worlds of palaeontology, archaeology and anthropology, it was discovered that Zinjanthropus lived no less than one and three quarter million years ago. It is therefore likely that it was about two million years ago in the plains of Eastern Africa that the ancestors of man took the step which for ever separated them from the rest of the living world. They took pebbles and they chipped them on two sides to make cutting tools for their own use. Thus began the Stone Age, the period of pre-history when man's weapons and tools were primarily made from rock. For perhaps one and a half million years skill advanced little and the simple pebbles, sometimes accompanied by other tools made from bone, are the only ones known.

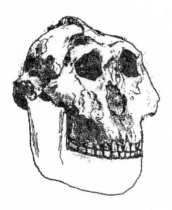 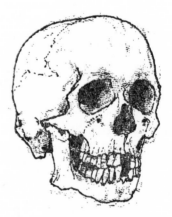

The skulls of Zinjanthropus and modern man compared. The skull of Zinjanthropus has been reconstructed from remains found in Olduvai Gorge.

HAND AXES

But about 400,000 years ago another major advance was made. The hand axes came into existence. These are large, pointed pieces of rock, obviously suitable for heavy work. They could be used as a heavy weapon to club to death animals, and perhaps even other members of

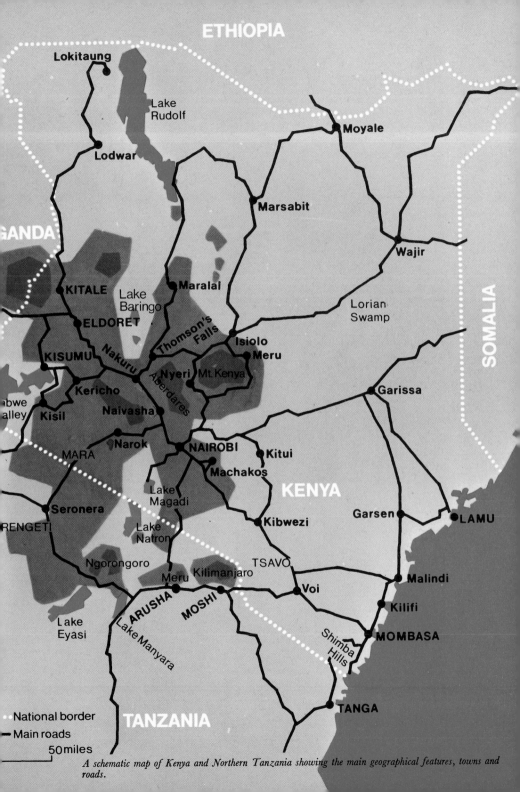

A schematic map of Kenya and Northern Tanzania showing the main geographical features, towns and roads.

The incomparable wild life of East Africa is famous throughout the world. Here zebras drink at a water hole in the Ngorongoro crater. Wildebeest graze in the background.

The coast of Africa is perhaps less famous than the game reserves but it is equally spectacular and offers some of the finest beaches in the world. Shown here are fishermen at Malindi. In the background is the famous Vasco da Gama pillar. The cross on the top of the pillar was left behind by da Gama in 1498.

East Africa is the home of the largest living land animal – the African elephant, seen here crossing the Uaso Nyiro River from the Samburu to the Isiolo Game Reserve.

TOP *Nowhere are there greater contrasts than in East Africa. These glaciers are near the summit of Kilimanjaro – 6010 metres high (19,340 feet) – the highest mountain in Africa.*

BOTTOM *At sea level the unspoiled beaches run along the coral coast. This is Silversands Beach, Malindi, on a typical crowded afternoon.*

man's own species. At this time the animals which were living were often similar to modern species in shape but several times larger in size. Sheep-like creatures, for example, were as big as modern buffaloes while pigs could be as big as modern cows. Good examples of the bones of these creatures can be seen at Olduvai, Olorgesaillie and in the National Museum in Nairobi. It seems probable that one method of killing these giants was to drive them into swampy areas where they became bogged down and could be clubbed to death. Another method may have been to hurl at them groups of three stone balls wrapped together by leather thongs. These would become wrapped around the animal's legs and bring it to the ground much in the style of the South America bolas. This idea has been suggested by the fact that frequently three smooth round stone balls have been found grouped together. Again good examples may be seen at Olorgesaillie.

Hand axes of a remarkably uniform type are found widely over Asia and Europe and Africa. Once the methods of making them were discovered the knowledge must have spread rapidly over the earth. Of course we can never know precisely where the original discovery took place but again it seems probable that East Africa was the scene. It is the approximate centre of the vast area over which hand axes are found and hand axes are more abundant here than anywhere else in the world. A superb and easily visited example of a hand axe site is at Olorgesaillie where they can still be seen literally in their thousands. The site is just over forty miles from Nairobi along the Magadi Road.

FURTHER DEVELOPMENTS

Marked regional variations among the races of mankind first became apparent about 50,000 years ago when the world-wide hand axe type of culture began to give rise to civilisations with marked local characteristics. These variations probably arose because of the interaction between man's rapidly developing ingenuity with the supplies of food, stone and other materials available in each local region. In East Africa by this time the grotesquely huge animals had largely become extinct and had been replaced by the species which for the most part we know today. Implements tended to become much smaller and were of a much greater variety. Scrapers, small axes which were probably hafted on to wood, and heads for spear-like weapons are found in abundance. Bone implements are also common and some of these appear to have been worn smooth by working with leather, suggesting that skins and other perishable materials were coming into extensive use. People who were responsible for this type of culture probably lived in East Africa until five or six thousand years ago or even later.

THE LATER STONE AGE

About ten thousand years ago there appeared here a type of culture which is still in existence in some areas. It is characterised by an immense variety of tiny tools, sometimes known as microliths. These are often made from obsidian, the jet black smooth volcanic glass which can be chipped to give a very fine cutting edge. There are vast numbers of scrapers, of tiny sharp arrow heads and of fine knives which were probably embedded in wood to make primitive types of scythe and sickle. Many of these implements have been found over a hundred miles from the nearest known source of obsidian suggesting that a primitive system of trackways for trading may have come into existence.

But the tools are not the only things which characterise the Later Stone Age culture. Pottery makes an appearance as do fine, large stone bowls with pestles which were clearly used for grinding things. The people were clearly interested in decorating themselves for ostrich egg beads, shell pendants and red ochre for rubbing on the hair and skin have been found in many places. Like the obsidian the ochre must often have come from many miles away, again suggesting trade. Finally these people were distinguished by the possession of complex burial customs and by having skulls virtually identical with those of currently existing races of men. Further south in Africa they developed brilliantly the art of rock painting but there are very few examples of this in Kenya and Northern Tanzania. It seems very probable that these Later Stone Age people lived in villages, kept domestic animals, gathered wild grain and perhaps even began to cultivate crops.

In this period of pre-history, change was obviously rapid and local variations in culture were marked. For example the interested visitor may find four very different varieties in the vicinities of Lakes Nakuru and Elmentaita in the Rift Valley less than a hundred miles from Nairobi. The best known sites are at Gamble's Cave and at Hyrax Hill just outside Nakuru. One burial at Nakuru seems to indicate a ritual in which slaves or wives were slaughtered when an important man died. At the bottom of a cliff eight skeletons were found lying at random as though they had simply been thrown there. Beneath these eight was a very carefully laid out skeleton covered in red ochre. Another form of burial was practised by the Njoro River Cave people not far away. The bodies, again smeared with ochre, were tied in a hunched up position. They were buried in a very shallow grave with a stone bowl, beads and ornaments. A large fire was then lit on top of the grave, converting the bodies to a form of charcoal.

Some East African tribes, like the Hadzapi and the Sandawe of the region south of Lake Eyasi in Northern Tanzania, appear to be still in the Later Stone Age. But most of the modern people of East Africa were transformed by the coming of iron, perhaps about two thousand years ago. The people who now live here and their histories will be described in chapters four and five.

❧ 3 ❧

Men and Migrations

For anyone interested in the development of mankind, in the growth of races, in past mixing and contact of peoples and in possible future changes, East Africa is one of the most fascinating areas in the whole world. Unfortunately as far as early history is concerned we have as yet appallingly little hard information on which to base our judgments. There are very few real experts in this field and of those few no two can certainly agree. The story told in the first part of this chapter is therefore very much a view through a mist. But the few certain glimpses we have are so fascinating that they are well worth describing.

THE CLASSIFICATION OF PEOPLES

In their studies of the origins and relationships of races, scholars place emphasis on a number of different criteria. In Africa five of these are particularly important and will be described in this section.

Physical Features

Early physical anthropologists spent much time measuring the shapes of heads and noses and faces. These characters are still held to be of considerable importance in tracing the ancestry of modern peoples. The head shape is characterised by the cephalic index, the ratio of the greatest breadth of the skull to its greatest length. Long skulls are much longer than they are broad, short skulls are almost round, while as might be expected, medium skulls are intermediate. The nasal shape is defined as the ratio of the breadth of the nose to its height and ranges from long and thin to short and wide. In studying the face, the degree of eversion of the lips and whether or not the jaw projects beyond the forehead are also important characters.

In recent years two other physical characters have been found to be highly significant and their importance is certain to increase as knowledge improves. The first is the blood group pattern. Everyone is now familiar with the concept of blood groups and has heard of ABO and Rh factors. There are however many other factors and a man's complete blood grouping pattern is almost as characteristic of him as an individual as is his fingerprint. Equally the pattern of blood groups found within a particular race is also highly characteristic. Closely related races have similar patterns while those which are distantly related usually have very different patterns. Thus by studying blood groups it is likely that in the future that the inter-relationships of modern races will be much more closely defined. The second character is the type of haemoglobin, the pigment in the blood which makes it red. Most human beings have one type but in a significant proportion of black people there is another type known as sickle cell haemoglobin. This can be of value to the person who possesses it as it seems to offer some protection against malaria.

Language

This is not quite so useful or so certain as a clear physical character since languages can be and are interchanged between peoples who have no physical relationship. But provided this limitation is borne in mind, language can be a very helpful guide. The main indigenous African languages fall into one of the following groups:

1. Sudanic. These languages are characteristic of the peoples of West Africa and of the upper Nile valley. Very many of the words are monosyllables and as in Chinese, a word which appears to be spelt in one way may have many different meanings according to the tone of the voice. Objects which are not biologically male or female are not given a sex gender. There is no attempt to make words (e.g. adjectives and nouns) 'agree' with one another by the use of prefixes and suffixes. The Nilotic languages of the Nile Valley probably have a distant common ancestor with the Sudanic.

2. Bantu. These languages are very roughly speaking spoken by Africans who live south of the Bantu line which runs approximately along the Equator. As in the Sudanic languages, nouns are not given a gender but in contrast they are divided into classes each characterised by a particular prefix. This prefix appears in every word in a sentence which agrees with the noun, giving a marked alliterative effect e.g. mtoto mdogo mzuri, a good little child in Swahili.

3. Hamitic. In these languages the nouns have both number and case which are expressed by suffixes. Verbs are conjugated by both prefixes and suffixes.

4. Semitic. These are closely related to the Hamitic and probably have an unknown common ancestor. They are distinguished by having 'triliteral verb roots' i.e. the root of the verb found in the third person singular almost always has three syllables.

5. Bushman. These languages have not yet been very well studied. They tend to be monosyllabic and make extensive use of suffixes. Their outstanding feature is the employment of many 'click' sounds.

Culture and Way of Life

Many different ways of life clearly went into the development of modern African cultures. However perhaps five forms are basic.

1. Hunters living in open country, moving from place to place and obtaining food by killing wild animals and gathering wild plants.

2. Hunters similar to the first group but living in thick forest.

3. Lakeside dwellers. These are basically fisherman and hunters but the relative stability of a lake tends to lead to permanent village settlement with much pottery and other not easily portable articles.

4. Forest agriculturalists who move into an area of virgin forest, fell and burn the trees, grow crops until the soil is exhausted and then move on. They possess no animals with the possible exception of dogs.

5. Pastoralists who live in open country, keeping animals such as sheep, goats and camels, but above all, cattle.

Remnants of all these primitive ways of living can be clearly seen in some modern African tribes.

Social Organisation

The type of social organisation of a people can fall into one of three basic categories.

1. Based virtually entirely on the 'extended family' i.e. including aunts, uncles and cousins, but with relatively little organisation outside

this extended family. This is a very early form of social structure and today exists only in a few remnant Bushman groups.

2. A society with an extensive super-familial organisation but with no central power basis and no autocracy. In this type of society many elaborate forms of democracy developed. This form of social structure was probably the most common in Kenya and Northern Tanzania before the coming of the Europeans.

3. A society with extensive super-familial organisation but also with strong central power vested in kings or chiefs. The old Kingdoms of what is now Uganda were of this type.

Most African peoples fall into the second or third groups and it is among them that the word 'tribe' has a real and definite meaning. A tribe may be defined as 'a group taking with a common name in which the members take pride, with a common language, with a common territory and with a feeling that all who do not share this name are outsiders' (Huntingford).

It is important to recognise that in Africa in all three types of society the so-called extended family is extremely important. To modern Europeans and North Americans who have come to regard the family as meaning parents and children, the concept can be quite a surprise although no doubt our nineteenth-century ancestors would take to the idea much more easily. Very roughly the principle means that brothers, sisters, uncles, aunts and cousins are all virtually on a par with parents and children. Each individual has extensive obligations to all the other members of his family. This can create very real problems when a European type of society interacts with the traditional African one. The modern African businessman or civil servant who does well may often find that much of his new prosperity disappears as all the members of his family make their legitimate demands upon the member who has done particularly well.

Oral Traditions

It used to be fashionable to dismiss oral traditions as useless in the study of history because of the obviously far-fetched nature of many of the stories. However it is now increasingly recognised that almost all myths have a real basis in actual events: the main problem is that the timing of these events is almost invariably distorted so that something which happened a mere two hundred years ago may be described as having occurred in the very dim and distant past. Many African historians are now seriously engaged in collecting these traditional tales before the old people who know them die and they disappear for ever.

THE FOUNDATION GROUPS

As described in chapter three it is now generally believed that man's Garden of Eden was in East Central Africa and that from this area he migrated outwards to colonise the rest of the earth. Some people, of course, stayed in East Africa: they became ever more closely adapted to their environment but were limited in their development by lack of exposure to new places and new materials for building and making tools. Others, in other parts of the world, were changed by their interaction with their new climates and surroundings to form Negroes, Semites, Hamites, Europeans, Indians, Chinese, Japanese, Indonesians and so on. In time, many of these peoples who had left East Africa tens of thousands of years earlier, and who had been changed almost out of all recognition began to move back into their original cradle area and to make their impact on those who had stayed behind. Much of the story which follows is speculation as yet again there are very few hard facts on which to base it but even if only half true it forms the basis of a remarkable saga.

It seems possible that about ten thousand years ago there were living here at least four different types of people who had evolved in East Africa itself. Perhaps the best known of these people were the hunters and food gatherers of open country whom we know today as Bushmen. At present there are moderate numbers of Bushmen in the Kalahari Desert area of Botswana and in the neighbouring countries and there is a very small group, the Hadzapi, living near Lake Eyasi in Northern Tanzania. Less well known are the forest dwellers although it is possible that the pygmies of the Congo forest may be their descendants. Other types of people who lived here at that time have disappeared completely and are known only from the remains they have left.

Then, over the next thousands of years, the East African scene was radically altered by the immigration of peoples from other places. By far the most important of these immigrants are the Hamites and the true Negroes. The Hamites are characterised by long heads, long thin noses, relatively light coloured skins, a pastoral way of life with a strong social organisation but no dominant central power and a characteristic group of Hamitic languages. Their place of origin is uncertain but they probably came from the Southern Arabian Peninsula or even further east and entered East Africa via the Horn of Africa in a series of waves.

The true Negroes probably originated somewhere in the Western half of Africa. They are characterised by round heads, broad noses, everted lips, dark skin and spiralled hair. They probably originally lived by forest agriculture but this gradually developed to give more advanced agricultural societies again with a strong social organisation but this time often with a strong central chief or king. Their original languages may have been of the Sudanic group.

The Invasions

The first waves of Hamites probably entered East Africa as early as six or seven thousand years B.C. They brought with them their physical features, their pastoral life, and their languages. They probably also brought weapons and a military organisation superior to that of the indigenous peoples whom they killed, drove out or interbred with. None of these early Hamites exist today in pure form but possibly as little as one thousand years ago or less, most of the people living in East Africa were hybrids resulting from interbreeding between these first Hamites and the ancient peoples of the area. Some of these hybrids retained a primarily Bushman way of life and are probably now represented by the Hottentots of Southern Africa and the Sandawe, south of Lake Eyasi in Tanzania. Others remained primarily forest hunters and may be represented today by the Dorobo groups, primarily found in forests in and around the Rift Valley. Others became lakeside dwellers and the El Molo who live life by Lake Rudolf may represent a remnant of them. Still others probably took to agriculture and lived in peculiar houses known as tembes, partially excavated below ground level. Remains of these houses are found over large areas of the Kenya Highlands and many of the modern tribes who live there have myths about the people who lived in these houses and whom the modern people displaced. Some of these hybrids may still exist in the form of the Iraqw or Mbulu people of the area between Ngorongoro and Lake Manyara who may still live in tembes and have a language with Hamitic features.

C

The early Hamitic invasions certainly did not stop in East Africa but went far westwards. In interaction with the true Negroes, the early Hamites produced three other types of people, the Bantu, the Nilotes and the Nilo-Hamites. It was in the forms of these peoples that the Negroes, already partially hamiticised, penetrated into East Africa.

1. The Bantu. These are peoples obviously related to true Negroes but who show varying amounts of Hamitic influence as indicated by facial features, language and culture. They are a very mixed group and are not at all racially pure but they are unified by their adoption of the Bantu languages, which may have originated somewhere in the Congo Basin. Most Bantu are predominantly agricultural but most also keep some form of animals as well, though not necessarily cattle.

2. The Nilotes. With respect to physical features, blood grouping and the presence of sickle cell haemoglobin, these people are much closer to true Negroes than are the Bantu. They probably originated in the Nile Valley. The remarkable thing about their culture is the extent to which they have adopted and developed the cattle cult. Cattle are very important in every aspect of life and in some of the tribes assume a semi-religious position. The Nilotes all speak languages distantly related to the Sudanic group.

3. The Nilo-Hamites. These are clearly related to the Hamites in every way, having long heads, long thin noses and relatively light skins and being almost exclusively cattle keeping. They all speak Hamitic languages and probably originated in Southern Ethiopia.

For the past ten thousand years the history of East Africa has been the story of successive invasions of Hamites, Bantu, Nilotes and Nilo-Hamites and of their impact on one another and on the indigenous populations whom they found living in the region. The original inhabitants are now found only as decimated remnants but in modern East Africa there are thriving groups of Bantu, Nilotes, Hamites and Nilo-Hamites, all of whom can be seen easily by the interested visitor.

Other Invaders

Finally in this section there must be mentioned other less widespread but nevertheless not unimportant groups which have entered East Africa and left something of their way of life behind. These other invaders are significant not so much because of any physical descendants

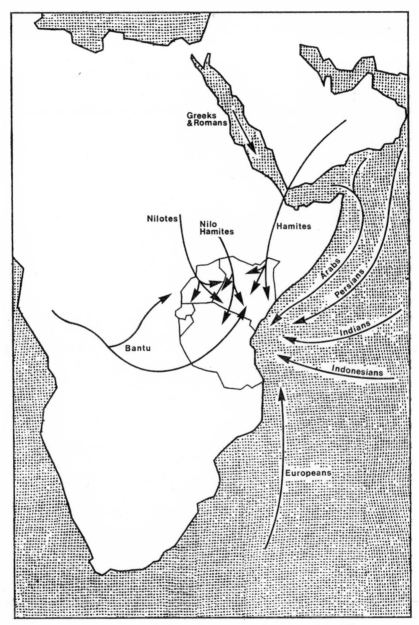

Map showing the various racial influences which impinged upon East Africa.

they have left behind but because of their effects on the culture and way
of life of modern East Africa.

1. Indonesian. Two or three thousand years ago, the great outrigger
Indonesian canoes ranged far and wide across the Indian Ocean. In
Africa their most important landfall was on the island of Madagascar
where they left many people, much of their language and much of their
culture. Only a few came to East Africa but they had an importance out
of all proportion to their numbers. They left here the coconut, the
banana, the design of their outrigger canoes, some words and possibly
some music. The extent of Indonesian influence in modern East Africa
is a fascinating topic which has yet to be fully explored.

2. Semitic. The Semites, like the Hamites, originated in the Middle
East and their can be little doubt that the two groups had a common
ancestor. The Semitic influence is however less important than the
Hamitic mainly because it is more recent and because it has not penetrated much beyond the coastal strip. However, the coast as seen today
is largely the result of the combined influence on Bantu peoples of
Indonesians and Semites. The Semites, predominantly Arabs, have
probably been on the coast for 1,500 years or more (see chapter 5).
There are perhaps 30–40,000 relatively pure Arabs on the East African
coast today, together with much larger numbers of Swahili, people who
are a relatively direct cross between Arabs and Bantu. The main significance of the Swahili is that their language looks like becoming the
first lingua franca of Africa which is of truly African origin. It is basically
a Bantu language although many of its words are derived from Arabic.
It is therefore readily learned by most Bantu although Hamites, Nilo-
Hamites and Nilotes have more difficulty. In Tanzania it is already a
true lingua franca. In Kenya and Uganda it is spreading rapidly and
many books, magazines and newspapers are written in it.

3. Persian, Chinese and Malaysian. All three groups have had some impact on the East Africa coast via the great trade routes of the Indian
Ocean. There is a good collection of Chinese pottery in the museum at
Fort Jesus in Mombasa and eight hundred years ago most of the families
in Canton had black slaves. Again the interaction between these
peoples and East Africa is largely an unexplored subject.

4. Indian. For two thousand years or more there may well have been
small groups of Indian traders living on the coast but most of the
obviously Indian people in modern East Africa have descended from

labourers brought in by the British at the end of the last century and the beginning of this to work on the railways, farms and in other industries. Almost every group found on the Indian sub-continent is also represented in East Africa but perhaps the most dominant groups are the Hindus, Sikhs, Goans and Muslims (especially the Ismailis who recognise the Aga Khan as the head of their community).

5. *Europeans.* Many visitors to East Africa fail to recognise how very ancient are the connections between this part of the world and Europe. Vasco da Gama was here soon after Columbus discovered America and the great Fort Jesus in Mombasa was established in the sixteenth century. Even older are the trade routes which linked through many intermediaries, the gold fields of Central Africa with the capitals of Northern Europe. Chemical assay has now shown, for example, that the first gold coins produced in the London Mint in the twelfth century were made from African gold. Having said this it is obvious that there was an explosion of European interest and involvement in the second half of the nineteenth century and even today in Kenya there are about 40,000 Europeans.

TABLE 1.   Peoples of Kenya and Northern Tanzania

Possible Foundation Groups
    Hadzapi
    Sandawe
    Dorobo
    El Molo
    Iraqw
    Coastal Forest Hunters (Boni, Sanye)
Hamites (Cushites)
    Somali
    Galla
    Boran
    Rendille
Nilo-Hamites (Eastern Nilotes)
    Turkana
    Kalenjin Group (Suk, Elgeyo, Marakwet, Kipsigis, Nandi, Tugen)
    Masai Group (Masai, Samburu, Arusha)

Nilotes
> Luo

Bantu
> Western Group (Luhya, Kisii)
> Central Group (Embu, Meru, Kikuyu, Kamba, Chagga)
> Coastal Group 1. Pokomo
>   2. Nyika (Giriama, Digo, Duruma, Segeju)

For reasons of clarity this simplified table omits many of the smaller tribes, particularly in the Bantu Group.

Note. *The account given in this chapter uses a traditional and familiar terminology. In recent years, however, partly because the term 'Hamites' has been used in the past in an unpleasant and racialist manner, it has been replaced by the term 'Cushites'. It has also been recognised that the so-called 'Nilo-Hamites' are probably a division of the Nilotic Peoples and so in the new terminology they are known as 'Eastern Nilotes'.*

4

The Modern Peoples

This section describes something of the life of the modern peoples of Kenya and Northern Tanzania. Even today we are painfully ignorant of most of the old customs and particularly among the Bantu and the Nilotes, the societies are changing so rapidly that much of what was written only a few years ago is now hopelessly out of date. A vast effort is required to record and work out the customs and inter-relationships of all these peoples but the number of research workers currently involved in this task is painfully small. Fortunately the Hamites and Nilo-Hamites are changing relatively slowly but for many of the Bantu and Nilotes it may already be too late. Table 1 shows the main African groups living in the region today. There are many other small tribes, particularly among the coastal Bantu, which have been omitted for reasons of simplicity.

THE POSSIBLE FOUNDATION GROUPS

These may be remnants of the peoples who lived in East Africa two to ten thousand years ago. They are few in number but because of their antiquity they are in some ways the most interesting groups of all.

1. Hadzapi. There are now only a few hundred of these people living near Lake Eyasi in Northern Tanzania. They are probably related to the Bushmen now living in Southern Africa and they have a clicking language. They grow nothing, keep no animals but dogs and live entirely by hunting and collecting. They have remained totally unchanged by contact with modern society and have vigorously resisted all efforts at development.

2. Sandawe. These people live south of Lake Eyasi, also speak a clicking language, and appear related to the Hottentots of the south. They may possibly be hybrids between Bushmen and the very first Hamitic invaders. A little over fifty years ago they were entirely hunters and collectors but they have recently been changed by contact with pastoral peoples and with Europeans. They now keep cattle and grow some crops.

3. Dorobo. The Dorobo also are hunters and collectors but they are primarily dwellers in forests rather than in open country. They are willing to learn from cultures with which they come into contact and they have lost their own language, all now speaking varieties of Nandi. They have become dependent on surrounding tribes for things which they do not manufacture themselves such as ironwork. Both the Nandi and the Masai have myths which regard the Dorobo as the original inhabitants of the world who were later dispossessed.

The Dorobo live in the forests on the hill tops in and around the Rift Valley north of Naivasha and south of Rudolf. They are famed as hunters and trackers and can follow game with uncanny accuracy. They are particularly fond of wild honey and have developed an astonishing relationship with small inconspicuous birds known as honey guides which also live in the forest. The birds too like honey and are clever at locating the nests of wild bees but they are quite unable to break these nests open to get at the honey. They will therefore fly to the nearest Dorobo who knows just what the bird wants and will lead him to the nest. He will then smoke the bees out, break open the nest and take the honey, but always leaving some for the honey guide. Honey guides have a similar co-operative relationship with the small animals known as ratels or honey badgers whose powerful claws can tear the nests open.

4. El Molo. These are the smallest of all the remnant groups and only about one hundred are left. They live on the shore and on small islands on the east side of Lake Rudolf near the oasis of Loyengelani. They live almost exclusively on fish from the lake which they catch by netting or spearing. Their houses are little more than hovels made of branches and weighed down by huge stones to stop them blowing away in the gale force winds which are an almost constant feature of their environment. They drink only the water of the lake which has a very high mineral content. They have obviously got many bone deformities which have variously been attributed to malnutrition, to in-breeding and to fluorine poisoning from the lake water. It seems possible that in the not far distant future these people may die out completely.

5. *Coastal forest hunters*. There are several of these groups, notably the Boni and Sanye, who live in the forest behind the coastal strip, particularly at the northern end. Very little is known about them.

6. *Iraqw or Mbulu*. These also are a group about which little is known. Their language has some Hamitic features and some still live in the houses known as tembes, pits covered with roofs made of mud mixed with dung. It is possible that the Mbulu are the last representatives of the people who used to occupy the Kenya Highlands where many remnants of their huts and farms can be found. Near Engaruka in Northern Tanzania there is a whole ruined farming village whose builders are unknown but who may have been Mbulu.

THE HAMITES (CUSHITES)

The pure Hamites live in what in colonial times used to be romantically called the Northern Frontier Province. There are four groups, the Somali, the Galla, the Boran who are closely related to the Galla and often grouped with them, and the Rendille. The administrative areas in which these people live now are the North Eastern Province and the northern part of the Eastern Province. Even very recent history illustrates the considerable Hamitic pressure coming from the Horn of Africa. The accounts of colonial administrators in this region are full of the problems of resisting invading groups of people from Ethiopia and Somalia. After independence there was a minor 'war' in this area as the tribes fought to consolidate their positions and in an effort to get part of the North Eastern Province transferred from Kenya to Somalia. Only recently has this struggle come to an end as the result of a new accord between Somalia and Kenya.

1. The Somali. The Somali probably began to enter Kenya only about one hundred years ago but now they occupy about the upper four fifths of the North Eastern Province. Most Somali are pastoral, camels being more important in the north and cattle in the south: the southern Somali also grow some crops. Some Somali are also vigorous traders and in pursuit of business they have spread far beyond the regions where the majority of their people live, even down into Tanzania. In particular they act as butchers. All Somali are Muslims. The Somali are especially interesting because they are clearly divided into two castes, the noble Somali and the Sab. The Sab may possibly be hybrids between the true Somali and the original inhabitants of the area they now occupy. The Sab themselves are divided into a number of groups, each one specialising in some particular trade. For example the Tumal Sab are smiths and iron-workers, the Yibir Sab are leather workers and conjurors while the male Midgan circumcise Somali boys and the female Midgan infibulate Somali girls (infibulation consists of excision of the clitoris followed by partial sewing up of the vulva). Sab until recently were not allowed to own any animals apart from sheep and donkeys and could not marry noble Somali.

The Somali, like all the Hamites and some of the Nilo-Hamites may often be seen carrying head rests made of wood. These are usually attached to the wrist by a strap and are used as pillows and also to keep the curly hair of the Somalis out of the sand. They are often finely decorated and some are carved with representations of snakes and scorpions which are supposed to protect the sleeper from the creatures represented on the head rest.

2. The Galla. The Galla constituted the wave of Hamitic invasion which preceded that of the Somali. They entered what is now Kenya about 700–1,000 years ago. One group pushed southwards and became the modern Galla. The other group pushed westwards primarily into what is now Ethiopia, and became the modern Boran. The Galla like all Hamites, keep cattle but they also now lead a relatively settled existence and grow crops. They have an extremely complex system of age sets and age grades some features of which seem to have been borrowed by other tribes in East Africa. An age set is a group which a man enters either at birth or at initiation and in which he then remains for the whole of his life. Among the Galla there are ten of these sets. An age grade in contrast is a temporary stage through which a man goes and in which he spends a fixed period of time. Among the Galla each man from birth passes through a series of five age grades each lasting eight years. The men of the fourth grade from the ages of 24 to 32 form their tribal government and one of their number is elected leader for eight years. After 40 the grading system ends although the men continue to belong to the sets into which they were born.

3. The Boran. These people are closely related to the Galla but have remained almost entirely pastoral and largely nomadic. They live mainly in the northern part of the Eastern Province. Those in the northern part of this region keep camels and are pagan while in the south the camels tend to be replaced by cattle and the Boran become Muslim. The main Boran movement into Kenya has occurred as a southward push from Ethiopia only within the last hundred years or so. There are about two million people in the tribe altogether and only about 150,000 of these live in Kenya.

The pagan parts of the tribe have some of the most complex and fascinating initiation ceremonies in all Africa. They have been well described by Joy Adamson in her book *Peoples of Kenya*. All male initiated Boran must have killed either a man or a fierce animal and must have become father to a male child. A plait of hair at the crown of the head shows that a man has accomplished these feats. Some sections of the pagan Boran worship snakes. The Sabo, for example, kill all snakes but puff adders which are tabu while the Gona kill puff adders but no other snakes. The two sections co-operate and when a member of one wishes to kill a snake which is tabu he calls on a member of the other section to do the job.

4. Rendille. This is a small tribe of about 6,000 completely nomadic people who live in the country south of a line from Marsabit to Lake Rudolf. They have relatively complex portable huts made from skins and poles which they can dismantle and put on camels. Their animals have around their necks large flat wooden bells which make an unforgettable sound. The Rendille follow the religion of Islam but have as yet been hardly studied by any outsiders. One of their most striking customs is that women who have borne their first son mould their hair into a large crest using a mixture of fat and red ochre. The crest is cut off only when either the son is circumcised or the father of the boy dies.

NILO-HAMITES (EASTERN NILOTES)

To people from outside East Africa the Nilo-Hamites are perhaps the best known of all the main racial groups because the famous Masai belong to them. The outstanding feature of the Nilo-Hamites is their primarily pastoral way of life with their devotion to cattle and milk. Milk is the major item of diet and in many groups assumes a semi-sacred status. It must always be put into a container made of vegetable material such as a gourd, a wooden bowl or, remarkably enough, a very finely woven and milk-proof basket. It must not be boiled, nor must it be drunk immediately after milking. Blood is also important in the diet although by no means such a staple as milk. When blood is required a tourniquet is put around the neck of a cow to make the great veins stand out. A masked arrow is then fired into one of the veins and the blood collected into a suitable container. The wound is then patched with mud and cow dung. The cattle themselves are of overwhelming importance and a man's wealth is assessed by the size of his herd: despite this for superstitious reasons there is a marked reluctance to make a precise count of the animals which a man owns. Much to the chagrin of modern farming experts it is extremely difficult to persuade many Nilo-Hamites that quality of cattle is more important than quantity. The attitude is well-summarised by the story of a young and enthusiastic agricultural officer who harangued a Masai elder on the virtues of having a smaller herd of high quality animals, urging him to cull the obvious weaklings. The old Masai confounded the officer by taking out of a pouch two twenty shilling notes, one crisp and new, the other dog-eared, dirty and torn. 'If these were yours, would you throw the dirty one away? Could you not buy with it just as much as you could with the new one?'

Most of the customs associated with cattle, milk and blood can also be found among the Hamitic peoples but in Kenya and Tanzania they reach their peak of development among the Nilo-Hamites. In the region there are three main groups of them, the Turkana, the Kalenjin Group and the Masai Group.

1. The Turkana. The Turkana occupy the arid region of Kenya which lies west and immediately south of Lake Rudolf. They are probably relative newcomers having pushed into Kenya from Uganda within the past hundred years. They are perhaps the most fierce of all the Nilo-hamitic tribes and are unusual in that they do not circumcise but do pierce the lower lip, filling the hole with a wooden or ivory plug. On ceremonial occasions they wear magnificent ostrich feather head dresses and if possible leopard skin capes. The women wear beaded skirts and numerous necklaces made of ostrich egg beads. Cowrie shells, the universal symbol in East Africa for the vagina are also worn by the women, even though the Turkana country is so far from the sea. Even today the Turkana retain their warlike behaviour and are frequently involved in fights, particularly with the Merille who live on the Kenya-Sudan-Ethiopia border.

2. The Kalenjin. This is a large group of tribes which includes the Suk or Pokot, Elgeyo, Marakwet, Kipsigis, Nandi and Tugen as well as other small peoples. They live in and around the central part of the Kenyan Rift Valley. Some of them are particularly interesting because they seem more adaptable than other Nilo-Hamites and illustrate the way in which the transition from a nomadic and pastoral life to a more settled form of existence may occur. The most striking changes have occurred among the Kipsigis, a warlike group who might have been expected to be fiercely resistant to new developments. Instead they have taken to settled crop and dairy farming with unusual vigour. As a result they have been able to support a rising population and to couple this with a rising standard of living. If they had remained primarily pastoral and nomadic, the rising population could only have led to starvation and falling living standards.

The Suk or Pokot attract attention because they are a living example of the ways in which the fusion of peoples to produce new hybrids may have taken place in the past. The Hill Suk are agricultural, settled, and irrigate their land. They have relatively substantial and permanent huts, grain stores and folds for their cattle. They are very closely related to the other Kalenjin groups such as the Nandi. The Plains Suk on the other hand are pastoral and partly nomadic, grow few if any crops and live in flimsy huts with none of the stability of a Hill Suk homestead. They are probably physically related to the Turkana group of tribes but were expelled from further north by the advance of the Turkana less than a hundred years ago. They then settled in the plains immediately below the Hill Suk country. The Plains Suk have now completely adopted the Nandi-type language of the Hill Suk but many of their customs remain different even though the two groups are now much closer than they were when first observed by Europeans.

The Elgeyo and Marakwet live in extremely hilly country on the edge of the Rift Valley. Because of the nature of their terrain, their 'fields' must be tiny. It might be expected that such steep land would be poorly watered because of the rapid run off of rain. In fact the land is well supplied by an extremely complex system of irrigation ditches. Oddly enough the Elgeyo and Marakwet did not devise this ancient irrigation system themselves but they found it when they first arrived in the area. No one knows who actually did build the channels but it has been speculated that they may have been related to the Mbulu people who now live between Lakes Manyara and Eyasi in Tanzania.

3. The Masai Group. This group consists of three closely related peoples, the Masai, the Samburu and the Arusha. They provide an interesting contrast: the Masai and Samburu are both very conservative pastoralists living a semi-nomadic life and depending entirely on their cattle but the Arusha are agriculturists, living in settled areas and growing crops as well as keeping cattle. They live in Northern Tanzania in the district around the town which bears their name. The Samburu live in the northern Rift Valley region between Isiolo and Lake Rudolf.

The Masai are an especially attractive and interesting tribe and many who have worked among them have caught the disease which in colonial times used to be known as 'Masaiitis'. They are a proud and independent people who feel no need to make concessions to the ways of life of others but nevertheless who are courteous and friendly to anyone who treats them on equal terms. They occupy a vast area stretching from the region of Nakuru right down into Tanzania. Many of the best known parks and reserves, Nairobi, Mara, Amboseli, Serengeti, Ngorongoro, Tarangire and Ngurdoto are in or on the edge of Masai country and so most visitors have the opportunity to see them.

But their present importance is as nothing to their former glory. Two to four hundred years ago they pushed south from the Lake Rudolf area and by 1850 had established a virtually total hegemony over all the open country in what are known now as central and southern Kenya and Northern Tanzania. Most other tribes lived in fear of the superbly fit and efficient Masai warriors and tended to confine themselves to the forests where Masai fighting tactics were relatively ineffective. The extent of the Masai land is demonstrated today by the place names which they have left behind in areas where they no longer live. Nanyuki and Laikipia north of the Aberdares, Ol Doinyo Sabuk near Thika and the names of the four main peaks of Mount Kenya, Batiaan, Nelion, Lenana and Sendeyo are all Masai words. Nairobi itself is a Masai word taken from the expression Ngare Nairobi which means cold water and refers to the Nairobi River. But in the second half of the nineteenth century their fortunes changed. Instead of being united the various sections of the tribe began to fight among themselves. In a famous battle near Nakuru, the warriors of the Laikipia section were totally wiped out by being driven to their death over the cliffs of the Menengai Crater. In 1880 a vicious outbreak of rinderpest decimated their flocks and in 1892 they themselves were hard hit by smallpox. Finally with the coming of the Europeans much of their grazing country in the north of Kenya, on the Laikipia Plateau, in the Rift Valley and around Nairobi was taken for farming. The surprising thing is that despite all these setbacks the Masai remain today a proud, virile and attractive people.

Most visitors are interested in the organisation of the tribe and in the various stages through which Masai pass during life. They are a democratic group and there is no real source of hereditary temporal power. There are however people whom Europeans tend to call medicine men or witch doctors because they are believed to possess supernatural powers and advise when the time is auspicious for a particular action to be carried out. But both these names are rather derogatory when applied to the dignified individuals who perform these functions and their Masai name of laibon is to be preferred.

All Masai males pass through three main stages. Each one is first a boy, then a warrior (moran) and then an elder. Boys are circumcised when they are between 14 and 18, the appropriate time for each generation being decided by the laibon. The older half of a circumcised group is known as the Right Hand and on reaching warrior status they used to form the front line troops. The younger half is the Left Hand and they used to form the reserve. On the morning of the circumcision ceremony each boy goes out very early in the morning and lies on the open ground in order to become cold. Cold water is also poured over him presumably in order to act as a form of anaesthesia. While the operation is being carried out the candidate must not flinch or cry out or he will become an object of ridicule. Immediately after the operation he remains in his mother's hut for four days and on emerging for the first time he wears female clothing.

Once the wounds have initially healed, all the circumcised boys black their bodies with charcoal and make a white pattern in chalk on their faces. Two ostrich feathers form a head dress and the boys roam the countryside in a group. They shoot the birds with bows and arrows and mount the feathers on a special wooden structure making a head dress which frames the face. They also shoot blunt arrows at girls of their choice. This is probably an extremely ancient custom as a similar practice is found among the Bushmen of the Kalahari Desert. Gradually during this period the hair is allowed to grow very long. Once it is of sufficient length to do up into plaits to make the various characteristic elaborate styles, the young men become full moran or warriors and remain so for about eight years.

The moran have no duties apart from defending their people and cattle against wild animals and enemies and on suitable occasions taking the offensive. They particularly hope to capture large numbers of cattle to form the basis of the huge herd which every Masai wants to own. The moran therefore form an instantly available and formidable standing army which in the past was responsible for the military dominance of the Masai but which has now lost much of its significance. During their period of warriorhood the moran live in a manyatta, a group of huts which is not surrounded by a thorn stockade. Each moran takes with him some of his father's cattle and a senior female relative to look after him. Also in the manyatta live a group of young girls of the same ages as the moran. During this period it is absolutely forbidden for a moran to have sexual relations with a married woman: anyone caught in this is later subjected to various forms of public humiliation.

After seven or eight years as warriors, the moran have their heads shaved and are allowed to settle down, marry and take their place as elders of the tribe. At this time two are elected from the group to act as the leaders and representatives of their generation. The elders with their wives and families live in a group of houses known as an enkang which differs from a manyatta in that it is surrounded by a tough thorn stockade into the centre of which the cattle can be driven at night for protection. The huts within the enkang are only about three or four feet high. Each consists of a framework of green and pliable branches on to which is plastered a mixture of mud and fresh cow dung which soon dries. Each man usually has a hut with an entrance room where young animals may be kept. This is followed by two main rooms, the first for the husband and wife and the second for the children and grand-mothers. The huts have no windows or chimneys and are incredibly dark and smoke-filled. The main advantage of this is that the flies which swarm in vast numbers around the cattle tend to be kept out.

All Masai have a basic diet which consists of milk. The cows are milked by the women directly into gourds. These gourds are specially treated by thrusting into them the smouldering twigs of a wild olive thus giving the milk a smoky olive flavour which is repulsive to most non-Masai palates and stomachs but which is a delight to the Masai themselves. Blood is drawn from animals particularly during times of drought and food shortage and may be taken alone or mixed with milk. Cattle are killed for meat only on important ceremonial occasions. The one exception to this rule is that groups of moran are sometimes allowed to drive fat cattle from their fathers' herds off into the bush to a place where a temporary shelter is constructed. Here the cattle are killed and the moran literally gorge themselves with meat, the process ostensibly being designed to make their bodies strong.

Surprisingly enough, with the exception of eland which they regard as wild cattle, the Masai do not kill any game for food. Nor do they kill for any other purpose any animals apart from those which molest either their cattle or their people. The only exception is the lion which used to be killed by moran in order to prove their bravery. Not surprisingly in modern Kenya and Tanzania this practice is forbidden. This respect for wild animals probably explains why the Masai have lived among them for so long without any apparent depletion of the stock: it is something which many others could learn from the Masai.

A major problem faced by the Masai since the coming of the Europeans has been that of overstocking their land with cattle. Formerly this did not matter so much for if the animals multiplied it was simple enough to invade a new area to provide the grazing. But when the limits of Masai expansion were clearly defined by the colonial government, this solution was no longer possible. The numbers of cattle rapidly became too great for the area to support. They grazed so heavily that grassland was destroyed leaving only bare dust. When the rains came much of this dust which had been valuable soil washed away. The lack of vegetation meant that particularly during periods of drought the cattle could be decimated with consequent severe starvation among the Masai themselves. The last very severe drought was in 1960–61 when it is estimated that about one-third of a million cattle died. This disaster did what no government could ever do: it emphasised the dangers of the old nomadic pastoral existence in times when the limits of tribal land have been clearly defined. Within the past decade there has therefore been a definite tendency towards the establishment of settled, enclosed ranches where the stock numbers and the grazing can be easily controlled. Some of these ranches may now be seen along the road between

D

Athi River and Kajiado. At last the Masai have radically begun to change their way of life and there can be little doubt that the pace will increase rapidly in the next few years.

THE NILOTES

The Luo are the only representatives of the Nilotic peoples in Kenya and Tanzania. Most of their near relatives live in Uganda or the southern Sudan. They pushed into the area they now occupy along the shores of Lake Victoria and known as Nyanza only three to four hundred years ago. When they arrived, like most Nilotes they were probably primarily pastoral but they rapidly adapted to their new environment with its lake, its heavy rainfall and its fertile soil. They developed settled agricultural holdings for the growth of crops and quickly learned to exploit the vast fish resources of Lake Victoria. Despite its fertility their environment is not an easy one in which to live: because of the climate and the relative abundance of still or sluggish water it is ideal for the development of both bilharzia and malaria. In spite of this the Luo have multiplied considerably, now numbering rather under two million people, the second largest tribe in Kenya. They have probably been helped to survive so successfully in this environment by the fact that a high percentage of them carry sickle cell haemoglobin, the unusual form of red blood pigment which seems to provide some immunity to malaria.

In the past the Luo were famed for the extravagance and splendour of their ceremonial clothing which made extensive use of black and white colobus monkey skins, hippo teeth and python bones. They, like the Turkana are one of the few Kenyan tribes which have never practised circumcision. Instead they knocked out the four lower front teeth but this practice has now virtually died out. The Luo today are an extremely progressive group and have provided many of Kenya's best scientists and doctors. Their capital is Kisumu on Lake Victoria which has a colourful harbour and is a terminus for the lake steamers. There it is sometimes possible to see the exciting boat races for which the Luo are justly famous.

THE BANTU

In numbers the Bantu are by far the most important of the major racial groups in Kenya and Northern Tanzania making up over three-quarters of the population. There are three main groups, the Western living not far from Lake Victoria, the Central living in a broad band from Mount Kenya and the Aberdares, down through the Machakos Hills to Kilimanjaro, and the Coastal group. The Western and Central groups are separated from one another by a broad band of Nilo-Hamites while the Central and Coastal Bantu are separated by an inhospitable tract of dry thornbush country. In the Western group the Luhya probably came from Uganda and ultimately from the Lake Chad area about 300 to 500 years ago while the Kisii probably came up from Tanzania about 200 years ago. Most of the tribes in the Central and Coastal groups have myths which say that they started off in the Taita Hill region on the edge of the modern Tsavo Park, then moved to the coast area somewhere near the present Kenya-Somalia border, and finally were pushed out and into their present areas by the advance of the Galla.

1. The Western Group. The Luhya are a large tribe whose country is split by the present Uganda-Kenya border. They number over a million and are the third largest tribe in Kenya. They contain many sub-groups including such people as the Tiriki, Maragoli, Hanga and many others. The Luhya were famous in the old days for the scanty clothing worn by their women: however missions have been very active in Luhya country for a long time and this feature is now a thing of the past. They are a settled agricultural people and some parts of their region have the highest rural population density in the country. Their most important town is Kakamega, famed for its large snake population. The Kakamega Forest nearby is an excellent place for bird watching.

The Kisii live in South Nyanza between the Luo and the Nilo-Hamites. They are centred on the town of Kisii itself and like the Luhya are primarily settled agriculturists. Even today their medicine men practise the Stone Age custom of trephining for headache and some types of mental disease. The trephine operation consists of exposing the skull and scratching away at the bone until a circular piece is removed, the rationale being to allow the evil spirit to escape from the brain. Many Stone Age skulls have been found with trephine holes which have obviously healed at the edges, demonstrating that the person must have lived for a long period after the operation. Among the Kisii today, survival after the operation seems to be usual and several people are known who have had repeat treatment and have several large holes in their skull covered only by loose skin.

2. *The Central Group.* This consists of many tribes, the most important being the closely related Kikuyu, Meru and Embu who live on the slopes of Mount Kenya and the Aberdares, the Kamba who live on the Machakos Hills and in the surrounding plains and the Chagga who live on the slopes of Kilimanjaro.

The Kikuyu are the largest single tribe in either Kenya or Tanzania now numbering over two million people. Nairobi was built on the borderline between the Masai and Kikuyu areas and although it attracts people from all over Kenya its population is primarily Kikuyu. The tribe has changed and is changing more rapidly than any other. This means that old descriptions of tribal structure are now largely out of date as accounts of modern society. They are nevertheless extremely important because they describe clearly the base from which recent developments have sprung. The best known, most authoritative and most readily available account is President Kenyatta's classic *Facing Mount Kenya.* One thing that has not changed is that the basis of all action remains the family. It is the family which owns land and even today it is the ties of the extended family which are the all important ones.

The movement of the Kikuyu into their present area, like that of most of the tribes, was relatively recent. In about 1650 they first became established near what is now Fort Hall in, as the roadside sign says, 'The Garden of Eden of the Kikuyu'. Here, myth says, the original couple, Gikuyu and Mumbi, lived: they had nine daughters who became the founders of the nine Kikuyu clans. From the Fort Hall region they spread out along the steep-sided parallel ridges of the Aberdares. These ridges are separated by very steep forest covered valleys with rushing rivers at the bottom and so it was the ridges rather than the valleys which formed the tribal unit above the family. From the Aberdares they spread to Mount Kenya and more recently all over the country. They have proved the most adaptable and thrusting of all the tribal groups and today they can be found as traders, farmers and even fishermen from the coast to Nyanza and from the tiny settlements in the northern desert right down to the Tanzanian border. Their original land on the slopes of the Aberdares is so steep that it is not easy to work by modern machinery and so most of it is still farmed by hand. As is usual in this part of Africa once a virgin piece of land has been initially broken in, most of the field labour is done by women. It is also the responsibility of the women to collect water and the firewood which is so important in giving warmth at night on these high and chilly hill sides. Most visitors are astonished by the phenomenal loads of wood and water which these women can carry by bands stretched across their foreheads. The Kikuyu are predominantly a settled agricultural people, growing maize for food and cash crops such as pyrethrum and coffee and more recently vegetables and flowers for income. They keep cattle and goats but in nothing like the numbers maintained by the pastoralists. However cattle are still an important sign of wealth and in a calculating one cow is estimated as being equivalent to 13 goats.

There are about one million Kamba and they are the fourth largest tribe in Kenya. The hills around Machakos where they live receive much less rain than the Aberdares. When the Kamba arrived there the country was swarming with game of all kinds and as a result the Kamba became famous hunters and trappers. Unlike the Masai however they were not selective in the animals they killed and so game of the larger varieties soon became scarce in their area. The Masai lived in the plains bordering the Machakos Hills and there were many stirring battles. As a result of their skill in fighting and hunting, coupled with their adaptability, the Kamba joined the police and army in large numbers and have proved themselves to be extremely competent.

About a hundred years ago the Kamba were primarily a pastoral, cattle keeping people with the growing of crops very much of secondary importance. As the Kamba and their cattle multiplied, the forest was first cut down to provide more grazing and the grassland was then destroyed by over use. This loosened the soil to a disastrous extent and every heavy fall of rain washed away thousands of tons of the best soil. But within the past 50 and especially within the past 30 years something of a revolution has occurred in the Kamba Hills. The hill tops have been recovered with forest and dams have been built to restrain the water. Old-fashioned pastoralism with large common grazing areas which could readily be over-used has largely disappeared. The cattle that are still kept are now enclosed by fences in fields where the degree of grazing can be readily controlled. But the growing of crops has largely replaced the keeping of cattle as a way of life. As in much of Kenya, maize is grown as the staple item of diet but most farmers produce cash crops as well,

particularly coffee, vegetables for the markets of Nairobi and fruit for
the canning and jam making factories near Machakos. Mua Hills jams
and marmalades are as good as any in the world. The Kamba are very
fond of honey. They encourage the wild bees by hanging hollowed out
logs up in trees where the bees can make their nests: many of these can
be seen from the main Nairobi-Mombasa road. The Machakos area is
missed by most tourists because it contains little game but it is very well
worth a visit by anyone who is interested in the scenery and in the
people of Africa. It is easily reached in an hour's drive from Nairobi
along a tarmac road, its landscape is striking and it is populated by a
friendly and welcoming people.

The Chagga are one of the most advanced tribes in Tanzania. They
live on the well-watered, forested slopes of Kilimanjaro with its rich
soil. However, although plentiful when calculated on an annual basis
the rainfall is very unevenly distributed throughout the year. In order
to supply water to their land during the dry periods the Chagga have
developed an astonishingly complex system of irrigation channels.
These often run for several miles along valley sides and over ridges,
taking water from the permanent mountain streams to large areas of
land which would otherwise be waterless except during the actual rains.
The length of these channels and the need for strict discipline in their
use in order to ensure that every farmer got his fair share forced the
Chagga to organise themselves in a co-operative way on a scale which
is virtually unique. This history of co-operation was to pave the way
for remarkable development in the years between the two world wars.
Before that the Chagga lived primarily from bananas and cattle. Because of the lack of grazing land the cattle were kept in enclosed stalls
and fed by vegetation brought to them. Just after the first great war, a
man who later became Sir Charles Dundas was put in charge of the
Chagga area and immediately saw how suitable it was for the growth of
coffee. Once he had demonstrated to the Chagga that they could grow
both coffee and their beloved bananas on the same plot, this progressive
people saw the opportunities and there was no holding them back. They
banded themselves together into what is now the largest co-operative in
East Africa for collecting, processing and marketing the crop. The
Chagga have used their wealth wisely, especially in providing
for education. They have made the slopes of Kilimanjaro with
its cheery people, its pleasant climate, its beautiful flowers and its

magnificent scenery one of the pleasantest places to visit in all East Africa.

3. *The Coastal Group*. The Coastal Bantu are divided into three main divisions, the Pokomo who live along the Tana River, the Nyika, so named because they all live in the bush country immediately behind the coastal strip, and the fishermen. The Nyika group is in fact made up of a very large number of small tribes, perhaps the most important being the Giriama, the Digo and the Duruma.

The Pokomo are a cheerful agricultural people who have been relatively little studied. In the relatively recent past they were ruled by secret societies of a West African pattern which are relatively unusual in East Africa. It is said that these have now virtually died out. In fiction and films the words 'secret society' have a sinister ring as almost all the stories about them told to Europeans are evil and terrifying. In fact this view is quite erroneous since the secret societies played a very important role in efficiently regulating the life of the tribe and in preventing individuals from behaving in a way which would be detrimental to the life of the people as a whole. For example in times of famine they would distribute food stores and ensure that people did not eat their stores of seed.

The Nyika have several customs which are unique among the Bantu of Kenya and Tanzania. Notable among these are the practises of having a central tribal council house and fortress or Kaya and of erecting carved wooden memorials to the dead. The tribal Kaya was usually built on a hill top in dense forest. It was often several hundred yards across and surrounded by a large stockade. Within its walls were cultivable land, housing for several hundred people and a central council chamber which could also hold several hundred people. Elders of the tribe were buried within the stockade. During periods of war or of discussion of great tribal issues most of the people would go to the Kaya. About a dozen Kaya still exist in a moderate state of preservation in the country behind the coast between Kilifi and Mombasa. Perhaps the easiest to reach is the Kaya of the Giriama, about seven miles north east of Mariakani which is on the main Nairobi-Mombasa road. Nyika graves are marked by carved wooden, stylised effigies of the human figure about three feet high and one foot wide. Small depressions are carved out of the wood and are then filled by pastes made from euphorbia tree resin mixed with white ash, red ochre or black charcoal: the mixture sets to an enamel-like consistency.

The fishermen of the coast are basically Bantu but who show evidence of hybridisation with Arabs and with most of the other peoples who have landed on this shore. Without expensive boats which can easily and quickly go far from land and without expensive modern equipment, fishing here is not easy. The sea is full of sharp coral which can easily tear nets to pieces. The fish are caught either in special traps or by hand lining them from an out-rigger canoe made of mango wood. Mango wood is very resistant to the degenerative action of salt water. The traps are of two types, small weighted baskets which are baited and sunk near the reef and much larger ones erected in narrow creeks along which the tide ebbs and flows. When the tide comes in the fish enter the trap but when it goes out again they cannot leave and find themselves trapped.

OTHER PEOPLES OF MODERN EAST AFRICA

Virtually every race on earth is represented in modern East Africa by at least a few individuals but the most important groups which have not yet been described are the Asians, the Arabs and Swahili and the Europeans.

The word 'Asian' in East Africa refers primarily to the people from the Indian sub-continent, most of whose ancestors were imported here during the early days of colonial rule. There are now about 200,000 of them in Kenya and Tanzania. During the colonial period they came to hold a position of dominance in retail trade and in office jobs, both in government service and in private industry. At the time of Independence they were given the choice of either opting for East African citizenship, thus foregoing any right to enter Britain, or of retaining their British passports which they believed would ensure them entry to Britain if at a some later date they were not wanted in East Africa. One group, the Ismailis, acting on advice from the Aga Khan, took out Kenyan nationality virtually *en bloc:* they have done particularly well as is shown by the flourishing Aga Khan Hospital and schools and by the number of important businesses which display the Aga Khan's portrait. Among the other Asians, notably Sikhs, Hindus, Goans and Muslims apart from the Ismaili group, the decision was made strictly on an individual basis. Some opted for East African citizenship immediately while others decided to retain their British passports. Understandably in recent years under pressure from its own unemployed people, the East African

Governments have severely restricted the issue of work permits to non-citizens and as a result many Asians have lost their employment. Unfortunately at the same time the British Government decided that it would have to do something to reduce the large flow of immigrants and it limited the number of permanent residence vouchers given to East African Asians to 1,500 per year. This is not nearly a large enough number to cope with the demand and so many of these people are now in a very difficult position.

The Arab and Swahili peoples live on the coast and merge into one another with no firm and precise distinction between the two. The Swahili are hybrids between Arabs and Bantu, like the Arabs are strict Muslims, and speak the full form of Swahili, often using many Arabic words. There are probably in the region of 40,000 relatively pure Arabs on the Kenya coast. Their society is found in its least changed form at Lamu in the north. Even today there are very close links between Southern Arabia and the Persian Gulf and East Africa because of the dhow traffic.

At the present time there are about 40,000 Europeans in Kenya and a very much smaller number in Tanzania. Some of them are citizens of the East African countries having been born there, and having decided to identify for good with the fortunes of these beautiful countries which like few others bind to themselves those who come to know them well. Other Europeans are foreign advisers, teachers, diplomats and businessmen who come for just a few years and then leave, mostly with regret. There are a number of Europeans outside Nairobi in the other main towns and cities and on farms, especially in north west Kenya and north of the Aberdares, but the vast majority live in Kenya's capital as will be apparent to every visitor.

5

A Brief History

This chapter is primarily devoted to the history of what is now Kenya. However, the present borders of Kenya are very recent creations compared with the events over the past two thousand years or so with which this section deals. Inevitably therefore many aspects of the history of East Africa as a whole will be covered.

One of the striking things about East Africa prior to the nineteenth century was the almost total lack of contact between what happened at the coast and what happened in the interior. The main cause of this phenomenon is the stretch of inhospitable thorn bush country which lies behind the East African coast and which was a formidable barrier for all but the most determined travellers. East Africa's low rainfall ensured that this barren country was not crossed by major rivers navigable by large boats. Thus until the mid-nineteenth century, all contacts between coast and interior were sparse and erratic.

A major problem facing the historian of East Africa, especially the one interested in the interior, is the lack of documentary evidence. The European historian is used to relying almost entirely on historical documents. The East African historian has to make use of all sorts of unfamiliar and as yet relatively undeveloped techniques. Oral traditions, customs, languages, the physical attributes of people, archaeology and many other things must all be studied. It is often surprising what a comprehensive picture can be built up using these seemingly difficult techniques. In many cases the result is history which is a more rounded study of what happened to a whole people rather than the traditional catalogue of the doings of kings, the makings of wars and the signings of treaties. In the future, document-orientated historians of countries which have a long tradition of recording events in writing may find themselves using these techniques to work out the histories of peoples as distinct from the histories of rulers.

THE COAST TO THE COMING OF THE PORTUGUESE

In the chapter on the peoples of East Africa it was pointed out that for a thousand years or more before the birth of Christ, ships from Indonesia, India, the Red Sea and the Persian Gulf had been making contact with the East African Coast which at that time was known as Azania. The first firm documentary evidence of such contacts is in a sailor-merchant's guide to the Indian Ocean ports known as the 'Periplus of the Ery- thraean Sea'. This was probably written in the second century AD by some rough, tough Greek who had travelled widely in search of trade. Places which are mentioned, though under different names, probably include the Lamu group of islands, Mombasa and Zanzibar. At this time there was only one major trading centre on the Kenyan or Tanzanian coast, a place called Rhapta, probably at a river mouth somewhere in central or northern Tanzania. The major imports of Rhapta were iron and goods made from it and the major export was ivory. The trade was organised by merchants from South Arabia and possibly India but unfortunately no useful information is given about the indigenous inhabitants apart from the fact that even at this time the merchants were interbreeding with them.

The next piece of firm information comes from Ptolemy's Geography, which was probably mainly compiled 200 to 300 years after the Periplus by scholars at Alexandria. Trade at Rhapta continued but the place had grown and had apparently developed tentative contacts with the interior. A great snow-covered mountain, which must be Kiliman- jaro, is described as lying inland from Rhapta, and far distant in the interior of Africa there are reputed to be vast lakes.

We know almost nothing about what happened at the coast in the next three hundred years. Trade with the Roman Empire via the Red Sea faded and died, probably because of the increasing dominance of Persian sea power. Contacts with Persia were facilitated by the pattern of winds in this north-west corner of the Indian Ocean. From November to March, the dry north-east monsoon winds carried ships directly and easily from South Arabia and the Persian Gulf to Africa. From April to October, the wetter south-east monsoon allowed the boats to return.

To the surprise of many, this trade has by no means ceased and many dhows still make the annual return journey. The boats, the sailors and even the cargoes seem to have changed remarkably little in over a thousand years.

This trade with South Arabia and the Persian Gulf seems to have been enormously stimulated by the Muslim explosion of the seventh and eighth centuries. To the Arabs the East African coast became the land of Zinj or Zenj. It still supplied ivory and now tortoiseshell, rhino horn and slaves. However, most of the slaves came from the Horn of Africa and there is little evidence to suggest that at this period they came from what are now Kenya and Tanzania. The flourishing of the slave trade is indicated by the fact that in the ninth century there were enough Zenj in Mesopotamia to stage a major rebellion and that even as far away as China Zenj slaves were in great demand.

During this period a new item appeared in the cargo lists, gold. Gold was mined in what is now Rhodesia and gradually found its way in considerable quantities to Sofala on the coast of what is now Mozambique. This gold then passed up the coast from trading centre to trading centre. It attracted southwards merchants bringing many items but especially textiles and pottery of various kinds. Financed by this lucrative merchandise there grew up on the coast a whole series of 'city states', all semi-independent, all with ruling classes from Persia and South Arabia, all almost perpetually struggling with one another for supremacy, and all reaching peaks of development between about A.D. 1000 and A.D. 1500. The most important of these states were a group on the Lamu islands (Lamu, Pate and Manda), Malindi with its associated city of Gedi, Mombasa, Zanzibar, Mafia and Kilwa. Kilwa, which was in southern Tanzania and which ruled Sofala was the richest of all. All the cities followed the religion of Islam and all built numerous mosques, the remains of some of which can still be seen. Just before the Portuguese came they were very rich and highly developed with a very extensive trade network. They could afford to import large amounts of pottery from China as can be seen from the collection in the Fort Jesus Museum. The importance of their trade network is shown by the fact that gold used in the London Mint in the thirteenth century came from Sofala. The precise route by which it reached the barbarian north is unknown but the bare fact that it did so is evidence of the size of the traffic.

THE COMING OF THE PORTUGUESE TO THE MID NINETEENTH-CENTURY

During the last two decades of the fifteenth century, Portuguese agents were surveying the possibilities of the Indian Ocean trade routes. In 1498, Vasco da Gama's fleet made its expedition to the East African coast and beyond. For the next two hundred years the history of this seaboard was to be involved with the Portuguese imperial adventure.

Vasco da Gama's first journey was a peaceful one. He undertook no major military expeditions. He entered into no alliances apart from a rather vague one with the Sultan of Malindi whom he agreed that the Portuguese would support against the Sultan of Mombasa. For the next hundred years or so, however, Malindi's friendship was to be the mainstay of Portugal's position on the Kenya Coast. In April 1498 da Gama set up there outside the Sultan's Palace, a cross. Not long afterwards it was placed where it still stands today, on a pillar on a promontory commanding a magnificent view of Malindi Bay.

Subsequent Portuguese visits to the coast were not to be so peaceful. Within the next eight years, using their vastly superior sea power and fire power they had militarily subdued every city state on the coast with the exception of Malindi with which they were allied. If the cities had banded together to resist they could surely have caused the Portuguese a lot more trouble even if they could not have finally defeated them. But their individual interests remained paramount and so they were picked off and laid waste one by one. Mombasa proved the most recalcitrant of all the states and had to be destroyed three times in 1505, 1528 and 1588 before being finally subdued.

Until the end of the sixteenth century, the Portuguese hold on the coast was relatively weak. This was primarily because the states were weak and great strength was not required in order to get out of them what the Portuguese wanted, trade and ports on the route to the Indies. But although weak, the hold blighted the whole coast and effectively destroyed Kilwa in the south which prior to the coming of the Portuguese had been the richest city of all. The reason for this blight was not military destruction but the fact that for two thousand years the whole pattern of trade had been northwards and eastwards. The Portuguese at a stroke channelled the most important exports and particularly the gold of Sofala southwards around the Cape. This decimated the old trade routes and reduced the cities to towns, the towns to villages and the villages to forest. During this century for reasons which are quite unknown the large and populous city of Gedi became deserted and overgrown by vegetation.

The event which forced the Portuguese to assert themselves in greater strength was the southwards extension of the Ottoman Empire. In the sixteenth century the Turks had taken Egypt and the Arabian Peninsula and in 1585 a Turkish ship came down the coast as far as Mombasa, urging the cities to revolt. Malindi, remaining loyal, summoned a powerful Portuguese fleet from Goa and the rebellion collapsed. In 1588 the Turks came again, this time with five ships. Again with the exception of Malindi, most of the coast revolted and the Portuguese garrison on the island of Pemba was massacred. The Portuguese feared that these were probings for a major Turkish advance. Again a powerful fleet came from Goa, picked up the Sultan of Malindi and sailed to Mombasa where they trapped the Turks and their new allies inside the walls of the rebellious city.

Then there occurred an extraordinary mischance which sealed the fate of Mombasa. Some years earlier the Zimba, a fiercely cannibalistic tribe originating somewhere in the Zambesi Basin, for no apparent reason set out on a wave of unprecedented destruction. At Kilwa they killed over three-quarters of the population of 4000, eating many of them. They then moved up the coast ravaging everywhere they went. They arrived opposite Mombasa just after the citizens and Turks had been besieged. The Zimba Chief sent a message to the Portuguese saying that they were the lords of the sea but he was the lord of the land and he would deal with Mombasa. The city was virtually wiped out, thus saving the Portuguese much trouble. But the Zimba-Portuguese alliance proved of the most temporary nature. The wild cannibals moved on to the protectorate of Malindi and were preparing to attack it when another extraordinary misfortune befell them. They were taken in the rear by the Segeju, another warlike but not cannibalistic Bantu group moving down from the north. For the first time peoples of the interior had decisively interfered in coastal events and on both occasions by chance the intervention had favoured the Portuguese.

The Portuguese were not to know that the thrust of Ottoman expansion had been largely spent and that no more Turks would appear. The Europeans felt that their whole East African position was in danger. They therefore decided to secure it by building a massive fort on Mombasa Island and in 1593 the construction of Fort Jesus was begun. The Sultan of Malindi was rewarded for his loyalty by being set up as Sultan of Mombasa. The Court moved south and Malindi fell into a sleep from which it is only now beginning to be roused.

But the partnership between the Sultan and the Portuguese was hardly an idyllic one. The Captains of the Fort made it clear in many humiliating ways that the Sultan was merely a puppet. In 1614 he fled into the Mombasa hinterland where, bribed by the Portuguese, the Nyika tribesmen murdered him. His son, seven year old Yusuf, was taken to Goa to be given a Christian name and a sound Portuguese education. In 1630 he returned to Mombasa to assume his father's throne. Almost at once he reverted to Islam and on the Feast of the Assumption, 15 August 1631, he personally stabbed the Fort Commandant. At this signal the townspeople rose and all but five of the Portuguese were killed. This could and should have been the signal for the whole coast to revolt but once again they failed to unite and their cause was lost. In 1632 a Portuguese fleet found the Fort deserted. Faction fighting had broken out among Yusuf's followers and he, like his father, fled. Until the end of the century the coast remained in Portuguese hands.

But Portuguese rule was not entirely undisputed. A new power, that of Oman, was rising in the Indian Ocean. In 1650 the Omanis threw the Portuguese from their Muscat base in South Arabia. Immediately the people of Mombasa sent a secret embassy to the Imam of Oman asking his help in freeing them from 'the iron yoke and injustices' of Portuguese rule. In 1652 the Imam raided Zanzibar and destroyed the Portuguese post there, thus beginning a running war in which the rulers of the coastal cities alternately rebelled and were beheaded as the tide ebbed and flowed. But Omani power inexorably grew and in 1696 the Sultan despatched a fleet and over 3,000 men to attack Mombasa. The Portuguese were warned of their coming and over 2,500 people were locked into Fort Jesus to defend it. By the beginning of 1697 bubonic plague had reduced this number to under 50 and the fall of the Fort seemed imminent. But the incredibly heroic little band held on until September 1698 when a small relieving force entered it. A larger force did not arrive until December. But they were too late. The Fort had fallen and Portuguese rule in Kenya was virtually over.

In 1728-9 they returned for a brief moment, profiting from the dis-
satisfaction of the townsmen with their new rulers and from a quarrel
among the Omanis themselves but they were quickly expelled. Today
Fort Jesus remains the principal evidence of the period of Portuguese
rule. But it was not the only thing they left behind: from South America
they introduced cashew nuts, cassava and maize, all important in modern
East Africa. Maize is the staple diet of the majority of the population.

For the next hundred years or so, although nominally under Oman
suzerainty and ruled by Omani nominees, the coastal cities and towns
were virtually independent again. In Mombasa the Mazrui finally
declared their independence from Oman and the Sultan of Oman,
occupied with trouble at home, could do little about it. But yet again
the cities failed to unite and their history again reverts to a long sad
story of petty quarrels and wars and family murders. Even more sadly,
it was probably about this time that the southern slave trade began to
be developed, particularly through Kilwa and to a lesser extent through
Bagamoyo and Zanzibar. This trade was to have a horrific effect on the
people of the interior because it rapidly took on the aspect of a civil
war with much of the actual slave collection being carried out by
Africans themselves, notably of the Yao tribe. The slave trade was also
the most important factor which helped the British to justify themselves
when a century later they began to exert their power.

This phase of East African history came to an end in 1806 with the
accession to absolute power in Oman, typically after the murder of his
brother, of Sayyid Said ibn Sultan. This powerful personality, after
firmly establishing his position at home, decided to assert his authority
in his East African possessions. It was in his life time that the British
first began to be seriously interested in East Africa, thus heralding the
modern period.

THE INTERIOR UP UNTIL THE NINETEENTH CENTURY

The study of the history of the East African interior is only just beginning as scholars develop their methods of studying events not recorded
in documents. The story at present is very much a shadowy one and
only general trends can be ascertained with any reliability.

As little as one thousand years ago it is probable that most of East
Africa was sparsely inhabited by hunters, lakeside dwellers and hybrids

formed as a result of interbreeding between the original inhabitants and the first wave of Hamitic infiltrators. In the Kenyan highlands there was probably a small group of Kalenjin peoples and in the far north of Kenya the ancestors of the Masai group of Nilo-Hamites. Waiting on the wings in the Horn of Africa were more Hamites, including the ancestors of the Galla, and in Central Africa were the Bantu.

By A.D. 1500 the picture had radically changed. Most of the hunting peoples had greatly diminished as had the original Hamitic-indigenous hybrids. They had been replaced in the central region by a rapid expansion of the Kalenjin, in southern Tanzania and along both the Tanzanian and Kenyan coasts by the Bantu and in the north east of Kenya by the Galla and Somalis. In the next five hundred years the scene was to change sharply again.

Many of the Bantu tribes of Kenya and northern Tanzania have mythical histories which place their origins in a region called Shungwaya near the present Kenya-Somali border. In the sixteenth and seventeenth centuries they were displaced from this area, partly because of a drying of the climate and partly because of the southward push by the warlike Galla. After extensive wanderings most of the tribes reached their present homelands somewhere between 1600 and 1700. In the last section it was mentioned how one of these wandering Bantu groups, the Segeju, saved Malindi by destroyed the Zimba cannibals. Inland, the major events of this period were the southwards advance of the Masai who displaced many of the Kalenjin and the movement into Nyanza of the Luo, the only Nilotes in modern Kenya.

Towards the end of the period, contact between the coast and the interior gradually increased. The impact of slave traders on Kenya was very small and the main merchandise was ivory. Most of this was collected by Kamba hunters and brought down to the coast in Kamba-organised caravans. Not until the time of Sayyid Said ibn Sultan was there any significant penetration into the interior by coastal travellers and traders.

THE NINETEENTH CENTURY,
PRELUDE TO COLONIAL RULE

The seventeenth and eighteenth centuries had seen the northern European powers well-established in north America, South Africa and India. In the nineteenth century they were to turn their attention to

E

the rest of Africa. East Africa seemed of particular importance because of its excellent ports serving the Indian Ocean and also because it was believed to hold the source of the Nile. It was a dogma in most European capitals at that time that control of the Nile's source was the key to the control of Egypt and the Eastern Mediterranean. It is against this background that events of the nineteenth century must be seen.

Right from the beginning of his reign, Sayyid Said made it obvious that he was going to take more interest in Africa. He made his base at Zanzibar, the only one of the major East African centres which had remained relatively consistently faithful to Oman during the preceding century. The first East African contact between Sayyid and the British occurred in 1811 when the rulers of India ordered a Captain Smee of the British Navy to investigate what was happening on the coast. The main reason was to ensure that no hostile power was likely to seize power in East Africa. The excuse was that there were many Indian traders in East Africa and that the Imperial Government had to look after the interests of its citizens. Smee found that as early as this period much of the trade was in Indian hands and that Indians were the main sources of capital. He noted that only Zanzibar and Kilwa recognised the rule of Oman and that the slave trade was developing rapidly in southern Tanzania and northern Mozambique. Clove plantations were being established on the islands and run by slave labour, and over five thousand slaves were exported annually to South Arabia, the Indian subcontinent and the French sugar plantations on Mauritius and Reunion.

It was not until 1822 that Sayyid Said felt secure enough at home to devote much of his force to Africa. In particular he wanted to subdue the powerful and rebellious Mazrui in Mombasa. The Mazrui, seeing the writing on the wall, twice sent to the British in India asking for aid and protection. Twice the British refused because they saw little value in ruling Mombasa nor did they see any virtue in needlessly antagonising Oman. But in 1824, the British ship, HMS *Leven*, commanded by the deeply religious Captain Owen, was engaged in survey work off the East African coast. It arrived in Mombasa at a critical moment when a large Omani fleet was attacking Fort Jesus. The Mazrui asked Owen for his help. He could not cable home for instructions and so he had to make up his own mind. As he saw it, British protection in Mombasa could abolish slavery there and provide a base for attacking it in the rest of the coast. Owen therefore lent his support and the fire power of his ship to the Mazrui, hoisted the British flag and left a tiny shore party to look after British interests before sailing away. The shore party was commanded by 21 year old Lieutenant Reitz, who soon died, leaving a midshipman in charge. Both the Imperial Government in India and Sayyid Said were furious with Owen. Neither wanted the intervention and in 1826 the British withdrew leaving Sayyid Said to settle his score with the Mazrui which he did not finally do until 1837. By 1840 he was master of the whole East African coastline and he settled permanently in Zanzibar, returning to Muscat only once just before his death in 1856.

The second half of the nineteenth century saw the full development of European interest in East Africa. But what is now Kenya was very much on the side lines. The main centres of attraction were Zanzibar, because that was the seat of the Sultan, what is now mainland Tanzania because that was the primary area in which the slavers operated, and Uganda because it was rich and worth exploiting, and believed to contain the source of the Nile. Most of the great explorers whose names are familiar to European children, men such as Burton, Speke and Livingstone, barely touched modern Kenya at all. The first Europeans to take an interest in the Kenyan interior were two German missionaries, Krapf and Rebmann. Krapf had come to Zanzibar in 1844 and made a very favourable impression on the Sultan who encouraged him to start his work near Mombasa. In 1846 Krapf was joined by Rebmann who in 1848 from the Taita Hills was the first person to see Kilimanjaro (The Shining Mountain). His reports of a snow-covered mountain near the equator were treated with derision in Europe and more scorn greeted Krapf's description the following year of another ice-capped mountain, Mount Kenya, this time almost on the equator itself. Armchair theorists insisted that such things were impossible but Krapf and Rebmann had seen them with their own eyes.

The German missionaries continued their quiet steady exploration of the hinterland of the Kenya coast for many years but what was to happen to that hinterland was being determined by events elsewhere. In Zanzibar, largely because of her efforts to stop the slave trade and because of her overwhelming sea power, Britain had established herself virtually as ruler with the Sultan as a puppet. In Uganda Protestant and Roman Catholic missionaries had become established amid much unpleasant faction fighting and the Church Missionary Society repeatedly requested the British Government to declare Uganda a Protectorate and formally to take over power. In the 1880's the Imperial British East Africa Company set up a chain of posts in Kenya, notably one at Machakos, in order to open up the way to the exploitation of Uganda. In 1885 the Germans sent a large naval force to Zanzibar and forced the Sultan to recognise their right to mainland Tanzania. By the mid 1880's it became clearly apparent to the German and British Governments at home that something would have to be done to regulate the activities of their often highly independent agents in East Africa, and in 1886 a Commission decided on the boundary between German and British spheres of influence. It is said that an important factor which determined the position of the boundary was a complaint by the Kaiser to his aunt, Queen Victoria. It was originally suggested that the border should run from the mouth of the Umba River to the point where the line of 1° latitude intersected the shore of Lake Victoria. But if this line were followed, the Kaiser petulantly claimed, Queen Victoria would have two snow-capped mountains in East Africa while he would have none. As a result it was agreed that the boundary should just skirt the northern slopes of Kilimanjaro so that Germans and British should have one snow-capped mountain each. Such were the considerations which governed the drawing of the borders of modern African states.

Both German and British Governments initially left the exploitation of their spheres of influence to their respective Imperial Companies. But both Companies soon ran into trouble for neither had the manpower resources or the capital to develop their vast domains. Both were immediately faced with extensive rebellion, the Germans particularly along the coast and in the south and the British particularly in Uganda. In 1891 the German Government was forced to declare itself responsible for what was later to be called Tanganyika while the British Government followed suit with Kenya on 1 July 1895. At first Kenya was known as the East African Protectorate and stretched from the coast only to the east side of the Rift Valley. The area west of this to the present Uganda border was administered by the Uganda Protectorate and was transferred to Kenya only in 1902.

COLONIAL RULE IN KENYA

The first problem which faced the British Government was the hopeless unprofitability of the East African enterprise. At that time the only part which seemed to be worth exploiting was rich and fertile Uganda, controlling the source of the Nile, but the transport costs of sending goods from Uganda to the coast and vice versa were astronomically high. As so often happens the only way to make the project at all feasible was to begin by spending still more money: either the transport system had to be improved or East Africa had to be abandoned. The first work on the railway from Mombasa to the port of Kisumu on Lake Victoria was done in 1895. The difficulties were fantastic. The first two hundred miles lay across almost waterless terrain and after that the broken mountains of the Rift Valley region presented enormous problems. Wild animals caused serious trouble, particularly the lions in the region of Tsavo Park which killed over one hundred railway employees. The most spectacular lion killing occurred in 1900 when the Railway Superintendent, Mr Ryall, was snatched from his bunk by a lion, the animal somehow having managed to pull back the sliding door of his compartment. In spite of everything the railway finally reached Kisumu in 1901. The final stage of transport to Uganda was then by lake steamer.

One of the by-products of the building of the railway was the founding of Nairobi on a site where no town or even village had existed before. Faced with the task of taking the rails over the Rift Valley escarpment, the engineers wanted to establish a temporary railhead with marshalling yards and workshops which they could use as a base for the most difficult part of the enterprise. Nairobi was chosen because it had already been established as a depot by a Royal Engineers survey and road building party. It had a reasonable water supply and its flat plain on the edge of the Aberdare foothills provided an ideal site for the establishment of workshops and sidings. There was no intention of making it a town and certainly not one of turning it into a capital city yet that is what happened. Nairobi soon attracted traders and settlers and became a thriving centre. Its new importance was finally recognised in 1907 when the seat of the Protectorate Government was moved to Nairobi from Mombasa.

Another important by-product of railway construction was an enormous influx of people from the Indian sub-continent, primarily to act as labourers, but also as traders and entrepreneurs. The entry of Asians to East Africa was nothing new. As was seen earlier, even during the first decade of the nineteenth century much of the business of

Zanzibar was financed by Indian traders. However, the numbers involved and the depth of their penetration into the interior certainly were new factors. Unforseen problems were thus created and these have yet to receive satisfactory solutions.

No sooner had the railway been properly started than it was realised that Uganda could not conceivably provide enough traffic to make the vast enterprise pay. Traffic had to be generated along the course of the line and since no minerals were in evidence, the main hope of increasing revenue seemed to be in the encouragement of immigrant European farming. Even at the end of the nineteenth century a few pioneers were pressing the Government to grant them land and in 1897 this small group received a rich and powerful ally and leader in the person of Lord Delamere who had entered Kenya overland from the north on a hunting and exploration trip. The Highlands with their pleasant temperate climate were ideal for European settlement and the farming lobby, virtually ignoring the wishes and even the existence of indigenous peoples, persuaded the Government to declare large tracts of land as exclusively for European occupation. One bizarre scheme, mooted in the first decade of the twentieth century, was a proposal to give part of the Kenya Highlands to the infant Zionist Movement for the establishment of a Jewish State. A party of Zionist leaders was given a conducted tour of the region. They were not over-enthusiastic to start with but when the settlers, who were perhaps even less enthusiastic, stage-managed various spectacular incidents with lions and other wild animals the Zionists decided that Kenya was not for them. It is fascinating to speculate as to what would have been the courses of African and Middle Eastern history had their decision been different.

The European settlers made steady progress until the 1914–18 war when many of them joined the fighting against the brilliant and courageous general, von Lettow Vorbeck, in German East Africa. Von Lettow Vorbeck won the respect of all who fought against him and in spite of facing enormous odds his forces remained undefeated when the war ended. As a result of the post war settlement, most of German East Africa was handed to the British, except for the two far western provinces of Ruanda and Burundi which were given to the Belgians. In order to distinguish their new possessions from their old East African Protectorate, the latter was given the name of Kenya while the old German area was called Tanganyika. Thus, virtually the whole of East

Africa came to be ruled by one power an accident of history which has had important consequences in facilitating co-operation between the various parts of the region.

The unity of East Africa would, however, have been much greater had the Kenya European settlers not existed. Uganda and Tanganyika were held very lightly; there was a minimum of investment of British capital and expertise but there was also a minimum of expatriate involvement in the processes of government and in commercial enterprise. In complete contrast, in Kenya and particularly in the area which came to be known as 'The White Highlands', the words of the settler organisations at times came close to being law. There was a vastly greater injection of capital and expertise but there were fewer opportunities for African advancement. In the long term this capital investment has proved to be much to Kenya's advantage but in the short term it was inevitably the cause of much discontent and misery which erupted in the famous Mau Mau revolt.

It must not be imagined that the settler path was roses, roses, all the way. The natural difficulties to be overcome, especially water shortages, diseases and the problems of finding the crops and animals which would thrive, were enormous. There were undoubtedly a few rich and dissolute layabouts who gave Kenya a bad reputation but most of the settlers struggled and worked extremely hard in order to make their farms pay. In the process many went bankrupt, while a few became very rich. The advantages the settlers brought to Kenya were the development of a strong agriculture and, perhaps more important, the nuclei of supporting industries, including engineering, manufacturing and construction. This industrial infrastructure which barely existed in Uganda and Tanganyika was a major factor in the extremely rapid take off of Kenya after independence.

However, the African Kenyans could hardly be expected to appreciate these long term advantages and the British yoke undoubtedly lay much more heavily upon them than it did upon the Ugandans and Tanganyikans. The restrictions and the oppression were particularly felt by the Kikuyu and the Luo, two large tribes with exploding populations, hungry for land and for employment with reasonable remuneration. The first African organisations for promoting African interests were founded between the two world wars. After the second war, these received tremendous impetus from the return and demobilisation of

many African troops who had seen service and obtained experience
overseas. These men were far less content with the *status quo* than they
had been before the war and new organisations with a wholly new
drive and determination were established. Most important among these
was the Kenya African Union. A middle-aged man named Jomo
Kenyatta became its President soon after his return from England
where he had spent the war years. Kenyatta, a man with a deep understanding of the roots of African society and of the African past, soon
dominated the scene and became the target for all the opposition of the
settlers.

Outwardly, for the Europeans the post-war years in Kenya seemed
idyllic. The economy was booming, crop prices were high and the farms
had never seemed more prosperous. But underneath, especially in over-
populated Kikuyuland, fires were already smouldering. Angry young
men felt that the British could be forced to think seriously about independence only if there was violent action against the settlers. Older
men, equally anxious to obtain independence, were more in favour of
peaceful pressure and negotiation. In the early fifties the situation
exploded. In 1952 a State of Emergency was declared and Kenyatta
and other leaders were detained. The Emergency continued until the
end of the decade with Jomo Kenyatta, although in prison, still continuing to dominate the scene. Active political parties were banned and
much political pressure was exerted indirectly by the Kenya Federation
of Labour under Tom Mboya, its young but brilliant and resourceful
Secretary.

During the last years of the Emergency it became obvious to all but
a small number of the settlers that the question was not whether
Kenya was to be given independence but when. When the Emergency
ended in 1960, two main political parties developed. The Kenya
African National Union (KANU) was an outgrowth of the old KAU
and supported mainly by the large tribes of Kikuyu, Luo and Kamba:
it was led by Jomo Kenyatta. The Kenya African Democratic Union
(KADU) was a union of the smaller tribes, fearful of what might happen
to them and of the erosion of their minority interests: it was led by
Ronald Ngala from the coast. The next three years saw many extremely
complex manoeuvrings between the British and the two parties until
in 1963 KANU won the pre-independence election. Jomo Kenyatta
led Kenya to Uhuru (freedom) in December of that year.

TANGANYIKA DURING THE COLONIAL PERIOD

Immediately after the Germans formally took over Tanganyika in 1886 they were faced with a series of military uprisings. Some of these, notably the Maji Maji Rebellion, were of major size and they were not fully overcome until 1907. The Germans attempted to exploit their new possessions much more vigorously than the British and were extremely active in introducing new crops, rubber, sisal and coffee being the most important. A number of settlers came, particularly to the areas around Kilimanjaro and Mount Meru but few were really successful. The war totally disrupted life and at its close, with the British takeover, the pattern of development was quite different. Progress was exceedingly slow because Tanganyika was a poor country and unlike Kenya did not receive much in the way of injection of private capital. Nevertheless it was one of the happier colonial partnerships and progress to independence in December 1961, was relatively smooth and painless. Then as now, the Tanganyikans were lead by Julius Nyerere at the head of the sole effective political party, the Tanganyika African National Union (T.A.N.U.).

KENYA AND TANZANIA SINCE INDEPENDENCE

Zanzibar became independent in 1963 and almost at once the Sultan's government was overthrown. The new Zanzibar Government united with Tanganyika and the union came to have its modern name of Tanzania. Since independence both Kenya and mainland Tanzania have been remarkable for their stability. In each case the achievement is largely the result of the wisdom and courage of one man, President Kenyatta in Kenya and President Nyerere in Tanzania. In Kenya, soon after independence K.A.D.U. decided that it could more effectively protect minority interests as part of the ruling party and its members joined K.A.N.U. They were treated generously and a number of ex-K.A.D.U. men are now Cabinet Ministers. Thus both countries became effectively one party states, Tanzania by constitution and Kenya by preference, although in Kenya it is still possible to form new parties.

The concept of a one party state is so unfamiliar to Europeans and North Americans that it is likely to evoke a somewhat shocked and antagonistic response. Yet it seems likely that this really is the best solution for Africa. Quite understandably, in most African countries which have possessed more than one party, the division has tended to be almost exclusively along tribal lines. This was certainly true of K.A.N.U. and K.A.D.U. in Kenya. Political parties therefore tended to deepen and exaggerate differences between tribes, splitting a country instead of uniting it. The answer seems to be to have only one party, embracing all tribes and all shades of opinion, but also to allow genuine democracy at the local level. This is achieved by several candidates, all with the same party label, standing for each parliamentary seat. The system was pioneered in Tanzania in 1965 and worked well in Kenya in 1969. It has several advantages, some of which might be valued by Western electors. Perhaps the main ones are that the impact of tribalism is reduced and that the electors in each constituency have a real choice: they can actually elect the *man* rather than the party whom they want to represent them in Parliament. For instance, in Kenya in 1969 as many as ten candidates stood for some constituencies. This is a freedom which might well be envied by many in Europe and North America where almost invariably the party label is overwhelmingly important when compared with the qualities of the man himself.

6

The Protection of Wild Life

Some people come to East Africa to see the scenery, some to catch big game fish and some to enjoy the magnificent coastal beaches with their sunshine. In a few years many more people may come for these things but at the moment there can be no doubt that it is the wild animals which attract the majority of travellers. Nowhere else in the world can they be seen in their natural surroundings in such abundance and variety.

WILDLIFE CONSERVATION

Virtually all wild species are protected in East Africa and only very few may be indiscriminately killed. The degree of protection however differs from area to area and roughly speaking four different types of control are exercised.

1. The National Parks. These are established by decree of the central government and inside their borders there is complete protection of wild life. Human beings may not live in the Parks and the human utilisation of land is forbidden. Protection of animals takes unchallenged precedence over all other considerations.

2. The Game Reserves. These are usually set up on the initiative of a local County Council with the encouragement of the central government. There is often a central core to the reserve where protection is as absolute as in a National Park. Outside this core, the protection of wild life is still the primary concern but both human habitation and the grazing of animals are allowed: however these are kept to the minimum and are confined to people resident in the area before the Reserve was established. New immigration of humans is not usually allowed.

3. Conservation Areas. Like the National Parks these are usually set up by
the central government. They are places where farming, usually of the
pastoral variety, and the existence of wildlife are allowed to continue
side by side. In the conservation areas many species are absolutely
protected (e.g. elephant, rhino, lion, cheetah) but farmers may be
allowed to kill up to a certain number each year of potentially destructive species such as zebra.

4. Hunting Blocks. In these areas almost all animals (with one or two
notable exceptions such as giraffe) may be killed by hunters equipped
with the appropriate licence. The licence must be obtained before the
hunting trip and it specifies how many of each animal may be killed.
A fee must be paid for each animal killed and this ranges from about
£50 for some of the larger species down to about 20 shillings for small
gazelle.

PROBLEMS OF CONSERVATION

It is important that the traveller should understand some of the
problems of the establishment of National Parks and Game Reserves
where the preservation of animals is the primary consideration. It is
essential to realise that in most of these regions there is a very real
conflict between the needs of the local residents and the needs of the
animals. If there were no such conflict, game would not have virtually
disappeared from most of Europe and North America. Non-African
conservationists who tend to agitate for the preservation of game are
therefore asking Africans to display a far-sightedness which was notably
absent in the ancestors of the Europeans and North Americans. Only
when seen against this background can the difficulties and problems of
game preservation be seen. It is a remarkably understanding peasant
farmer who can appreciate the value of preserving elephants for foreign
tourists when a large old bull is devastating his crops. Too many conservationists perhaps fail to appreciate the very real difficulties faced
by the person who must stay in daily contact with the game all the year
round. The tourist is likely to enjoy the magnificent wild life even more
if he understands the sacrifices which have been made and the difficulties which have been surmounted in establishing these protected areas.

Perhaps the major problem in establishing a game park is the fact
that the animals do not stay in one place all the year round. Like birds

they migrate over long distances in search of good food and perhaps even more important in East Africa, in search of good water. In the dry seasons the animals are heavily concentrated around the few places where there is a permanent water supply and not many can be found anywhere else. It is for this reason that game viewing is particularly easy during the dry season. The animals are concentrated together in spots which are well-known and easily located. Almost all the major parks and reserves therefore have at their centre at least one major permanent source of fresh water which attracts the animals during the dry weather.

But in the vicinity of permanent water there is not nearly enough food to be had to keep the animals alive all the year round. If they are not to die of starvation during the wet season when water and fresh grazing may be found almost everywhere, they must disperse over wide areas of country. No game park could contain both the areas of dry season concentration and wet season dispersal although the vast Tsavo National Park in Kenya and Serengeti National Park in Tanzania perhaps come closest to this ideal. Most of the parks are therefore surrounded by extensive conservation areas in which animals and man must live side by side especially in the wet season. It is in these areas that wisdom and tact are most needed if the local inhabitants are not to be hopelessly antagonised by the concept of game conservation. If the conservation areas were to be lost to the game the animals would be forced to stay in the parks all the year round. Because of the lack of sufficient food they would probably completely destroy what grazing and browsing there is in a desperate effort to eat. The end result could only be starvation and death on a massive scale with finally the park supporting only a small fraction of the animals which it could previously carry.

POACHING

At the moment one of the most serious problems which the Game Departments of East Africa must face is that of poaching. It would probably not matter very much if this were confined to local residents killing game for meat and skins to meet their immediate needs. But the poachers work in large mobile gangs and there is considerable evidence that these gangs are financed from outside East Africa. The real organisers of the poaching appear to be extremely clever and most of the evidence against them would not stand up in court but there are few senior game officials who are not convinced that if the outside finance could be stopped then the poaching would rapidly be reduced to negligible proportions.

The main drives behind the poaching are the insatiable thirst of man for rhino horn, for ivory and for beautiful skins. It seems incredible in the twentieth century that an ancient Far Eastern superstition about the aphrodisiac properties of rhino horn should be bringing these magnificent beasts close to the risk of extinction. Yet there can be no doubt that the trade is still going on because rhino are regularly found dead with simply the horn removed, the rest being left to rot. Elephants too are often found with just their tusks torn out, and the rest of the carcase acting as food for maggots and insects and vultures.

Perhaps the most reprehensible type of poaching is the trade in skins, particularly the beautiful coats of leopard and cheetah, for Europe and America. The men who finance it are never likely to be caught because it is all too easy to cover their tracks. Yet it is ironic that the passing fashions of the developed nations should put in jeopardy so great a heritage of these emerging countries.

❧ 7 ❧

National Parks and Reserves of Kenya

Kenya is extremely rich in National Parks and Game Reserves. New areas are regularly being set aside for the preservation of game and of the natural environment. Recent ventures include the Marine National Parks near Malindi and the Lambwe Valley Game Reserve in western Kenya. In this chapter each park or reserve is described in some detail.

ABERDARE NATIONAL PARK

The Aberdares are a long range of mountains stretching almost from Nairobi to Thomson's Falls. On the west they are bordered by the Great Rift and on the east by the fertile high plateau which separates them from Mount Kenya. The two highest mountains are Satima in the north (just over 13,100 feet) and Kinangop in the south (just over 12,800 feet). Running between these two is a magnificent stretch of open giant heather moorland criss-crossed by clear streams in which trout flourish. Eland, various types of small antelope, and rhino are the commonest animals up at this level.

Surrounding the moorland at a rather lower altitude is a thick zone of forest which in many parts consists primarily of bamboo. Over most of the park only the upper zone of forest is within the boundaries. The exception to this is the wedge on the eastern side which goes right down through the forest zone and which contains the famous Treetops Hotel. In the forest large animals, elephant, rhino, buffalo and giant forest hog, are abundant. Waterbuck are common. Not uncommon but elusive and rarely seen is a large antelope known as the bongo, rich chestnut in colour with creamy white vertical stripes down its sides.

The park is reasonably well supplied with tracks. Three enter it from the east, two from Nyeri and one from Mweiga. There is only one on the west coming from Naivasha and the Kinangop Plateau. There are a number of camping sites on the high moorland. There are three main ways of seeing the park.

1. A stay at one of the hotels which specifically set out to show visitors the animals of the Aberdares. There are two of these, Treetops (where incidentally Queen Elizabeth was staying when she learned of the death of her father) and The Ark, a new venture built in a dramatic position overlooking a floodlit water hole. At both places visitors can sit up all night in a luxurious atmosphere on the verandah watching the constant stream of animals coming to drink. Elephant, rhino, buffalo and many smaller animals are virtual certainties while the fortunate may see bongo or leopard. Nights up at this altitude are cold and warm clothing is essential. Treetops is associated with the Outspan Hotel at Nyeri and the Ark with the Aberdare Country Club, both comfortable hotels just outside the park and ideal centres for exploring the Aberdares and the surrounding countryside. Trout fishing is available at both.

2. A drive up on to the moorland either from Nyeri or Naivasha. The tracks are very steep and at most times of the year only four wheel drive vehicles can travel around with certainty. Before attempting to go up to the moorland it is essential to enquire about the state of the roads either at the Bell Inn at Naivasha or the Outspan at Nyeri. Apart from colobus and other monkeys in the forest, not many animals are likely to be seen in the daytime but the scenery is magnificent. It is possible to make a day round trip from Nairobi. One goes first through the densely populated Kikuyu-land to Nyeri, then over the middle of the Aberdare Range to Naivasha and then back to Nairobi via the Rift Valley and the escarpment. This is an excellent way of getting within a few hours some sense of the atmosphere and tremendous variety of Kenya.

3. Camping at one of the moorland sites. This is probably the best way of all in which to appreciate the wild beauty of this lovely mountain range. The nights are very cold and it is imperative to take a good sleeping bag and several sweaters.

ALIA BAY NATIONAL PARK

This is the newest of all Kenya's National Parks, having been set up in late 1970. It is exceedingly remote, being situated rather more than half way up the east side of Lake Rudolf. At present it can be reached by air or by an exceedingly crude track. There is no accommodation whatsoever and visitors must be completely self-contained. Alia Bay was set up for two reasons. First it is one of the most exciting of the recently discovered sites where skulls of man's possible ancestors have been found. It is currently being intensively investigated by a team from the National Museum under the direction of Richard Leakey, Professor Leakey's son. Second, it is a totally unspoiled game area, particularly rich in dry country antelopes and also in birds. For some time to come reaching Alia Bay by any route other than by air promises to be something of a feat of endurance but for those who are prepared to face it, the overland journey through the northern desert is one of the most exciting trips in Africa.

AMBOSELI GAME RESERVE

Amboseli is one of the largest of Kenya's Parks and Reserves being 1,259 square miles in area. It is administered by the Masai tribe themselves working through the Kajiado District Council. Scenically it is probably the most dramatically attractive area of all since it is everywhere dominated by the shining, snow-covered cone of Kilimanjaro, Africa's highest mountain. Kibo, the highest peak is 19,340 feet above sea level and about 16,000 feet above the flat hot plains of the Reserve. There is something extraordinarily splendid about this vast mountain, isolated and alone rising to such an astonishing height from the burning plateau. It is one of the great experiences of Africa to sit beside a fire outside one of the lodges on a clear night, with the moon shining on the great ice cap high above and the lions roaring not so very far away.

Most of Amboseli consists of hot, dry thorn bush country. Animals in this part are relatively scarce but two are especially interesting. These are the beautiful fringe-eared oryx with its black and white face and long straight horns and the shy but graceful long-necked gerenuk which often browses from bushes while standing up on its hind legs. Both animals are well adapted to resist dehydration and can go without water for long periods.

However, most visitors spend their time in the south eastern corner of Amboseli in the area immediately around Ol Tukai. Here there are

F

three quite different types of habitat, small permanent lakes with accompanying lush swamp, Acacia woodland, and open plains. Also here is Lake Amboseli which except in the height of the wet season is a vast shimmering plain of fine white dust. During the dry season this Ol Tukai area contains one of the most remarkable game concentrations to be seen in all Africa. It is perhaps most famous for its large numbers of rhinos but elephant, buffalo, lion, cheetah, giraffe, baboons, monkeys and plains game are all common.

Around Ol Tukai and going through the swamps and woodland is an extremely intricate network of tracks. A Ranger Guide is essential to lead the visitor around these. Without him the tourist may see nothing but with him he is almost guaranteed to spend some of the most exciting hours of his life.

Amboseli may be approached from Nairobi by two different routes.

1. Along the tarmacked Mombasa Road to just past Emali about 80 miles from Nairobi. This road runs for the most part through vast open plains split up to form large cattle ranches. At Emali one turns right on to a dirt road which can be very wet during the rains. The first part of this road goes again through plains but again dry thornbush country is soon encountered and the road goes through this until the Ol Tukai area is reached about 160 miles from Nairobi.

2. Via Namanga. The route goes along the Mombasa Road as far as Athi River, sixteen miles from Nairobi. At Athi River is a huge cement factory whose chimney can be seen for miles around. It also has the main slaughter house of the Kenya Meat Commission to which animals can be seen being driven from far and wide. At Athi River you turn right for Kajiado (50 miles from Nairobi) and Namanga (104 miles from Nairobi). Until Kajiado the road goes through the open Athi Plains where much of the game from the Nairobi National Park grazes during the wet season but thereafter bush country is traversed. Plains game, giraffe and ostriches are often seen. At the time of writing the road is unsurfaced but when this book is published the Athi River-Kajiado section should be tarmacked with the Kajiado-Namanga section following two to three years later. About twelve miles before Kajiado is Isinya, a Masai Rural Training Centre where the Masai can learn about better methods of keeping cattle. This is a good place to buy beads, necklaces, mats, spears and leatherwork. The quality is good and prices are reasonable. Masai goods are also available at Namanga.

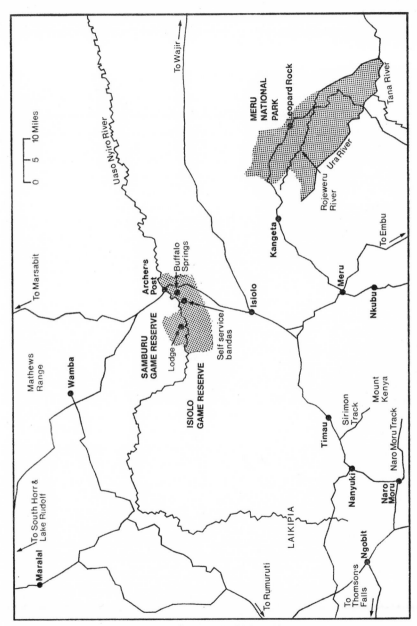

Kenya immediately north of Mount Kenya

From Namanga you turn left off the main road on to the Park tracks. Ol Tukai is just under fifty miles away.

There are five types of accommodation in Amboseli.

1. Amboseli New Lodge. This is a luxury lodge at Ol Tukai consisting of chalets in beautiful Acacia shaded grounds. Birds are abundant coming in large numbers to pick up table scraps.

2. Amboseli Safari Camp. Also at Ol Tukai this gives the atmosphere of a luxury hunting safari. Each tent is equipped with its own shower and toilet. Standards of comfort are high and the food is good.

3. Namanga Hotel at the west entrance to the Park.

4. Ol Tukai Lodge. This is a series of self-service bandas (huts) equipped with basic furniture. It is cheap and primarily intended for Kenya residents.

5. Camping. There are several good sites. As always in Africa camping is likely to be an unforgettable experience with at night elephant and other big game approaching to within a few yards of one's tent.

LAMBWE VALLEY GAME RESERVE

This new reserve has been founded with three main aims, to preserve in its natural state some of the small quantity of uncultivated land still remaining near the shores of Lake Victoria, to protect the herds of roan antelope and Jackson's Hartebeest, both rare in Kenya, which live there, and to make Western Kenya more attractive for visitors. The reserve is a little bigger than Nairobi Park, being 46 square miles in extent. As well as the antelopes it has a rich bird life and is likely to become a favourite with ornithologists. It is reached by taking the road which runs westwards from Homa Bay towards Sindo, Luanda and Mbita. At Mbita there is a ferry across to Rusinga Island at the entrance to the Kavirondo Gulf.

MARINE PARKS

There are two Marine National Parks, one at Watamu and one just south of Malindi. They are linked by a stretch of National Reserve and are described in chapter 11.

MARA GAME RESERVE

Like Amboseli, Mara was established as a reserve by the Masai tribe. It was set up in 1961 and comprises an area of about 700 square miles. Many local residents feel that Mara is the best of all the Kenyan parks and reserves as far as animals are concerned. The sheer abundance of game is truly awe inspiring and one has the impression of going back 10,000 years to the dawn of man's history before his technology had made much impression on the environment.

The Mara Reserve has two sections, a developed area around Keekorok Lodge and an outer undeveloped section. In the developed area are good murram roads which are continually being extended and improved in order to increase the amount of country which can be seen from an ordinary car. No human habitation is allowed in this central area and the grazing of Masai cattle is banned. In the outer undeveloped area, the Masai can graze their animals: most of the tracks in this area are suitable only for four wheel drive vehicles. Camping is allowed in the outer area but only by those in properly organised parties which have booked beforehand at the Game Department in Nairobi. No hunting is allowed, of course, but the outer part of Mara is a favourite place for photographic safaris.

Most of Mara consists of rolling grassland and savannah, lightly covered with acacia trees and with some dense bush thickets. North of Keekorok however there are some superb open plains with vast herds of buffalo, wildebeest, zebra, gazelles and topi. Along the river beds, and especially along the Mara itself which is a large permanent stream, there is thick forest. Near the lodge there are several dams and the resident herd of seventy or so elephants may often be seen drinking at one of them. Almost all the East African mammals and a very large variety of birds can be found in the Mara area but apart from the vast numbers of plains game visitors are usually most interested in the elephants, the hippos in the Mara River, the buffaloes which are often seen in the immediate vicinity of the lodge and above all in the large prides of lions, more abundant here than anywhere else in Kenya.

At the moment, apart from camping in the undeveloped area, it is possible to stay in Mara only at the luxury Keekorok Lodge. This is a first class hotel of international standard. It consists of a central eating, bar and administration block with cottages arranged around it. On the lawn in front of the lodge is a swimming pool and just across a little stream which forms the boundary of the lodge grounds buffalo and elephant are frequently seen. Zebra regularly come on to the lawn at night and occasionally more dramatic encounters occur. Not long ago a waiter taking around the early morning tea came face to face with a large male lion. Needless to say, the tea was spilt but fortunately the potential victim escaped.

The main route to Mara leaves Nairobi via the Nakuru Road. It climbs through Kikuyuland to the escarpment and then twists down to the floor of the Rift Valley. Soon after reaching the valley bottom there is on the left a road marked Narok. This passes the new Mount Margaret Satellite Communications Station and goes between Longonot on the right and Suswa on the left. Narok is a small but now quickly growing settlement which is the 'capital' of this part of Masailand. From Narok the road goes through increasingly open and better watered plains until Keekorok is reached about 170 miles from Nairobi.

There are three other less used routes. From Nakuru the road goes first through rich farmland, past Njoro and then up to the forested Mau Escarpment at Mau Narok. It then steadily descends to Narok itself and from then on the route is the same as the one from Nairobi. The other two very beautiful routes go south to Mara from near Sotik and are described in chapter 13. There is an excellent airstrip at Keekorok which can take quite large aircraft and more and more visitors are now escaping the long and dusty drive and going by air.

On leaving Mara visitors may return the way they came. More usually they go south entering the Serengeti and Tanzania at Sand River.

MARSABIT GAME RESERVE

This, centred on Marsabit 350 miles from Nairobi, is one of the most remote of the Kenyan parks and reserves. Until recently visitors were forbidden to travel to this area because of danger from Somali shifta (bandits) but with the settlement of the Kenya-Somali border dispute the area is now reasonably quiet. In mid-1970 the Government felt able to remove all restrictions on travel and no permits are now required. Visitors are simply requested to sign the book at the barrier at Isiolo, 170 miles south of Marsabit.

The road from Isiolo to Marsabit used to be one of the worst in East Africa but it has now been remade as part of the Ethiopian Highway. It is not surfaced with tarmac but it is a high quality, all weather, murram road: before it was constructed travel was particularly difficult in the wet seasons when there was a risk of flooding. Even now there are few vehicles on the road and there is no water for long distances so that cars are strongly advised to travel in pairs. The route goes through country occupied by the Samburu, Rendille, Somali and Boran. It is a jagged, spectacular and frightening landscape. One section of the road goes through a true desert, the Kaisut.

Marsabit Mountain, almost 5,000 feet high, is a well-watered and welcome oasis in a vast dry area most of which is only 1,500 to 2,000 feet above the sea. The 'mountain' is in fact a series of dramatic extinct volcanoes, heavily forested and full of game. There is a beautiful crater lake, aptly known as Paradise. The main things which persuade people to make the tough journey are the attraction of the remote, the reticulated giraffe, the rare birds, the greater kudu and perhaps above all the truly magnificent elephants. Nowhere in East Africa are the tusks so large and until recently ones of over 100 pounds were fairly common. Unfortunately they seem to have diminished in numbers recently, perhaps because of poaching.

There is a small self-service lodge beside a swamp in one of the craters: this operates on a first come first served basis. There are good camp sites but as yet there is no accommodation for those who are not prepared to rough it a little. Some would prefer to keep it that way for the area round Marsabit is one of the few areas in the world which have hardly changed for many, many years.

MERU NATIONAL PARK

This lies north east of Mount Kenya about sixty miles from Meru town. It is a hot dry area but it is well supplied by rivers there being nine permanent water courses. Meru is the home of Elsa and other members of Joy Adamson's famous lion family.

The park is split into two areas by the Rojeweru River. North of this is relatively open savannah country with the beautiful doum palms wherever there is water. Doum palms are unusual among palm trees in that they have trunks which repeatedly branch: they bear nuts which are as hard as stones. The soil in this section is mostly black cotton, an expression feared by all experienced East African motorists. Perfectly reasonable to drive over when dry, when wet it is converted into a sticky mass which can bog down even a tank! South of the Rojeweru the country is quite different. The soil is sandy and for the most part the vegetation is thick thornbush. The Ura and Tana Rivers which form the southern boundary of the Park are large and partially navigable.

The animals are typical of the drier northern areas, elephant, lesser kudu, gerenuk, oryx and Somali ostrich and reticulated giraffe being usually seen. One animal here which is unique to Kenya is the white rhino. A small number were introduced a few years ago. They now seem to be successfully established and can be seen in the vicinity of Park Headquarters at Leopard Rock. The bird life in the park is quite outstanding, hornbills of several kinds being especially conspicuous.

There is now no hotel accommodation in the park, the old Kenmare Lodge having closed. It is hoped that a new hotel may be built in the near future. There are several camp sites and there are also self-service bandas at Leopard Rock. Bookings must be made through the Game Department in Nairobi.

The main route to the park is via Meru town and is well signposted. The road first travels up into the Nyambeni Hills and the village of Kangeta. From the road there are superb views northwards of arid plains dotted with extinct volcanoes. From Kangeta the road goes steadily downwards again to the main gate of the park at Murera. This gate is about six miles from the Park Headquarters at Leopard Rock. The roads within the park are good and many new ones have recently been made so that existing maps are unreliable.

There is another route which at the moment is not recommended as it is difficult to find and very rough in places. However there is active road building in progress and it should soon be reasonable. The route leaves the main Embu-Meru road about 45 miles from Embu along a track marked to Chiokarige. It then goes to Gatunga and Kanjero, finally entering the park at the Ura River Gate about 40 miles from the main road. When the route has been improved this will be the preferred approach from Nairobi.

ᴛᴏᴘ *The Teleki Valley seen from Mount Kenya. This is a typical high altitude moorland with giant vegetation much in evidence.*

ʙᴏᴛᴛᴏᴍ *Kilimanjaro from Ol Tukai Lodge, Amboseli. The whole shape of the mountain can be clearly seen. The main peak, Kibo, is on the right while jagged Mawenzi is on the left.*

TOP *A Masai market on the rim of the Ngorongoro crater.*

BOTTOM *The fine features of a boy herdsman; they carry spears from an early age.*

TOP *An El Molo village near Loyengelani on the east side of Lake Rudolf.*

BOTTOM *A young Masai warrior. The ostrich feathers are part of complex initiation rites.*

Picking tea on a plantation near Kericho. For Kenya tea is becoming an increasingly important export commodity.

TOP *Masai cattle on the floor of the Ngorongoro crater in the early morning. These cattle are of central importance to the whole Masai way of life.*

BOTTOM *A typically colourful market scene. This one is at Malindi.*

The peaks of Batian, Nelion and the Lewis Glacier on Mount Kenya. Mount Kenya is one of the world's most dramatic mountains.

The proud head of a lioness. More perhaps than by any other wild animal, visitors to the National Parks are attracted by the lions which are common in most of the parks.

ɔP *The self service bandas at Ol Tukai Lodge, Amboseli, seen in the very early morning. The trees are splendid examples of the yellow-barked acacias.*

ɔTTOM *The new Lobo Wildlife Lodge in the Serengeti, built dramatically in the rocks on top of a hill.*

TOP *Lake Natron with flamingos by the shore and wildebeest and zebras in the foreground. This is one of the most remote and most beautiful places in the whole of East Africa. It is on the floor of the Rift Valley.*

BOTTOM LEFT *The lake at Hunter's Lodge, 100 miles from Nairobi on the Mombasa road.*

BOTTOM RIGHT *An old male baboon sitting on an appropriate notice in Nairobi National Park.*

MOUNT ELGON NATIONAL PARK

This park, forty five square miles in area, takes in most of the mountain above the 8,000 foot contour. Much of the park consists of dense forest in which there are many elephant, buffalo, monkeys, forest hogs and leopards. Above the forest is open woodland with giant vegetation: eland are not uncommon at this level and a small group of Masai, the Elgon Masai, graze their cattle up here. The crater is perhaps the largest true crater in East Africa: being four miles across it is bigger even than that of Kilimanjaro. The paths on the mountain are good and the gradients are not very steep and especially above the tree line this is an ideal mountain for walkers. It may be climbed at any time of the year but the wet months, April, May, August and September should be avoided partly because of the bog underfoot and partly because of the mist which blocks out any view. There are three main routes up the mountain, from Mbale in Uganda and from Kitale, Endebess and Kimilili on the Kenyan side. The tracks are described in the Mountain Club of Kenya Guide.

MOUNT KENYA NATIONAL PARK

The lucky visitor arriving at Nairobi Airport early on some bright clear morning may be unimpressed when he is met by someone who enthusiastically points to a hill on the northern horizon and says 'That's Mount Kenya'. He may be a little more impressed when told that the hill is about three thousand feet higher than Mont Blanc and is about a hundred miles away from the air terminal. Like most of the other East African mountains, Mount Kenya or Kirinyaga was once an active volcano. It differs from most of the others in that it has no crater at its summit. The old crater has been completely eroded away and the present summit is the fractured plug of lava which once filled the vent. The peak is therefore much more dramatic and Alp-like than are the smooth craters of many African mountains. As a result it attracts climbers from all over the world. But it is by no means only a rock climber's mountain. It is true that the two main summits of Batian and Nelion can be reached only by those skilled in rock work but the moorlands and the lesser summits offer magnificent views and splendid walks to those who simply like the sensation of being in high places.

The National Park boundary is the 11,000 foot contour which encloses an area of about 227 square miles. There are three main zones within this region. Just within the park boundary is a rim of dense forest, rich in bamboo and with the trees characteristically festooned with long lichen streamers. Buffalo and elephant are very common indeed and rhinos are not at all unusual. Bongo may be seen, usually at dusk or dawn, by the very fortunate. Above the forest is a wide moorland zone characterised by marshy grassland peppered with giant varieties of familiar European plants, heathers, groundsels and lobelias. Sunbirds are common in this zone feeding on the flowers of the giant vegetation. Rock hyrax are also common among the boulders: their cousins, tree hyraxes are very common in the forest and terrify the uninitiated by their weird screams. Finally, above the moorland, is the zone where plant life is virtually non-existent, a country of cliffs, rocks, scree, glaciers, moraines and snow.

Information about climbing the mountain is given in chapter 21 and in the Useful Information section.

NAIROBI NATIONAL PARK

One can say without any fear of contradiction whatsoever that Nairobi is the most remarkable National Park on earth. No where else is it possible to see genuinely wild lions on a kill only fifteen minutes after leaving one's hotel in the centre of a major capital city. The park boundary is a mere four miles from Nairobi's main highway and is fenced only for safety's sake at points where it impinges on main roads: the whole southern boundary is wide open. The park has five gates. The Main Gate is reached by going out on the Langata Road past Wilson Airport. The Mombasa Road Gate is out on the Mombasa Road between Nairobi City and the airport. The other three gates, the Cheetah Gate at Athi River and the Banda and Langata Gates along the Magadi Road are primarily used by local residents.

The great majority of visitors enter the park via the Main Gate. Here there is a Wildlife Education Centre and the Animal Orphanage (chapter 9). In the orphanage which is a particular favourite with children, many of East Africa's animals may be studied at close quarters. Because of its relatively small size (44 square miles) and its very extensive network of roads with regular patrols which keep in radio contact with park headquarters, the warden at the gate usually knows where the animals of outstanding interest such as lion and cheetah may be found. The park has a comprehensive system of numbered posts whose positions are shown on the map. The warden will tell you near which numbered post the animals in which you are interested are most likely to be seen.

Although so small and so close to a major city, the park contains most of Kenya's important animals with the exception of the elephant. It is also an excellent place for bird watchers and more species have been recorded here than in the whole of the British Isles. The outstanding animals almost certain to be seen by the casual visitor are lion, cheetah, rhino, giraffe, eland, waterbuck, warthog, Thomson's and Grant's gazelle, hippo, baboon, silver backed jackal, kongoni, wildebeest, zebra, impala and bushbuck. The person who does not see most of these after a couple of visits can consider himself unlucky. The outstanding birds are vultures, ostriches, secretary birds, kori bustards, guinea fowl, francolin and, during the rains, male paradise whydahs with their fantastic tails.

Like all the parks, Nairobi is at its best during the dry season when animals come from far and wide in search of water. The months immediately before the long and short rains, February and early October respectively, are possibly the best for seeing the greatest concentration of animals. The other dry months (June to September and December and January) are also good although immediately after the rains long grass tends to obscure the view of the smaller animals. There are animals to be seen however, even at the height of the wet season: at this time an extension of the Ormanye circuit (22, 21, 29A, 29, 27B, 27A, 30) often seems to be rewarding.

There is a strip of highland forest along the western edge of the park on the rim of a plateau with a commanding view of the park itself and of the Athi Plains beyond stretching to the Kamba Hills and down to Tanzania. Most of the park is open grassland dissected by river valleys along which there is a plentiful growth of vegetation, particularly of acacia trees. Most of the rivers are seasonal but there is permanent water in the Athi which forms the greater part of the southern boundary of the park.

Immediately on entering the park the road passes through a small patch of forest. Here there is a resident herd of impala and bushbuck,

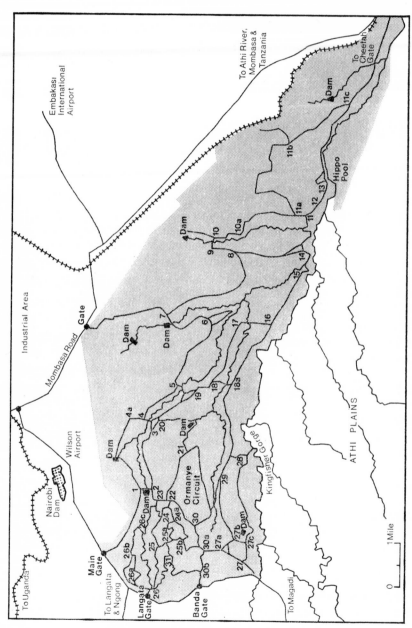

Nairobi National Park. See text for key to numbers.

giraffe and warthog are frequently seen. At a point marked by an elephant's skull, one comes out of the forest and has a splendid view of the plains below, with the largest dam in the park immediately in front. This is a good place to stop and to scan the scene with binoculars, looking for the animals themselves or for the tell-tale stationary cars which suggest that something interesting has been located. From this point you can take whatever track you choose. Every one has something worthwhile to see. Lion may be found everywhere, even in the forest which they particularly frequent during the wet times of the year. Cheetah are found in the open plains, often resting during the daytime under a solitary tree. Rhino are seen increasingly frequently particularly at the south west corner. Giraffe are usually apparent browsing on the trees along the water courses. Leopard are rarely found but they are there, especially in the forest and in the yellow-barked acacias along the Athi. Hippo and crocodile occur by the Athi River hippo pools. But no matter what animals you are interested in you can hardly fail to enjoy your visit to Nairobi Park.

LAKE NAKURU NATIONAL PARK

The National Park comprises the whole of Lake Nakuru together with a strip of the surrounding land. Its primary purpose is the preservation of the feeding grounds of the hundreds of thousands of flamingos which thrive on the algae which grow in the lake's alkaline waters. It has been calculated that when they are there in maximum numbers, the flamingos remove from the lake one hundred and fifty tons of algae per day. The visitor should not expect invariably to see vast numbers of the birds for they are very demanding creatures which move from lake to lake in East Africa depending on which one has the most abundant algal growth at any particular time. But they do seem to like Nakuru particularly and when they are present in full numbers they have been described as the most breathtaking sight in the world. There are two sorts of flamingo (see chapter 18) the much more abundant and much redder lesser and the much bigger and much paler greater. The young of both varieties are almost white. Both species when in flight stretch out both legs and neck.

But Nakuru should not be regarded only as a flamingo sanctuary. It is an outstanding place for watching water and waterside birds of many types. The non-ornithologist will perhaps find the pelicans, spoonbills and avocets the most interesting of these. Spoonbills are large white birds with long black bills shaped, surprisingly enough, like spoons. Avocets are smaller black and white wading birds which have the distinction of possessing a long and delicately upcurved beak. The keen ornithologist will find literally hundreds of other different varieties: about four hundred species have now been recorded in the vicinity of the lake and new ones are added most years.

The animals of Nakuru, while not a major feature, are also interesting. Waterbuck, bushbuck and impala are always to be seen on the grassland by the lake and Nakuru is perhaps the best place in Kenya to observe the Bohor reedbuck. This antelope is reddish-brown in colour, about thirty inches high at the shoulder and gallops along in what has appropriately been described as a 'rocking horse' type of motion. There is a small colony of hippos in freshwater spring-fed pools at the north east corner of the lake. They may be reached by a woodland track which goes off to the left just before the main entrance to the park. After about three miles there is a car park with an observation post mounted high in a tree from which the waters of the lake can be scanned. From the main entrance of the park, the main track goes right along the western edge of the lake. From this track there are numerous side tracks going off to the left which go right down to the shore and form ideal vantage points for observing the flamingos.

OL DOINYO SABUK GAME RESERVE

This forest covered mountain near Thika is described in chapter 9.

SAMBURU-ISIOLO GAME RESERVE

This is really two game reserves in one, Samburu on the north side of the Uaso Nyiro River and Isiolo on the south side. The two are linked by a concrete causeway a couple of miles upstream from Samburu Lodge. On the edge of the old Northern Frontier Province, their arid landscape with its backing of jagged mountains, their abundant dry country wild life and their nomadic peoples provide a real taste of the romance of the desert.

Most of the country in both reserves is dry thornbush interspersed with small areas of open plain and, in Samburu, with thick forest on the tops of the hills. Along the permanent watercourse of the Uaso Nyiro is dense vegetation characterised by the strange branching doum palms. Buffalo Springs in the Isiolo section form an abundant additional source of fresh water. Between the springs and the river there is a swamp which remains green all the year round. One of the springs has recently been deepened to form an unusual informal swimming pool.

Although almost the whole gamut of East African wildlife may be seen in the parks, the animals of particular interest are elephants, crocodiles, Grevy's zebra, Beisa oryx, gerenuk, reticulated giraffe and the blue-legged Somali ostrich. Grevy's zebra are frequently seen in the company of common or Burchell's zebra when the distinction between the two may be clearly seen (chapter 16). Reticulated giraffe are fairly widespread wherever there are acacia trees but are perhaps most likely to be seen near Buffalo Springs and in the swampy areas near the Buffalo Springs bandas. Gerenuk are common in the thornbush country. Beisa oryx are most frequently seen in the shade of trees near the small patches of open plain, particularly those just south of Buffalo Springs. Lions are not uncommon but the nature of the country makes them difficult to find. The reserves are magnificent bird haunts: the striking red-tailed and white headed buffalo weaver is particularly common.

The usual approaches to the reserves are by air (the strip is just south of the causeway across the river) and by road via Nanyuki and Isiolo. It is also possible of course to approach from the north along the Marsabit Road or via several rough tracks which enter from the Rumuruti and Maralal country to the west. There are three possible places to stay.

1. Samburu Lodge. This is a luxury lodge beautifully situated on the bank of the Uaso Nyiro just downstream from the causeway.

2. Buffalo Springs bandas. These are self-catering bandas which, somewhat confusingly are not at the springs themselves but about four miles further west. There are four of them, each consisting of a large verandah with gas cooking facilities, a bedroom and a bathroom. Two beds are usual but two more can be put up in each banda.

3. Camping sites. There are several of these, mainly situated along the south eastern edge of the Isiolo Reserve.

SHIMBA HILLS GAME RESERVE

This beautiful little reserve is situated on the range of hills behind the coast and south of Mombasa. The rolling country with its splendid views both over the coastal plain and inland is particularly attractive because of its trees and because it remains green all the year round. The main entrance is just off the Mombasa-Tanga road, a mile or so after the little market and administrative centre of Kwale. The main road to Tanga leaves the coastal tarmac strip about four miles south of Likoni Ferry. The first few miles of this road are deep mud when wet and deep soft sand when dry: both make approaching heavy lorries a considerable hazard. It is perhaps therefore better to go a further six or seven miles along the coastal road as far as the village of Tiwi and there to turn right along a road marked Kwale. This joins the main road after the worst stretch of the latter is over. Going along the main road, at the bottom of the hills one comes to the East Gate. The Main Gate is reached after climbing up the hill to Kwale. There is also a South Gate via which it is possible to get back to the coast and so make a circular trip.

The Shimba Hills Reserve was founded primarily because it is the only place in Kenya where the beautiful sable antelope with their magnificent swept back horns are to be found. Elephant are fairly common and leopard and lion occur but are almost never seen. In 1970 another attraction was added with the introduction of a herd of the rare roan antelope. The herd originally lived near Thika but it was felt that it was unlikely to survive long there and so it was trapped and transferred. Sable and roan antelopes are very easily confused. The male sable is a very dark brown with very long swept back curved horns and is unlikely to be mistaken but female sables with their smaller horns are difficult to differentiate with certainty. They are a reddish-brown as opposed to the roan's beige brown. Roans have long ears with tufts of hair at the end, very stout horns and a black patch stretching from beneath the eye right round under the posterior part of the lower jaw. In sables the posterior part of the lower jaw is white.

At the gates it is possible to buy for a shilling a sketch map which shows by stippling the places where sables are most likely to be seen. All the likely areas can be covered within a couple of hours and it is very unusual for any visitor not to see the sables. One place in the reserve which should not be missed because of its splendid views over the coastal plain is Giriama Point: the sables and some elephant are very often in the vicinity of this place.

TSAVO NATIONAL PARK

Tsavo National Park is Kenya's greatest game sanctuary and one of the largest areas in the world devoted to game preservation. It is over eight thousand square miles in area and is roughly half way between Mombasa and Nairobi. It is bisected by the main road and railway and travellers by both routes are often rewarded by the sight of some of Tsavo's famous elephants. The region to the south and west of the road is known as Tsavo West and that to the north and east as Tsavo East.

This is a dry land and the greater part of the park is covered with thorn bush which does not make game spotting easy. There are, however, examples of most of the other typical East African habitats including open plains, Acacia woodlands, rocky outcrops, dense forest (particularly on top of the Chyulu Hills) and most important as far as the game watcher is concerned, a palm-rich vegetation along the several permanent watercourses. The park has two major river systems. The Tsavo rises west of Tsavo West, flows through Tsavo West and joins the Athi just east of the Tsavo Gate. The Athi is the same stream as the one which flows through Nairobi Park. It runs for a short distance through Tsavo East before joining the Tsavo to become the Galana or Sabaki. There are also two important seasonal rivers in Tsavo East, the Voi in the south and the Tiva in the north.

Tsavo is so huge that many of its areas have not yet been developed to cater for visitors. This applies particularly to the area north of the Athi-Galana in Tsavo East and that south of the Voi-Taveta road in Tsavo West. Most of Tsavo consists of a plain underlain by very old rocks. The major geological features are the Yatta Plateau whose escarpment forms an impressive backing to the Athi-Galana, the Chyulu Range of volcanic hills in the northern extension of Tsavo West, and the very numerous rocky outcrops which occur wherever harder groups of rocks have resisted the steady weathering of the plain. The Chyulu Hills form one of the most recent volcanic ranges in the world. They were vigorously active within the memory of tribal oral traditions as the name of the highest peak, Shaitani, suggests. It is

G

probable that vigorous eruptions occurred during the past few hundred years. The higher reaches of the hills are thickly forested and very beautiful. The tracks to Chyulu are normally closed to the public at present but permission to use them can be obtained from the Warden at park headquarters between the Mtito Andei Gate and Kilaguni. There are no permanent watercourses on the hills. Most of the water seeps down into the earth and as the result of an accident of geology emerges many miles away at Mzima Springs in the midst of an otherwise dry valley. The immense flow of crystal clear water (approximately fifty million gallons a day) gushing up into what is almost a semi-desert is one of the great sights of Africa. Some of the water goes into the Tsavo River and some is piped to Mombasa about 150 miles away.

The outstanding game feature of Tsavo is undoubtedly its elephant population. The park contains in the region of twenty thousand of them. They can be seen in small groups along all the rivers but there are three places where they concentrate in large numbers in situations where they can be easily observed and photographed. These are the celebrated water hole just in front of the verandah at Kilaguni Lodge, the dam at Aruba Lodge where every morning and evening large numbers come down to drink, and Mudanda Rock, just off the track which leads from the Manyani to the Voi Gates in Tsavo East. Mudanda can be the most spectacular place of all in the right season. It is a long whale-shaped rock outcrop. The rain which falls on it runs off, mainly on one side, into a natural dam where huge numbers of elephants come to bathe and to wallow. It is possible to drive up to the rock on the opposite side to the water, to climb up some steps to the top and to sit in comfort watching the elephants below. Mudanda is at its best in the dry period soon after the rains. During the wet season the animals have plenty of water elsewhere and at the height of the dry season there is often no water in the dam.

Tsavo is also famous for its hippos which can be observed in uniquely favourable conditions in Mzima Springs. The spring water gushes up with tremendous force and then forms a palm-fringed river full of hippos, crocodiles and fish. Elephants are frequently to be seen grazing on the vegetation. At the Springs there is an underwater glass-walled chamber into which visitors can descend and from which they can observe fish and hippos at close quarters. Cars are parked a little way from the Springs and an excellently laid out nature trail giving interesting information about animals and plants is followed on foot.

Most of the other East African animals can be seen in Tsavo although the smaller ones are often difficult to spot because of the thick vegetation. Crocodiles occur along most of the rivers but are most abundant at Crocodile Point just below Lugard's Falls in Tsavo East. It is frequently true that crocodiles are particularly common below waterfalls: it is probable that they feed on fish and animals which are washed over with the water and killed. Lugard's Falls consist of a series of rapids rather than a single large fall. The Galana River has worn the rocks into fantastic shapes and at one point it is so narrow that it is possible to stand astride the rushing river. However this is not recommended as it is very easy to slip and once inside the water there can be no hope. At least one recent fatality has occurred in this way.

Rhinos are common and large but lions, although common, are frequently not seen by those on a short visit: the same is true of cheetah and leopard. Tsavo is a good place to see gerenuk and oryx, both animals of dry bush country. It is the best place in Kenya to see the beautiful lesser kudu: these graceful antelopes are most frequent in the country around Voi and along the Galana.

By far the most developed area of Tsavo is the section of Tsavo West which lies west of the main road between Tsavo and Mtito Andei Gates. This contains two luxury lodges, Kilaguni and Ngulia and a group of self-service bandas, Kitani Lodge. There is an extensive network of tracks particularly around Kilaguni and Mzima Springs. The road from Kilaguni along the Tsavo River to Tsavo Gate is often rewarding.

In Tsavo West the area which is best developed is the quadrangle bounded by the Manyani Gate, the Voi Gate, Aruba Lodge and Sobo by the Galana. It is an enjoyable day's circuit to go from Voi along the Voi River to Aruba, north to the Galana at Sobo, along the Galana via Lugard's Falls to Manyani and back to Voi via Mudanda Rock.

The main Nairobi-Mombasa road bisects the park and most visitors enter by one of the gates along this road, Mtito Andei or Tsavo for Tsavo West and Voi or Manyani for Tsavo East. More recently two new entry points have been opened up making Tsavo easier to visit. One road goes from Amboseli to Tsavo West enabling visitors to see both parks on a circular tour from Nairobi without any retracing of steps.

Another road goes from Malindi along the Galana River to Tsavo East. This opens up a short cut to Malindi from Nairobi and also makes it easy for people who have come to Kenya primarily for a coastal holiday to spend a day or two in big game country.

There are many places to stay in or near Tsavo:

A. Luxury lodges inside the Park.

1. Kilaguni. This is the oldest of the luxury lodges and one of the most famous game viewing spots in East Africa. Its major feature is its magnificent verandah, which houses both the dining areas and bar. The verandah overlooks a popular water hole to which elephants, zebra, antelopes and other animals come all day long: it is quite common for elephants to approach to within a few feet of the verandah. At night the water hole is floodlit and predators such as lions and hyaenas are frequently seen. The verandah has a beautiful view of the Chyulu Hills and in the morning and evening the great snow-capped dome of Kilimanjaro may be seen in the distance. Kilaguni is also a paradise for ornithologists for the birds are exceptionally tame. Weavers nest in the trees in the lodge grounds and many varieties of brilliantly coloured birds, including hornbills and golden-breasted starlings, visit the verandah at meal times.

2. Ngulia Lodge. This is a recently built lodge in Tsavo West. It stands on top of a rocky outcrop commanding magnificent views of the plains. Many good game viewing trails have now been established in the vicinity.

3. Voi Safari Lodge. Like Ngulia this is a recent addition to the park and is built on a hill with splendid views. It is a good centre for exploring Tsavo East. Lesser kudu are frequent visitors to the water hole.

4. Tsavo Tsafaris Luxury Tented Camp. This is in the undeveloped part of Tsavo East north of the Athi Galana at a place called Kitani Yandundu. It is sixteen miles from Mtito Andei and offers a good opportunity to see a National Park in the very earliest stages of its development.

B. Self-service establishments.

1. Kitani Lodge. This is in a palm-fringed area close to Mzima Springs. Elephants are frequent visitors and often scratch themselves against the walls of the bandas.

2. Aruba Lodge. This is in a magnificent situation on the shore of Aruba Dam. The bandas here are exceptionally well constructed and equipped. Elephants are always to be seen in the vicinity and animals of all varieties, including lions, come down to the dam at night. Kills are not infrequently made right at the lodge boundary and the night sounds at Aruba are some of the most impressive to be heard anywhere. The dam is also a good place for birds. Boats can be hired at the lodge and enable visitors to approach drinking game very closely.

3. Bushwackers Safari Camp. This is not actually within the park but is close to it in very similar country. It is reached by turning east from the main road at Kibwezi, 127 miles from Nairobi. The camp consists of bandas beside the Athi River, sixteen miles from Kibwezi. Camp sites are also available.

C. Camping sites.

There are camping sites at the Voi and Mtito Andei Gates and at Aruba Lodge. The one at Aruba is particularly well equipped with excellent toilet and washing facilities.

D. Hotels on the edge of the Park.

The Tsavo Inn at Mtito Andei and the Park Inn at Voi are both pleasant hotels which form good bases for exploring the park.

8

National Parks and Reserves in Northern Tanzania

Northern Tanzania is exceptionally rich in parks and reserves of which there are seven, Arusha, Kilimanjaro, Lake Manyara, Mkomazi, Ngorongoro, Serengeti and Tarangire. Even the country outside these areas offers excellent game viewing. Good little guides published by the Tanzanian National Parks are available for Arusha, Lake Manyara, Ngorongoro and Serengeti. They may be obtained at the park gates.

ARUSHA NATIONAL PARK

Potentially this is a park as remarkable as that of Nairobi. The nearest point on its boundary is only nine miles from the centre of a town which as the capital of the East African Community may one day become a major international city. The park has plenty of game and although lion are absent this is more than compensated for by an abundance of buffalo and elephant.

The park contains three quite distinct areas. The dirt road from Usa River to Ngare Nanyuki divides Meru Mountain on the west from the Ngurdoto Crater and Momela Lakes on the east. The main gate (Ngurdoto Gate) with its museum may be reached by going to Usa River (13 miles from Arusha and 36 from Moshi) and going north along the Ngare Nanyuki Road for about four miles. The Momela Gates and the Park Headquarters are reached by continuing for a further seven miles along the same road. The Momela Gate is the only entry point for the Meru Mountain section of the park.

The Ngurdoto Crater is a beautiful little caldera about one and a half miles across. At one time it was a subsidiary vent on the slopes of Meru and it collapsed as the molten rock inside its cone flowed away. It now forms a unique sanctuary within a reserve for no one is allowed down on to the crater floor. The animals may wander there completely undisturbed even by well-meaning visitors. However they are certainly not unseen as around the crater rim there are two tracks, each with many viewing points, where visitors are encouraged to leave their cars in order to sit and watch the game hundreds of feet below. Buffalo, warthogs and baboons are the animals seen in the greatest numbers on the crater floor but elephant and rhino are also common. The beautiful black and white colobus monkeys occur in the forest and leopards may occasionally be spotted by the acutely observant. From the place called Mountain View on the southern crater rim there is a good view of the summit of Kilimanjaro.

From the Ngurdoto Gate another track leads northwards to the Momela Lake region. This passes through varied country with forest, acacia woodland, open glades, grassland, swamp and a few small lakes. Many animals may be seen but bushbuck, reedbuck, waterbuck, buffalo, giraffe, elephant and hyaenas are particularly common. In the Momela Lake region there is a group of seven significantly sized lakes of varying freshness and alkalinity. Because of their different mineral contents each supports a different type of algal growth and this gives each a different colour. Lake Rishateni is a particularly brilliant emerald green. The dominant animals are buffalo, elephant, waterbuck, reedbuck and hippo but the lakes are particularly notable for their abundance of bird life. This is especially so from October to April when they are crammed with thousands of wildfowl which spend the summer months in northern Europe and Asia.

Meru Mountain was added to the park relatively recently. Meru (or Socialist Peak as it is officially called) is one of East Africa's great mountains, being very nearly 15,000 feet high. It would undoubtedly have been much higher but for a tremendous event which occurred about 250,000 years ago. At that time the crater was perfect and was probably filled by a crater lake. The volcano had shown little activity for many years. Then suddenly in a tremendous series of fantastic explosions, the whole eastern wall of the crater was blown away and a mass of water, mud, rocks and lava cascaded down the eastern side of the mountain. The remains of this can clearly be seen today in the tortured country on the lower parts of the eastern slopes. The Momela Lakes were formed by depressions in the drying mud. Since this great

explosion there have been many subsidiary eruptions and these have
formed the Ash Cone, 12,030 feet high, in the floor of the main crater.
The most recent eruption occurred in 1879 and there is plenty of evidence
in the way of steam vents and hot springs that Meru should be considered
as dormant rather than extinct. The Jekukumia River whose mineral-rich
water comes from the crater sometimes flows hot and sometimes flows
cold presumably due to shifting volcanic activity far below.

There is now a reasonable track up Meru Mountain which for most
of the way runs through thick forest. Four wheel drive vehicles are
undoubtedly an advantage. The track first passes the subsidiary hill of
Tululusia: on the right a side track leads to a fine waterfall. The main
route continues through a remarkable arch made from wild fig trees and
eventually climbs to a flat area known as Kitoto about 8,000 feet above
sea level. From Kitoto very rough tracks lead up towards Meru Crater
and the impressive waterfall in the gorge of the Ngare Nanuyki River.
It is just possible to drive along these in four wheel drive vehicles when
the weather is dry but they are more suitable for walking If you do
want to walk it is advisable to take a guide from the Momela Gate as it
is quite easy to become lost It is certainly well worth the effort to get into
the crater as the cliffs and views are outstanding. From Kitoto the crater
may be reached by walkers in about half an hour. For those who want
to climb to the summit of Meru itself there are three main routes, one
from the National Park via Little Meru, one on the west side via
Olkokola Farm and one on the north via Pyrita Farm. Details are given
in the Mountain Club of Kenya Guide, *Mountains of Kenya.*

There is at present no accommodation within the park although a
hotel is planned. There are several very beautiful camp sites in the
Meru section (including one in the crater) and there are two at Momela
beside Lake Kusare. Outside the park are the Momela Game Lodge,
just by the Momela Gate, where the film *Hatari* was made, and the
Mount Meru Game Sanctuary and Hotel Tanzanite at Usa River. The
park can also be easily visited by those staying at Arusha or Moshi.

It is usual to approach the park from the Arusha-Moshi road. However those coming from Kenya may prefer to take the road to Ngare
Nanyuki which leaves the Namanga-Arusha road about sixteen miles
before Arusha and skirts the north side of Meru. About two miles past
Ngare Nanyuki turn south towards Usa River and enter the park via
the Momela Gate.

KILIMANJARO

The Kilimanjaro Reserve consists of all the mountain above the 6,000 foot contour. The lowest part consists of Chagga shambas but above this is a thick forest zone where animals are plentiful but rarely seen. Perhaps the most obvious are the colobus monkeys with their long black and white coats and harsh calls. Unlike the mountains in the Kenya Highlands, Kilimanjaro has no bamboo zone and the forest merges first into scrub and then into open moorland. The rarest animal on Kilimanjaro is the Abbot's duiker which lives only in mountain forests in northern Tanzania. It is reddish brown, about thirty inches high at the shoulder and nocturnal so that it is hardly ever seen. As yet the game viewing possibilities of Kilimanjaro have not really been developed. Its main attractions at the moment are the pleasant resort village of Marangu (chapter 15) and its climbing (chapter 21). There is excellent fishing on the mountain which is controlled by the Kilimanjaro Fishing Club. Arrangements should be made through the club or through the Kilimanjaro Tourist Association at Moshi. The Marangu hotels make good bases for trout fishermen.

LAKE MANYARA NATIONAL PARK

In Northern Tanzania, the east wall of the Rift Valley is not clearly defined. Instead of breaking in two places as in Kenya, here the earth's crust split only once, giving a very steep western escarpment but only a gradual slope on the eastern side. This formation can be clearly seen in the Manyara area with its sheer Rift wall. Manyara is a typical alkaline Rift lake, shallow and varying considerably in area depending on the rainfall. The National Park boundary contains the northern and western shores of the lake, the strip of flat country between the lake and the Rift wall and the escarpment itself.

Undoubtedly the most famous of Manyara's animals are its tree climbing lions. There have been many guesses as to the reaons for this strange behaviour – and it certainly is odd to find a lion staring at you from a broad branch twenty feet above the ground – but as yet none is well established. The various explanations include escape from the heat, escape from the worst of the biting insects, escape from the large herds of buffalo and elephant which crash around Manyara, or the

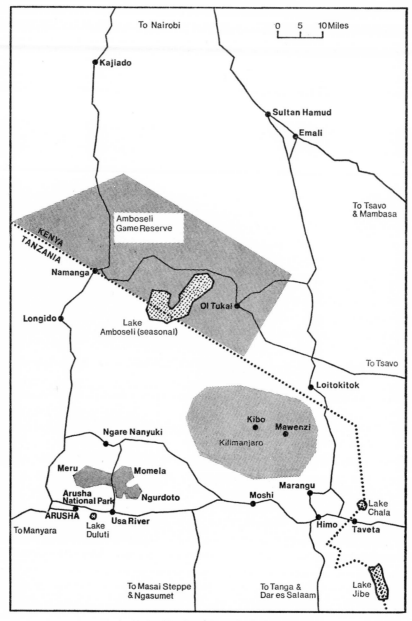

Arusha National Park and the Amboseli Game Reserve.

securing of a better vantage point in which to laze away the day. One explanation which because it is so simple may well be the right one is that the Manyara lions climb trees simply because the Manyara trees are easily climbable by big cats which are not particularly well adapted for that sort of thing.

Apart from the lions, Manyara has a rich animal life including baboons, monkeys and most of the usual types of antelope. The most conspicuous animals are undoubtedly the large herds of elephant and buffalo. When bull buffalo become old, they leave the herd and live either in small groups or alone. These solitary animals live on the shore where food is fairly plentiful and soft. Herd buffalo are often shy and rather cow-like in behaviour, rarely causing trouble, but solitary bulls are often of uncertain temper and can be extremely cunning. They should therefore be approached with considerable caution and on no account provoked. Leopard are not uncommon in the park and may be seen resting in the acacia trees or hunting in the early morning or evening.

Like all the Rift lakes, Manyara is outstanding on account of its bird life. Most of the East African water and waterside birds may be seen here with flamingos, pelicans and spoonbills especially conspicuous. The lake is fed by springs and streams coming down from and out of the Rift wall. It is nowhere very deep and in the dry season it may shrink to only a few square miles in area leaving vast areas of shimmering soda around its edges.

The two outstanding geographical features of the park are the Rift wall and the lake. There is one main park track which runs the length of the park between these two. From the main gate at the north end to the hot springs of Maji Moto at the south end is a distance of about twenty five miles. At the gate (there is only one) is an excellent little museum. Guides can be obtained here and those unfamiliar with the park are strongly advised to take one. Especially after rain some parts of the lake shore which look firm are, in fact, very swampy and can easily bog down a vehicle: the guides know the dangerous places and can warn you about them. Apart from this the guides are, of course, familiar with all the best places for spotting the wild life (especially the tree-climbing lions) and you are likely to see much more if you take one.

On going into the park you immediately enter a zone of very unusual vegetation for this dry part of Africa. This is thick forest which closely resembles rain forest even though the average annual rainfall is very low. Such thick forest could obviously not grow without water and this comes not from above but from below. Many springs and streams arise as the result of water flowing through the volcanic rock of the Rift wall and emerging at the bottom. In places there is too much water even for the forest trees to grow, giving rise to patches of true swamp. Animals are naturally difficult to spot in this zone. The most obvious are the large troupes of baboons. Elephants are also common and leopards are not rare although infrequently seen.

About two and a half miles from the gate the road forks. The main track goes straight on but the left hand fork is probably more rewarding. It leads to a large open space known as Mahali pa Nyati where a herd of about 400 buffalo is usually to be seen. The lake shore here can be very swampy and care is advisable.

After about five miles the forest thins out and runs into more open bush country with some fine patches of acacia woodland and also areas of grass. The lions are usually found in the acacia trees keeping an eye open for the zebra, antelopes, buffalo and gazelle which feed on the grass and form their prey. Along the water courses are some fine palm trees. This sort of country continues right through to the hot springs at Maji Moto. The water is fresh and has a temperature of about 140° Fahrenheit. There is no exit at this end of the park and it is necessary to drive back to the main gate. However there are so many small and interesting side tracks that if you are with someone who knows the park well it is possible to return almost without retracing your path.

The park gate is 76 miles from Arusha. The first fifty miles are tarmac to Makuyuni. From Makuyuni a murram road heads west to the small town of Mto wa Mbu (Mosquito River) 25 miles away. The park gate is about a mile after Mto with Mbu on the left hand side. Coming in the other direction, Lake Manyara is about 34 miles from Ngorongoro. The only accommodation in the vicinity is the luxury Lake Manyara Hotel. This is reached by passing the park gate and continuing along the road up the Rift Wall. The hotel is in a magnificent position on top of the escarpment with incomparable views of the lake and the Rift Valley. There is a swimming pool and a pleasant lawn from which it is possible to watch the activities of elephants, buffalo, rhino and other creatures far below.

MKOMAZI GAME RESERVE

This reserve is immediately south of the Kenya border between Kilimanjaro and the sea. It is almost an extension of Tsavo West and has a large population of elephants. The Reserve consists of hot dry thornbush country and as yet is undeveloped for visitors.

As in many of the dry areas of East Africa, its bird life is an outstanding attraction and most of the few people who visit Mkomazi at present are ornithologists. Mkomazi is also a good place for the dry country antelope, oryx, lesser kudu and gerenuk. Moshi and Lushoto are the nearest centres where good class accommodation is available. Tanzania Wildlife Safaris will arrange camping trips to the reserve and these may soon be put on a regular routine basis.

NGORONGORO CONSERVATION UNIT

This is an area of about 2,500 square miles between the Serengeti and the Rift Valley. It used to be part of the Serengeti National Park but in 1959 it was detached from the park in order to preserve the rights of the ten thousand or so Masai who live within the unit. At present, three main areas are of interest to visitors, the short grass plains which adjoin those of the Serengeti and which provide wet season grazing for hundreds of thousands of wildebeest, zebra and gazelles, Olduvai Gorge where so many important tools and animal and human fossils have been found, and the great crater of Ngorongoro itself. The short grass plains are described in the Serengeti section while Olduvai is described in a section of its own.

Undoubtedly the centre piece of the Unit is the Ngorongoro Crater itself with its huge resident populations of plains game and other animals. Like many of the craters in this part of the world, Ngorongoro is really a caldera, the remains of a volcano which collapsed when the molten lava inside the cone flowed away. Because the crater itself contains sufficient water and grazing all the year round, the animals are unusual in that they move relatively little and can be found in the crater during any month, wet or dry. It is this which makes the crater such a sure attraction for irrespective of the time of the year animals will always be seen. And the setting in which the animals are seen is incomparable. The vast caldera, almost ten miles across, over a hundred square miles in area and 2,500 feet deep is one of the few sights which truly deserve that overworked epithet, breathtaking.

The crater walls are unbroken and all the hotels and offices are up on the crater rim, 7,500 feet above the sea in a cool, damp, thickly forested area which is a favourite with elephant, buffalo, leopard and many smaller fry. Elephant and buffalo are very frequently seen in the immediate vicinity of the hotels. The crater floor far below has a very different climate, much drier and much hotter. Nevertheless, the vegetation in the floor is abundant because it receives by way of springs and streams much of the water which falls as rain on the crater rim. The rim and the floor are linked by three tracks. The north eastern one is little used by visitors and links the crater to the highlands further north. The western one, the Sendeto Descent, is a one way downward track and is the route by which most people enter the crater. The southern one, the Lerai ascent, is a one way track for vehicles climbing out. There is a light airstrip on the floor of the crater and arrangements can be made with the hotels for vehicles to meet incoming planes. Only four wheel drive vehicles are allowed down into the crater.

Several different types of habitat are found on the crater floor. The predominant one is open grassland. There are also large areas of swamp, some freshwater streams and pools, a patch of acacia woodland, the Lerai Forest, in the south, and Lake Magadi, a soda lake which typically is not more than seven feet deep and whose area fluctuates enormously depending on the amount of rain. Visitors normally descend Sendeto at about 8 a.m., have a picnic lunch in the Lerai Forest at about 12.30 p.m. and return to the crater rim at about 2 p.m. The main animals likely to be seen are wildebeest, zebra, kongoni, reedbuck, gazelles, hippo, eland, rhino, elephant, lion, hyena and all three species of jackal. With Amboseli, Ngorongoro is the best place in East Africa for seeing rhino. Its large lions are also famous for their black maned males. The crater has enormous numbers of hyaenas which unlike most of their fellows do not seem to be primarily nocturnal in habit. They may therefore be seen at all times of the day often lying in pools and at the edge of the lake. It has recently been discovered that in Ngorongoro the traditional relationship between lions and hyaenas is partially reversed. It is always taught that hyaenas scavenge on lion kills. In Ngorongoro it is now known that the lions obtain about 25 per cent of their food by chasing hyaenas away from kills which the

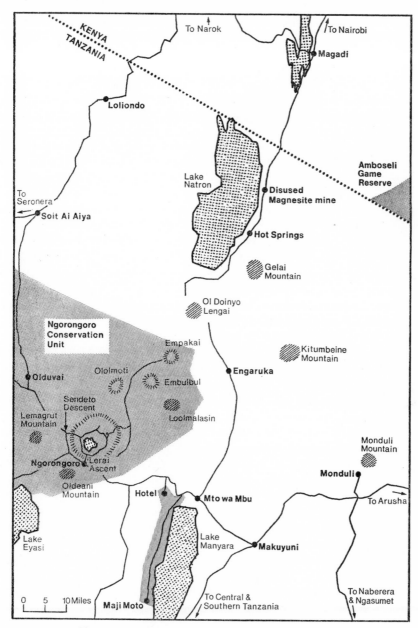

Ngorongoro Conservation Unit, Lake Natron and Lake Manyara.

hyaenas themselves have made. The bird life in Ngorongoro is also abundant. Flamingos are almost always to be seen on the alkaline lake, while geese, ibis, spoonbills and many others are common around the swamps.

Many visitors are surprised to find that Masai people live within the crater itself. There are around a hundred and fifty Masai on the crater floor and they own something approaching two thousand cattle. They do not interfere with the animals and the animals rarely interfere with them, an astonishing example of the remarkable harmony with wild life which the Masai have achieved (chapter 4).

Other areas of the Unit are hardly visited by tourists yet at least two are of outstanding interest. These are the south west area around the huge soda lake, Eyasi, and the north eastern highlands rising to almost 12,000 feet at Loolmalasion. Lake Eyasi region is where the interesting Sandawe and Hadzapi peoples live (chapter 4). The highlands contain several other craters, Empakai being particularly beautiful and rich in animal life. The road from Ngorongoro to Empakai has now been greatly improved and the journey takes only two to three hours. It is strongly recommended as being of outstanding beauty and totally unspoiled. From Empakai there are views of Lake Natron and the active volcano, Ol Doinyo Lengai.

Most visitors enter the Ngorongoro Unit from the Serengeti or from Arusha and Manyara. From Manyara the road travels through rolling farmland where most of Tanzania's wheat is grown. This region is inhabited by the Mbulu (Iraqw) people who are probably one of the oldest indigenous groups in East Africa. Their traditional pit houses or tembes, are now rarely built. The tembes are made by excavating an area and have only very low walls and a flat roof above ground level. Those with sharp eyes should be able to see a few existing examples of tembes from the road. The route rises steadily and passes for some way through lichen-hung mountain forest before reaching the crater rim and going round it to the village of Ngorongoro itself. On this southern rim on a site commanding a magnificent view of the crater is a memorial to Michael Grzimek who did so much for the wild animals of Ngorongoro and Serengeti. Tragically he was killed in an aircraft accident while flying over the area he loved so much.

The visitor coming from the Serengeti crosses a long stretch of open plain before climbing steadily to the crater over the north east shoulder of Lemagrut Mountain. Just before the crater is reached, the track traverses the Sendeto Depression, an extremely beautiful grass bowl, sometimes mistaken for the crater itself by those who have not seen the latter's vastness.

There are now many places to stay within the Unit ranging from luxury hotels to camping sites.

1. Ngorongoro Crater Lodge and Ngorongoro Wildlife Lodge. These are both luxury hotels on splendid sites with wide views over the crater. The former is the oldest game lodge in East Africa while the latter is new having come fully operational only in 1970.

2. Kimba Lodge. This is much simpler but nevertheless provides good accommodation on the crater rim.

3. Ngorongoro Forest Lodge (Dhillon's Lodge). This is situated on the south side of the crater rim road looking down a valley in which buffalo and elephant are frequently seen. It is primarily intended for local residents. It is possible to have full board, to cook one's own food or to bring one's own food and have it cooked by the Lodge staff. It is a very informal and friendly place.

4. Lake Ndutu Tented Camp. This is situated at Lake Ndutu, an alkaline lake on the border of the Serengeti Park and the Ngorongoro Unit. It is reached by driving from Ngorongoro towards the Serengeti. About thirty miles from the Unit Headquarters is a sign on the left pointing along a track to the camp. The camp is about fifteen miles from the sign. The camp operates in the drier parts of the year only.

5. Ngorongoro Youth Hostel. This consists of a large dormitory which is reserved for educational parties and a small annexe for casual visitors. Bookings are not accepted for the annexe.

6. Camp sites. There are two of these, one, Simba Camp, on the crater rim and one down in the crater itself. In order to use the latter special permission must be obtained from Park Headquarters.

OLDUVAI GORGE

This is within the Ngorongoro Conservation Unit but is so important and so different that it should be separately described. The gorge is about two hundred feet deep and has been formed over tens of thousands of years by river erosion. The river is now dry for most of the year but at one time was probably more permanent. The gorge is difficult to see

H

from the surrounding plain until you are right on its edge as the unfortunate Dr Kattwinkel found in 1911 when he almost fell into it (chapter 3). The importance of the gorge lies in the fact that in its walls are exposed a unique series of deposits in one of the few areas of the world where man and his ancestors have lived for two million years or more.

The floor of the gorge is composed of lava which was probably deposited about two million years ago during one of the recurrent violent periods of volcanic activity. Above this floor is a complex series of sedimentary beds which have been laid down in the succeeding years. Bed I, the lowest, consists of layers of volcanic ash alternating with clay: this may indicate that at that time Olduvai was on the shore of a lake whose level fluctuated with the climate. It was in this bed, about one and three quarter million years old, that Zinjanthropus and the first known man-made tools were found. Bed II consists mainly of clay and sand probably deposited from the waters of a shallow lake: it contains numerous hand axes indicating considerable technological development. Bed III, very obviously red, consists of alluvial material washed down from Lemagrut Mountain: the climate at this time seems to have been very harsh and few tools have been found. Bed IV consists mainly of stream-deposited clays and contains numerous beautifully made hand axes, far superior to those from bed II. The gorge is then topped by a wind-blown deposit of sand and volcanic dust indicating a desert period with little or no habitation.

Many different sites in the gorge have been excavated, almost exclusively by Dr and Mrs Leakey and members of their family. Several of these have been prepared so that they may be observed by visitors. They include the sites where most of the important human skulls and animal skeletons have been found. One of the most interesting sites is a stone circle. possibly representing one of man's earliest attempts to shelter himself: it was found at the base of Bed I.

Olduvai is reached by a three and a half mile track which leads off the main Ngorongoro-Serengeti Road. The turn off is about 25 miles from Ngorongoro. At the rim of the gorge are a guide hut and ticket office, a small museum and a viewing point with a good view over the whole gorge. Guides will drive with you down into the gorge and show you all the sites in which you are interested. For those with a little imagination, able to clothe dry bones with flesh, this is one of the most thrilling places in Africa.

SERENGETI NATIONAL PARK

The Serengeti is a huge National Park, over six thousand square miles in area. It is perhaps the best known big game area on earth having been made famous by many books and films such as *Serengeti Shall Not Die*. Its fame is entirely justified. The animals, the scenery and the light, which one feels Impressionist painters would have found entrancing, are all utterly unforgettable.

The Serengeti has four major areas, the plains of the south east, the central savannah, the bush of the northern section and the mixed country of the western corridor. Within these major sections are many smaller areas of different types of habitat including riverine vegetation, swamps, alkaline lakes, freshwater dams and the prominent rock outcrops known as kopjes.

There are two important sub-divisions of the vast plains in the south east Serengeti. The short grass plains are in the extreme south and east of the park and continue into the adjacent Ngorongoro Conservation Unit. To the north and west of them are the long grass plains. On the long grass plains the grasses reach heights of two to four feet but the short grass is usually less than a foot high even if it is not grazed. The boundary between the two is roughly in the region of Naabi, the prominent hill where the southern gate of the Serengeti is situated. Both short and long grass plains are green and provide first class grazing from mid-November to mid-May when there is sufficient rainfall. The short grass seems to be particularly attractive to the animals and fantastic numbers are to be found on the plains in the wet months: smaller numbers are in the less attractive long grass area. The two together contain at this time about 350,000 wildebeest, 180,000 zebra, over half a million Thomson's and Grant's gazelles, smaller numbers of other antelopes such as topi and kongoni and a large following of predators, lion, cheetah, hunting dog, hyaena and jackal, which make an easy living from the vast herds.

But at the onset of the dry season in May the short grass withers completely. There is no permanent water available and so most of the wildebeest and zebra which must drink very regularly move off to the northern and western sections of the park. The predators leave too and soon the short grass area is almost totally devoid of animal life. The visitor entering the southern Serengeti during the dry season should not therefore be surprised that this famous game sanctuary is apparently empty of animals. The long grass does not wither so totally and within its area there are a few poor sources of water. In consequence, some of the drought-resistant species such as kongoni, topi and Grant's gazelle may be seen in the long grass area even at the peak of the dry season.

Notable features of much of the Serengeti but particularly conspicuous in the wide open plains are the kopjes. These are hard outcrops of rock which have resisted the steady erosion of the plateau and which over millions of years have come to stand clearly above the level of the surrounding country. The rocks have been split and broken by weathering and form many fantastic shapes. The kopjes provide a slightly cooler and sometimes slightly damper environment than the surrounding country and different plants and a few shrubs are enabled to grow there. Rock hyraxes and dik-diks are usually found around the kopjes. The rock crevices are a favourite haunt of snakes.

Towards the centre of the park at Seronera, the long grass plains become much broken up by acacia woodland along the numerous seasonal watercourses and beyond Seronera they merge into savannah country with scattered trees. At all times of the year the Seronera area is splendid country for seeing the big cats, lion, leopard and cheetah. Seronera is famous for its large prides of magnificently maned lions. At least one family of cheetahs is usually to be observed on the plain near the airstrip. The river beds, especially that of the Wandamu River, provide outstanding opportunities for seeing in daylight that most difficult of the major predators, the leopard. The leopards here have become fairly used to vehicles and normally allow themselves to be photographed without fleeing into the undergrowth. Seronera is also a good place to see hyaenas and jackals: silver backed and side striped jackals are fairly common and the golden jackal is occasionally seen.

Seronera is the most developed area in the park with the Park Headquarters, a museum, two lodges, camp sites and the Serengeti Research Institute which attracts scientists from all over the world. The SRI as it is often called is perhaps the most important single game research station anywhere and is continually providing interesting new information about the habits of animals and their interaction with the environment. Banagi, at the foot of a hill eleven miles north of Seronera, was the original Park Headquarters and still has some scientists' houses.

Not far from Banagi at the junction of the Orangi and Seronera Rivers are some fine hippo pools.

The western corridor of the park extends from the Banagi-Seronera region to within five miles of Lake Victoria. It contains extensive ranges of hills, a substantial permanent river, the Grumeti, and a varied range of habitats. The western end of the corridor consists of black cotton plains which are a misery to drive through during the wet season. The rare and beautiful roan antelope is found in small numbers in the corridor and several varieties of monkey are common in the forest sections. There are some exceptionally large crocodiles in the river.

The section of the park from Banagi northwards is much more densely wooded than further south. There are also some stretches of open plain and savannah and some fine ranges of hills. The northern section contains permanent water in the Mara and its tributaries and in the headwaters of the Grumeti.

The dominant animals in the Serengeti are undoubtedly the vast herds of wildebeest and zebra. Their seasonal migrations over great distances provide much of the Serengeti's extraordinary interest. The migrations are relatively easy to understand once it is appreciated that the short grass which springs up in the south east in the wetter half of the year is particularly attractive, but that the area where it grows is totally waterless during the dry season. Permanent water but much less attractive grazing is to be found in the Mara and Grumeti and their tributaries in the northern and western sections of the park. So the animals spend from December to May in the short grass areas and from June to November in the north and west. In November and December they trek south while in May and June they go north again. The most spectacular scenes are usually sometime in May when the short grass is withering and the wildebeest form up into immense columns of tens of thousands of animals. All around are large numbers of predators, lion, cheetah, hyaena, jackal and hunting dogs, just waiting for the weak or unwary to fall by the wayside. This is one of the few times and places when and where visitors can be reasonably sure of seeing hunting dogs, elusive animals which normally roam widely.

Most of the wildebeest young are born in the short grass area in January and it is then that the smaller predators, the hyaenas and jackals have a wonderful time feeding on infants which die and on the afterbirths. Four months later when the migration begins the young animals are remarkably strong although inevitably a few weaklings fall. Rutting takes place in May just before and during the migration. Male wildebeest set up territories based on a stamping ground where the bull paws the earth and does his best to look impressive while he gathers around him a harem which he hopes to serve. The whole process is incredibly complex and bewildering to the observer and, judging from their behaviour, one suspects to the wildebeest themselves. The territories and the harems are in a constant state of flux as the herds move irregularly on. The whole incredible performance is a sight not to be missed.

There are three main routes into the Serengeti. From the north there is a good road from Keekorok in Kenya's Masai Mara Reserve which enters the Serengeti at the Klein's Camp Gate. From the south there is a much used but rough and dusty road from Ngorongoro: this enters through the short grass plains and the barrier is on Naabi Hill which can be seen for miles around. From the west a road from Mwanza enters via the Ndabaka Gate but this is difficult to use in the wet season because of the black cotton soil. In addition there are a number of minor roads. One from Loliondo enters the east side of the park and another from Musoma enters the eastern end of the corridor north of Banagi: this road passes near Ikoma Fort, an old German administrative centre which was the scene of a battle in the first world war. The Fort is now being turned into a lodge. A third road heads south west from Seronera to the Shinyanga district where Tanzania's diamonds are found.

The three main roads meet in the Seronera – Banagi area and it is here that the system of game viewing tracks is best developed. These are so complex that as usual you will waste less time and see more if you take a guide. Another extensive system of tracks is now being opened up in the Lobo area in the north of the park: these promise to provide first class game watching especially in the dry season. The Lobo area is the place par excellence for watching buffalo for the herds there are often over one thousand animals strong.

At present there are three main places to stay in the Serengeti:

1. Seronera Lodge. This is the oldest established of the three and consists mainly of a tented camp, all the tents having their own washing facilities and being shaded from the sun by makuti shelters. The lodge gives the visitor a taste of what a full scale luxury hunting safari is like. Animals are all around and buffalo and gazelles frequently wander

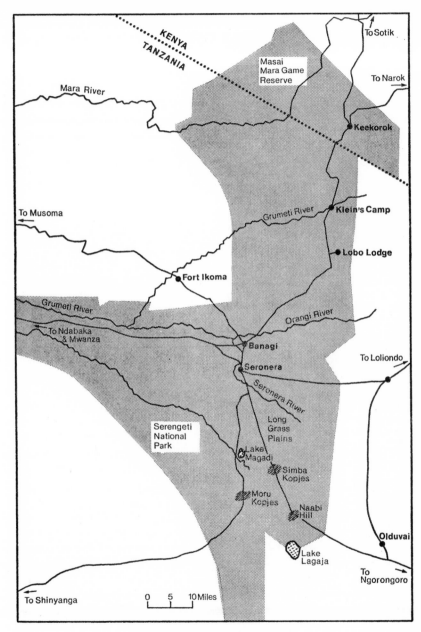

Mara Game Reserve and the Serengeti.

through the camp. Lion are not rare visitors and when I was there last a cheetah made a kill on the short cut grass immediately in front of the tents. The Lodge is also an excellent place for birds. Perhaps the most conspicuous are the starlings, superb, Hildebrandt's and Ruppell's long-tailed. Hildebrandt's is very similar to the superb starlings but lacks the white chest band of the latter. Perhaps the most remarkable birds around the Lodge are the d'Arnaud's barbets which are likely to wake you in the morning with their loud rattling call as male and female sit in a tree displaying to one another. They are green, speckled, starling-sized birds with a reddish patch at the base of the tail. They are unique in that they nest at the bottom of a vertical tunnel two to three feet deep which they excavate themselves. You may be startled to find a bird suddenly flying up from its hole between your feet.

2. *Seronera Wildlife Lodge.* This new luxury hotel promises to be a splendid addition to the accommodation available in the Serengeti. It should prove very popular.

3. *Lobo Wildlife Lodge.* This is perhaps the most remarkable hotel in East Africa for several reasons. First is its superb site right on top of a large hill commanding extensive views over the plains. Second is its architecture: it has been built in and around the jumble of vast rocks on top of the hill. You drive into it through a Petra-like cleft and are likely to spend your first hour or so there wandering through the building marvelling at the brilliant way in which the natural rock formations have been incorporated into the main rooms of the hotel. This is the only game lodge in East Africa which it is worth travelling a long way to see for its architecture alone. Third is the food and superb service provided by the most cheerful and friendly staff I have come across anywhere. Fourth is the fact that all this is deposited in the heart of some of the remotest big game country in Africa with a rapidly developing and extensive system of viewing tracks. Lobo, opened in 1970, is a venture which deserves to be outstandingly successful.

There are several camping sites in the park. The best developed are at Seronera about two miles from the lodge. These sites are often exceedingly exciting as they are a favourite haunt of lions. There is another site at Klein's Camp at the northern end of the park. Camp sites should be booked in advance through the Head Office of the Tanzania National Parks at Arusha. At Ndabaka Gate are two self-service rondavels, primarily for the use of those who arrive at the gate too late to reach Seronera the same day. At Seronera Lodge a few rooms are available for local residents to use on a self-service basis. Drinking water for self-service and camping accommodation is not available except at Seronera Lodge.

A new and luxurious hotel is being built on the basis of the old ruined German Fort Ikoma. The setting is dramatic and although just outside the Park itself, it offers a new base for exploring the Serengeti.

TARANGIRE NATIONAL PARK

This new and as yet virtually undeveloped park promises to be one of the best in Tanzania. It is on the east side of the Great North Road about eighty miles south from Arusha. It is predominantly dry country but it has permanent water in the Tarangire River and so during the rainless months attracts vast numbers of animals from the adjacent Masai Steppe. It is a first class place for observing rhino, lesser kudu, gerenuk and oryx. A tented camp operated by Tanzania's Wildlife Safaris is now open. Those interested in seeing what a National Park area is like when it is more or less in its original state should take the opportunity of visiting this new sanctuary.

❀ 9 ❀

Nairobi and Kenya East of the Rift

Compared to the coastal towns, Nairobi has existed but for a brief moment yet already it is one of the most important cities on the continent. To most visitors Nairobi is a surprise, a busy metropolis full of sophisticated shops, first class hotels and soaring new buildings, set down in the heart of Africa. It is also a delight, a city of flowers, with bougainvillaea, golden shower, oleanders and many others blooming everywhere.

As mentioned in chapter 5, the siting of the city was largely pure accident. A party of Royal Engineers under Captain Sclater were driving a rough road through towards Uganda. As a depot for this road, a Sergeant Ellis chose Nairobi, probably because of its permanent water supply in the Nairobi River and the apparent absence of indigenous inhabitants in a region which was on the boundary between Masai and Kikuyu land. When the railway arrived, a depot was required from which an assault could be made on the very difficult terrain of the Highlands and Rift Valley. Ellis's depot with its water and flat plains suitable for the construction of marshalling yards seemed ideal. Thus was Nairobi born. Appropriately enough the line of the track which Sclater drove through is still known as Sclater's Road, while the Sergeant is remembered in Sergeant Ellis Avenue, an important road in the centre of the city.

Once the railway had decided on its depot, events moved more quickly than anyone had planned. In no time at all there was a settlement of two thousand camp followers living near the railway. Despite the vast wide open spaces all round, as so often shanties were built hopelessly crowded together and very quickly a typical slum developed. In 1901 plague broke out. Colonel Patterson, the Railway Administrator, was a man of action rather than words: he gave the inhabitants of the bazaar one hour to clear out and burned the place to the ground. Plague broke out again in 1904 and it became clearly apparent that the Nairobi River was totally inadequate to supply the water needs of the rapidly growing population. At this time there was much talk of moving the city to a better and higher site, perhaps near Limuru, where both water supply and climate would be better and where much of the city would not be standing on the glutinous black cotton soil which is such torture during the rainy season. But the problems of moving proved insurmountable and in 1907 the Government recognised the *fait accompli* and moved the capital from Mombasa. Since then the city has grown at an ever increasing rate until now it is a thriving place with over half a million inhabitants.

Nairobi is a fairly easy city in which to find one's bearings if one remembers that the most important areas are arranged around the cross formed by Uhuru Highway and Kenyatta Avenue. Uhuru Highway is a six-lane dual carriageway running approximately in a north-south direction. West of it is a primarily residential area with hospitals, schools, churches and the President's official home, State House. Immediately to the east of the Highway are the shopping and industrial areas, the National Assembly (Parliament) buildings and most of the Government offices. Kenyatta Avenue crosses the centre of Uhuru Highway at right angles. East of Uhuru Highway, Kenyatta Avenue is Nairobi's premier shopping street while west of the Highway it rises up the hill to the Anglican Cathedral, various other churches, the Panafric Hotel and the State House. Most of the important streets run parallel either to Kenyatta Avenue or Uhuru Highway.

SHOPPING IN NAIROBI

Nairobi is a paradise for shoppers whether they are interested in ordinary curios, in rare and excellent examples of traditional or modern African art, in items from the Middle East, Persia, Pakistan or India brought here by the dhows, or in the most sophisticated western goods. Almost all the shops of interest to the visitor lie within a quite small area bounded by Koinange Street to the west, University Way to the north, Government Road to the east and Queensway to the south. Most of the exclusive shops tend to be in Kenyatta Avenue, Kimathi

Street, Standard Street, York Street, or Queensway. There are innumerable curio stores selling carvings, skins, spears, clothing, baskets, beadwork and a myriad other examples of African handicraft, and it would be invidious to mention any individual ones. The market in Muindi Mbingu Street contains a high concentration of curio stalls while Bazaar Street is perhaps the best place to buy clothing and goods from the East. One place where high quality goods are on sale and which is often missed by the tourist is the shop of the Maendeleo wa Wanawake, the national women's organisation. This is at the Uhuru Highway end of Kenyatta Avenue, directly opposite the main post office. Those who want to obtain really high quality and therefore expensive examples of traditional or modern African art should try one of the galleries listed in the Useful Information section.

Perhaps the items most sought after by visitors are the following:

1. Carvings in wood, particularly of animals, made primarily by craftsmen of the Kamba tribe.

2. Makonde ebony carvings from the Tanzanian coast. These, although truly traditional are remarkably 'modern' in the western sense. Many of them consist of intertwined groups of human figures with distorted features. Some are truly abstract and almost all show a high level of artistic ability. They are very much in demand and good examples are expensive.

3. Kisii carvings from Western Kenya. These are of many varieties but there are two specialities, stools carved from a single piece of wood and decorated with beads, and soapstone vases and animals. Soapstone is very soft, pale in colour and workable with a knife. It produces a very smooth surface.

4. Beadwork, particularly from Masai and Kikuyu areas. Favourite articles are tough and durable table mats and pendants, both backed with leather.

5. Gourds are fruits found in many shapes and sizes, some rounded, others long and thin. They are a natural form of 'pottery' and are used for many different purposes. They may be bought plain or decorated with beadwork and scorch marks.

6. Jewellery, bags and other articles made from game trophies. These are very plentiful. It is important to know that when you buy one of these articles you should be given an export licence which will indicate that you have purchased the goods from a recognised trader. The sale

of game trophies is very carefully controlled in order to ensure that the wild life is not over-exploited.

7. Clothing and other articles made from cloth. Many very colourful patterned materials are available made up into many different sorts of clothing. Very high quality batiks with African motifs are now made in Kenya. This ancient art of printing cloth by waxing the parts of the material which are not to be coloured came originally from Java. Tie and dye materials are also locally made and rapidly increasing in popularity.

8. Arab chests. These come from the coast and good examples are very expensive. Quite a small one may cost twenty pounds or more.

9. Persian carpets brought in by the dhows. These too are expensive but often are of very high quality. However it is not advisable to buy one unless you know something about them yourself or are advised by a friend who is an expert.

There are of course innumerable other items which you can buy but those just listed are the most popular. In most of the curio shops prices are not fixed and a little bargaining is part of the game. Even in shops where price labels are attached to goods it is often possible to obtain a good discount simply by asking for it. Nothing brings the price down faster than walking towards the door!

NATIONAL MUSEUM AND SNAKE PARK

The National Museum is one of the best organised and most attractive in the world and many visitors are surprised by its sophistication. The most important collections to be seen are the animals in the main hall, the birds in the Gandhi Room, Joy Adamson's superb collection of original paintings of African heads, a display of traditional tribal goods, and a room showing the finds which have been made in East Africa which illuminate the earliest history of mankind.

The Snake Park, just opposite the museum has a good collection of snakes and reptiles. Every Wednesday at about 5.30 p.m. the snakes are milked for their venom which is then used for the manufacture of antiserum. Visitors are welcome to watch this fascinating procedure.

The Museum and Snake Park are both to be found at the north end of Nairobi's central area, just off Ainsworth Hill.

RELIGIOUS BUILDINGS

These are to be found in abundance in this tolerant city which has welcomed people of all religions. Perhaps the most striking are the following:

1. The domed Jamia Mosque in Portal Street, the centre for Sunni Muslims.

2. The Khoja Mosque in Government Road, the centre for Ismaili Muslims. Visitors are welcome at both mosques but must remove their shoes at the door.

3. The Sikh Temple just off Duke Street.

4. The new and very striking Roman Catholic Cathedral at the west end of Sergeant Ellis Avenue. It is largely constructed of reinforced concrete and has some fine stained glass.

5. All Saints Cathedral of the Highlands, the old Anglican Cathedral just off Kenyatta Avenue on the west side of Uhuru Highway.

6. The Synagogue at the junction of University Way and Uhuru Highway.

7. The Presbyterian Church, a modern glass-walled building, at the end of University Way west of Uhuru Highway.

8. A number of churches on the hilly part of Kenyatta Avenue west of Uhuru Highway and including Greek Orthodox and Pentecostal.

GOVERNMENT BUILDINGS

Nairobi has many fine local and central Government buildings most of which have sprung up in very recent years. The most important and interesting are the following:

1. Parliament Buildings. These were started in 1954 and completed in 1965. They are architecturally interesting, decorated with many examples of African art and surrounded by attractive gardens. Tours can be arranged when the National Assembly is not in session by contacting the Sergeant at Arms (telephone 21291, ext. 256). Perhaps the highlight of the tour is the magnificent view of Nairobi from the top of the twelve-storey tower. While Parliament is in session debates can be heard from the Public Gallery by applying at the Harambee Avenue entrance.

2. City Hall. This lies between Queensway and Sergeant Ellis Avenue west of Wabera Street. It is a large complex of buildings containing

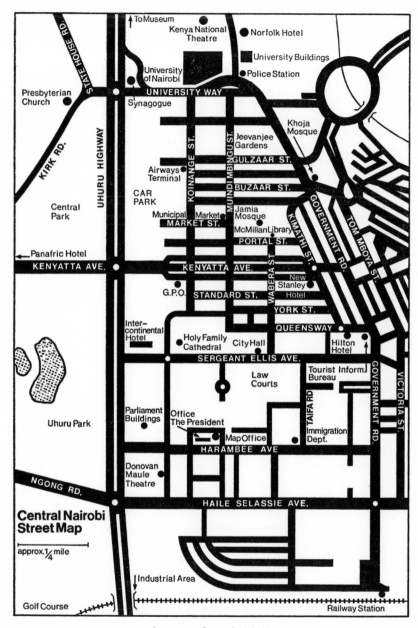

*Street map of **central** Nairobi.*

most of the city offices. It also has halls for public use which are often employed as conference centres. There is a pleasant open air restaruant where one can be refreshed while sitting in cool shade. A tour of the Hall can be arranged by contacting the Public Relations Officer.

3. The Law Courts. These impressive neo-classical buildings stand in City Square immediately south of Sergeant Ellis Avenue.

4. Harambee Avenue. Many of the major Civil Service offices are in this fine thoroughfare. They include the Office of the President and the Immigration Department.

EDUCATION

The most important single educational institution in Nairobi is the University of Nairobi at present catering for about 2,500 students but expanding all the time. Until 1970, the University College was a constituent college of the University of East Africa which included Makerere College, Uganda and University College, Dar es Salaam. In that year, three separate national universities were formed. The main campus of the University of Nairobi is immediately north of University Way and consists of an attractive building complex with some fine modern pieces of sculpture: the whole area is beautifully decorated with flowers and shrubs. Other important parts of the University are the Veterinary School at Kabete, the Medical School at Kenyatta National Hospital on top of Nairobi Hill and the Biological Sciences Complex off Riverside Drive at Chiromo. The playing fields and hostels are immediately west of the north end of Uhuru Highway.

Nairobi has many excellent schools far too numerous to mention. Other educational establishments which visitors may note are the Kenya Institute of Administration at Kabete, the Kenya School of Law on Girouard Road, the Kenya Science Teachers' College on Ngong Road near Dagoretti Corner, Strathmore College on St. Austin's Road and Kenyatta College out on the Thika Road. The impressive buildings of the Science Teachers' College were donated by Sweden in an attempt to ease the severe shortage of science teachers in the country. Kenyatta College and Strathmore College are both boarding establishments where the best school students from all over Kenya can come to complete their education under first class conditions.

LIBRARIES AND CULTURE

The most important library open to the public is the McMillan Memorial Library in Portal Street. As well as a lending section it has a superb collection of books and journals relating to Africa. Another library with a rapidly expanding African books section is the one at the University of Nairobi. This is not normally open to the public but scholars seeking a particular work can usually obtain permission to consult books from the Librarian. The National Museum has a good selection of books on African natural history which may be consulted after enquiring at the office. A list of other libraries in Nairobi is to be found in the Useful Information section.

Nairobi is fortunate in having two theatres. The National Theatre in College Road is primarily used by amateur groups and also for concerts. The Donovan Maule is a small professional repertory theatre with a pleasant and cosy building, a club and social centre and a high reputation: it is a club with a very reasonable day membership fee. The Kenya Cultural Centre opposite the Norfolk Hotel also has a little theatre where plays, puppet shows and other performances are put on from time to time.

PARKS AND GARDENS

Nairobi is fortunate in its Parks Directors and particularly in having for so long retained the services of Mr Greensmith who was largely responsible for the attractive appearance of Uhuru Highway and many of Nairobi's other public places. The main open spaces are:

1. Central Park between Uhuru Highway and Kirk Road north of Kenyatta Avenue.

2. Uhuru Park between Uhuru Highway and Cathedral Road south of Kenyatta Avenue. This contains a car park, lakes and a reviewing stand where most of Kenya's important public open air ceremonies take place. The hill in Uhuru Park is an excellent place from which to take a panoramic photograph of the city.

3. City Square. This is the region between Sergeant Ellis and Harambee Avenues. It contains the Law Courts.

4. Jeevanjee Gardens. A small restful oasis between the bustle of Muindi Mbingu Street and Government Road.

I

5. City Park. This is in the suburb of Parklands, just over two miles from the city centre along the Limuru Road. Much of the Park has not been touched and gives a good impression of what the area must have been like before Nairobi was founded. Its wildness even today is shown by the fact that in 1970 a passing motorist was astonished when he killed a full grown leopard which bounded out of the trees in front of his car. Boscowen House inside the park contains a comprehensive collection of exotic plants. The City Nurseries, noted for their unrivalled collection of varieties of bougainvillea can be visited by prior arrangement made by ringing 55371.

6. Jex Blake Memorial Gardens. This attractive hilly little garden on the south side of the Ngong Road as it goes up Nairobi Hill commemorates a woman who introduced many of the exotic and colourful plants which now grace Kenya.

7. Ainsworth and War Memorial Gardens. This peaceful little spot between the National Museum and Uhuru Highway is always well worth a visit because of the multitude of flowers which always seem to be in bloom.

8. Uhuru Highway. The verges and roundabouts of this major traffic artery form a park of their own as they display to the passer-by many of Kenya's most attractive flowers and shrubs. The Highway is particularly attractive in October when the jacaranda trees are in full bloom.

9. The Arboretum. This relatively little known area is one of Nairobi's great heritages. It consists of about eighty acres of beautifully laid out woodland, gardens and shrubberies containing an immense variety of native and foreign trees and plants, almost all of them clearly labelled. It is only about a mile and a half along State House Road from the centre of the city. As well as being of interest to the gardener and botanist the Arboretum is also a delight for the bird watcher. The gardens are particularly colourful on Sunday afternoons when many members of the Asian community, the women in their colourful saris, go there to walk and to picnic.

NAIROBI NATIONAL PARK AND ANIMAL ORPHANAGE

Nairobi is the only city in the world which has a National Game Park within its city boundaries. And although fairly small (44 square miles in extent) it is a real game park where almost all the important game animals of East Africa (the major exception being the elephant) may be seen. Contrary to common belief the animals are not fenced in. There are fences along the roads to protect both animals and passing motorists but the whole southern border is entirely open. The Park itself is fully described in the Game Park section of the book. Many tour organisations run half day trips from Nairobi to the Park.

The Animal Orphanage is found by the Main Entrance to the Park along the Langata Road. It is a great favourite with the children of Nairobi residents. It contains animals from all over Kenya which have lost their parents or which have been found ill or abandoned. It also has a collection of adult animals, many of which were kept as pets by Kenya residents until they grew too big or until their owners left the country. Feeding time for the carnivores is usually about 4 p.m. On Sundays visitors can buy a can of food for the animals but otherwise feeding them is forbidden. Perhaps the favourite animal in the Orphanage is Sebastian the chimpanzee who is always ready to perform some trick such as smoking a cigarette.

SPORT

Facilities for almost every kind of sport can be found in Nairobi. Golf, riding, sailing, swimming, motor racing and small plane flying are all very popular. Addresses and telephone numbers are given in the Useful Information section.

EXCURSIONS FROM NAIROBI

The excursions described in this section can almost all be done in a single day from Nairobi. Most can be done reasonably comfortably in this time but others like the ones to Nanyuki and the north side of Mount Kenya would be very exhausting if done in such a hurry and it would be better to spend at least one night somewhere *en route*.

Ngong Hills

The return trip is about 35 miles. The walk has been described in the section on mountain walking.

Karen Blixen's Farm

The Danish writer Karen Blixen (Isak Dinesen) lived for many years on a farm in the shadow of the Ngong Hills and the suburb of Karen is named after her. Her book *Out of Africa* about the life on the farm is a classic about Kenya's early period of European settlement. The farmhouse has been opened to the public by courtesy of the Danish Government. Part is a domestic science college but arrangements to see it can be made by telephoning Karen 2366.

Ngong Hills Circular Tour

This is about 50 miles return. For the most part the road is very rough and the trip should not be attempted in the rainy season. During the dry season there is no water at all and it is advisable to take plenty of liquid refreshment. The journey offers some splendid views, a steep drive down to the floor of the Rift Valley and out again and good opportunities to see Masai and game animals outside a game park. Leave Nairobi by the Langata Road and after passing Nairobi Game Park on your left, turn left along the Magadi Road. The tarmac continues for about three miles until it abruptly ends at a gully bottom. The dirt road passes through African shambas and past Kiserian Roman Catholic Mission before climbing on to the southern shoulder of the Ngong Hills where there are magnificent views in all directions. This is a good place to see buffalo, especially in the early morning. The road then bends to the right and in a great semi-circle below the Ngongs it drops down into the Rift Valley. Giraffe are very common here and several Masai villages can be seen. At the small trading post of Olepolos it is possible to buy Masai beadwork, spears and gourds. Here you leave the main Magadi Road, turning right to travel along the bottom of the Hills. Bear right at every junction and eventually after climbing out of the valley at the northern end of the Hills you will be brought back to Ngong Village.

Olorgesaillie

This is about 85 miles return. Olorgesaillie is one of Kenya's less typical National Parks, being one of the prehistoric sites excavated by the Leakeys. The road is very steep in places and very dry and it is imperative to ensure that your car is in good condition. Punctures are not uncommon and it is advisable to carry two spares or an effective puncture repair outfit with adequate tyre levers. The road is a spectacular one dropping in a series of steps towards the floor of the Rift. Game animals and Masai with their cattle, donkeys and goats are usually seen. Elephant have recently appeared in the region in considerable numbers. The track off to Olorgesaillie on the left is very clearly marked by a large notice.

Olorgesaillie is a site which is unique because of the sheer abundance of stone tools found there. During the hand axe period (chapter 3) the valley bottom was filled by a lake which attracted both humans and animals. The animals were mostly of the giant varieties which became extinct fifty thousand years ago or more. Early man may have killed many of them by driving them into swamps at the edge of the lake and then battering them to death. Hand axes and giant animal bones have been found here in abundance but as yet no human bones have come to light. Also found here were several sets of three rounded stones lying close together: these stones were probably originally held together by skin thongs and used to bring animals down in the manner of the South American bolas. Many of the original excavated sites have now been covered by open grass-roofed buildings so that bones and axes may be seen as they were found. One area in particular which may have been a stream bed contains literally hundreds of large hand axes scattered around. A low causeway has been built over this so that visitors can easily see the axes without disturbing them.

Olorgesaillie is extremely hot and it is advisable to make a very early start from Nairobi if you want to see the site in comfort. Alternatively there are very simply furnished self-service bandas which can be booked through the National Parks Department in Nairobi. It then makes a very pleasant trip to leave Nairobi about 4 p.m., spend the night at Olorgesaillie and go round the site first thing in the morning, returning to Nairobi again before it gets too hot.

Minor features of Olorgesaillie which fascinate many people are the large numbers of conical depressions in the sand, each with a little hole at the bottom. These look as though they could have been made by rain drops dripping off a roof but rain is unusual here and the holes are often seen where no such explanation is possible. The pits are in fact built by the larva of the ant lion fly: they are so constructed that unwary ants who come past fall over the edge and into the jaws of the ant lion. The ant lion may be caught by taking a twig and moving it in a circle around the bottom of the hole.

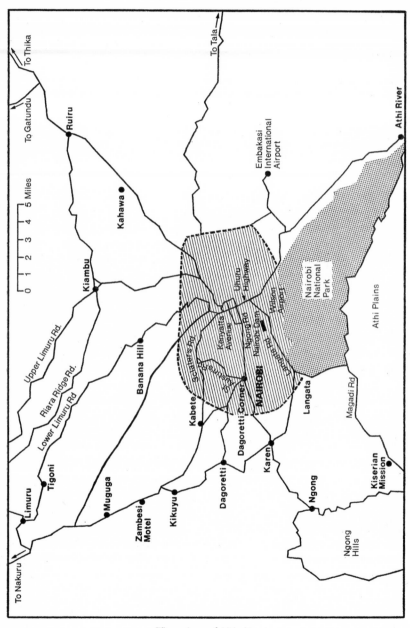

The environs of Nairobi.

Lake Magadi

This is about 170 miles return. Magadi is a 'lake' right at the bottom of the Rift Valley which consists almost entirely of solid and semi-solid soda, giving a vast white mass of pungent-smelling chemical. The soda is a valuable product and is extensively mined. As a result a remarkable town has sprung up on the shore of the lake. This is supplied by an airstrip, a good murram road and a railway whose main function is to take away the soda.

The route to Magadi by road is initially the same as that to Olorgesaillie but instead of turning left at the Prehistoric Site sign one goes straight on. The road is on the whole good but there are occasional fearsome pot holes caused by the intrusion of soft white diatomaceous earth. Not long after Olorgesaillie there is on the left a sandstone gorge at the bottom of which is a muddy stream. This is a favourite watering place for Masai cattle which are brought from miles around, each herd stirring up an enormous dust cloud. The road then continues through inhospitable dry country, descending further and further and becoming hotter and hotter. At last Lake Magadi can be seen and after rounding a corner the road crosses an old part of the lake bed with evaporating pans on either side. It then goes up a steep hill to Magadi Town which to me always conjures up visions of a place which Graham Greene might have used as the setting for one of his novels. At the top of the hill if one turns right and then bears left down the other side of the hill, one reaches the factory and the causeway which goes right across to the other side of the lake. The causeway is worth driving along just to get an impression of what hell must be like. On the other hand if one turns left at the top of the hill the scene is quite different. The road goes along a ridge first passing the flats of the workers and then the houses of the managerial staff and engineers. Finally there is an airstrip and a rather desperate golf course with its 'greens' made of black earth. If one perseveres, the rough road descends again and eventually comes to the best part of Magadi. The southern end of the lake consists of several arms which are supplied by hot springs and which usually have a shallow layer of water in them. This area is the haunt of myriads of flamingos and other water birds which are not shy and which can be seen at very close quarters. Animals such as zebra, giraffe and wildebeeste are common, the latter often wading through the lake itself. This region is about five or six miles south of Magadi Town, but the extra journey is well worthwhile.

Magadi is one of the hotest and driest places in Kenya. It is good to know that ice cold drinks are usually available at the duka. Petrol can also be obtained but it is not unknown for the pump to be dry and so enough for the round trip should be carried.

Lake Natron

This is most definitely not a day trip from Nairobi but it is included here because it is reached by continuing along the road which runs south of Lake Magadi. The track is very little used and two vehicles, preferably both four wheel drive, are essential. It is important to bear left at all the track junctions south of the lake. The route passes alternately through bush and more open savannah country packed with game. This is an excellent area for seeing both gerenuk and oryx. Eventually the track climbs up on to a wide high grassy ridge with a splendid view of Lake Natron and of Ol Doinyo Lengai, the active volcano which dominates the southern end of it. The track then descends to the side of the lake to the site of an old disused magnesite mine which is actually in Tanzania. Beyond the mine the track deteriorates fast but it is still readily discernible until some hot springs about half way along the side of Natron. The springs attract Masai, their cattle, and a magnificent variety of bird life. South of the hot springs the road is barely detectable and becomes more of a cross country route, steering a course between the lakeside marshes on the right and the worst of the volcanic boulders thrown from Mount Gelai on the left. Despite the roughness of the terrain (and despite the instructions given in the Mountain Club guide) this is now probably the best way to approach Lengai from Kenya. South of Lake Natron one reaches a system of vast wide ash rivers coming down from Lengai. During the dry season it is possible to drive across these at high speed. By driving up the westernmost river one can approach the base of the mountain most closely in preparation for a climb.

Kamba Hills

These hills form one of the most beautiful regions in Kenya, yet although they are less than an hour's drive from Nairobi on a good tarmac road they are very rarely visited by visitors or by residents of other parts of Kenya. This is a pity because the scenery is splendid and the people are warm-hearted and friendly.

TOP *Olduvai Gorge in Northern Tanzania, the site of Africa's most famous fossil finds.*

BOTTOM *One of the small but dramatic craters which are a distinctive feature of East Africa.*

TOP *Kilimanjaro from Amboseli with a group of Burchell's (common) zebras in the foreground.*

BOTTOM *The Ngong Hills seen from Nairobi National Park.*

TOP *The mysterious ruins of Gedi, now being rescued from the forest which enveloped them for over three centuries.*

BOTTOM *Olorgesaillie prehistoric site. The 'stones' littering the ground beneath the catwalk are, in fact, hand axes.*

TOP *A golden shower at Keekorok Lodge.*
BOTTOM *The blossoms of a flame tree.*

TOP *Frangipanni at Malindi.*
BOTTOM *The blue jacaranda blossoms which transform Nairobi in October and November.*

TOP LEFT *General view of Nairobi from Uhuru Park.*

TOP RIGHT *Nairobi's colourful indoor market.*

BOTTOM *One of the many fine new buildings that have recently been erected in Nairobi – part of the new University.*

The walls of Fort Jesus, Mombasa. Started in 1593, the Fort saw military activity for almost three hundred years.

TOP *Ol Doinyo Lengai, Tanzania's active volcano to the south of Lake Natron.*

BOTTOM *Typical bush country of East Africa; long grass, trees and distant mountains.*

TOP *The sea front at Lamu.*

BOTTOM *A man working amongst felled mangrove logs at Lamu. Traders come in dhows from South
Arabia to buy them. Note the dug-out canoe in the foreground.*

A typical evening scene on the East African coast.

In order to reach the Kamba Hills take the main Mombasa Road out of Nairobi. After about 30 miles turn left along another tarmac road to Machakos Town, the capital of the region. From Machakos there are innumerable tracks leading up into the hills and in order to make the best of these the 1/250,000 map of the Nairobi region is essential. Those with limited time to spare could take the Kangundo Road northwards out of Machakos. After about two miles a sign on the right points to a Forest Department station: a few miles drive up this track gives a good impression of the region. Those with a full day at their disposal should take the road southwards from Machakos which is signposted Mombasa. After about five miles fork left and go through Makaveti and Kiatineni to Mbooni. From Mbooni you may either return the same way or continue on along a circular route to Utangwa, Kivani, Kola, Mumandu and so back to Machakos.

The Kamba Hills are inhabited by the Kamba people and today form one of Kenya's most important fruit growing areas in spite of the fact that not long ago they were regarded as an agricultural disaster (chapter 4). Their present thriving and beautiful landscape offers considerable hope for the future.

Kiboko (*Hunter's Lodge*)

This is about 100 miles from Nairobi on the main Mombasa Road. The route passes through many different types of country. First, vast sweeping ranches and plains are to be seen. Then the route skirts the Kamba Hills with their closely packed shambas. After Emali it emerges briefly into open plains from which on a clear day Kilimanjaro can be seen and then it enters dry and dense bushland. In this bushland at Kiboko is a beautiful acacia-shaded oasis where a stream has been dammed to form a lake. Beside the lake is Hunter's Lodge a favourite place of refreshment. Boats may be hired for fishing for Tilapia and Barbus on the lake and the good road makes this a perfectly feasible day trip from Nairobi.

Limuru and the Rift Escarpment

This is a favourite afternoon outing for Nairobi residents. Nairobi is left either along the Ngong Road (bearing right at Dagoretti Corner along the Nakuru Road) or along Sclater's Road which can now most easily be reached by going northwards along Uhuru Highway. The two routes come together at the Kabete roundabout near the Veterinary Faculty of the University of Nairobi. From Kabete the road climbs steadily upwards through red-soiled and intensively cultivated Kikuyu country. Maize and pyrethrum are perhaps the most obvious crops although cattle, sheep and goats are everywhere in evidence. All along this road boys and young men are to be seen encouraging the passing motorist to buy sheepskins, mats, stools, fruit, vegetables and baby rabbits. Eventually the road climbs out of the cultivated country and runs through the forest before suddenly and incredibly emerging into open country overlooking the escarpment of the Rift Valley at one of its deepest points. The view, looking along the sharp edge of the escarpment and out to the extinct volcanoes of Suswa and Longonot rising from the valley floor is surely one of the world's finest and cannot adequately be described in words. Scale has recently been added to the view by the construction of a satellite tracking communications station in the valley floor. From the view point the huge white dish looks little bigger than a pin head. There is a place to stop and look right at the top of the escarpment by the roadside. However about half way down on the left a small track leads to a signposted Forest Reserve Picnic Site. The view is still spectacular and away from the rushing traffic on the road one can enjoy it to the full.

The return to Nairobi can be made the same way or by an almost parallel route which gives a quite different impression of Kenya. About four miles from the escarpment edge there is a colourful little market on the east side of the road. From here a tarmac side road goes to Uplands and Limuru. Almost immediately one passes through the little town of Limuru itself and then after a short stretch of small Kikuyu shambas one enters a different world of large farms and estates devoted to dairy farming to tea or to coffee and of immaculately kept and opulent residences. At the appropriately named Banana Hill there are again small shambas. Finally the road goes through some of Nairobi's richer suburbs before entering the city itself. In a brief afternoon it is thus possible to see a cross-section of Kenya unparalleled in its variety. Refreshment is available on the way at the Farm Hotel near Limuru or at the Kentmere Club six miles from Nairobi on the Limuru Road.

Longonot

This is the volcano which dominates the view from the top of the Rift

Valley escarpment. From the viewpoint there is a long winding descent to the dry grassland on the Rift floor. Here there are many thorn trees and euphorbias. Euphorbias are the trees which look a little like giant cacti: they have no leaves and are very resistant to dry conditions. Near the bottom of the valley is a small chapel built by Italian prisoners of war while they were working on the construction of the road. After reaching the valley bottom there is a long, gradual climb towards the shoulder of Longonot with the new satellite communications station clearly visible on the west side of the road. Full instructions for climbing the mountain are given in the mountaineering section. The climb is in fact very easy and involves no rock work.

Naivasha and Hell's Gate

The road described in the previous section continues over the shoulder of Longonot. On reaching the highest point of the road it is possible in the distance to see Lake Naivasha surrounded by hills. The tarmac road to the lakeside turns off to the west just before the main road reaches Naivasha town. Off this road are several clubs and marinas, a hotel and various farms offering camping and mooring facilities. All these places have boats for hire although the Lake Hotel is perhaps the best organised for the casual visitor.

The lake itself is extremely beautiful and is a paradise for the bird watcher, fisherman, yachtsman or motor boat enthusiast. Crescent Island which encloses a stretch of water opposite the Lake Hotel is particularly attractive. Both bird watcher and fisherman will find it profitable to drift slowly along the edge of the reeds and papyrus by the island shore. The lake level fluctuates considerably. The water has risen many feet in recent years hence the drowned and dead trees on which the pelicans perch. Many of the recently flooded areas are shallow and support a profuse growth of magnificent blue water lilies and papyrus fronds. The shallow waters also conceal a number of dangerous underwater obstacles such as fencing posts. Anyone who goes out in a motor boat, particularly one with a fibre glass hull, should first seek local advice as to which parts of the lake should be avoided.

The tarmac on the lake shore road ends after a few miles but a perfectly reasonable dirt road continues right around the lake, returning to the main Nairobi-Nakuru road on the north side of Naivasha town. The town itself is quite small. There is a good hotel, the Bell, with an excellent line in sandwiches and snacks. Just on the Nairobi side of the town is a splendid grove of yellow barked acacias or 'fever trees'.

Hell's Gate may be reached from the lakeside road. About nine miles after leaving the main Nairobi-Nakuru road there is a small crudely signposted track off to the left. During the wet season ordinary cars should not attempt this route. Soon the track passes between high cliffs which are the haunts of many different types of birds and an isolated conical rock known as Fisher's Tower comes into view. Unless you want to look at the tower itself, bear right when the track forks. The road continues for several miles along a flat open valley between towering rock walls and then enters scrub woodland where it becomes very narrow and deeply rutted. Eventually it terminates at a tiny clearing where there are excellent views down into Hell's Gate Gorge. A footpath leads down into the gorge to a place where there are some hot springs.

Hell's Gate may also be approached from the other end. After descending the escarpment on the road from Nairobi but before rising up towards Longonot turn west along the Narok Road. About fifteen miles from the junction on the north side of the road there is a signposted track to Akila Ranch. The bottom end of Hell's Gate Gorge may be approached this way. The track runs through private land and it is essential before proceeding to enquire at the ranch itself.

Kinangop and Sasumua Dam

The Kinangop is a wide plateau above and to the east of Naivasha. It is a huge step on the descent from the summits of the Aberdares to the floor of the Rift. In colonial times it was a stronghold of the European settlers and there were many huge farms. After independence, as a showpiece the large farms were all bought out, split up into smaller units and handed over to landless African farmers. The old farmsteads and the English pub at South Kinangop are now deserted and a quite different but vibrant life rules on the plateau. An interesting tour may be made by taking the road to South Kinangop which leaves the main Nairobi-Nakuru road about a mile and a half north of the Longonot railway crossing. From South Kinangop turn northwards to North Kinangop. From North Kinangop one may either turn west to Naivasha or continue northwards along a track which skirts Kipipiri Mountain and eventually returns to the main road at Gilgil. The road which leads south from South Kinangop cross roads within a couple of miles reaches the huge Sasumua Dam. This is a good place for trout fishing and the major supplier of Nairobi's water. For the intrepid, a little used and poorly surfaced but most beautiful and interesting road runs from South Kinangop over the top of the southern Aberdares and down through Kikuyuland to Gatura Market and Thika.

Thika

Thika is twenty six miles from Nairobi along the main road which heads north eastwards. It is an important industrial centre but is also famous for its sisal estates and pineapple fields. It has been immortalised in Elspeth Huxley's famous book about the early European days *The Flame Trees of Thika*. For the visitor the pleasantest place in Thika is the garden of the Blue Posts Hotel with its view of the Chania Falls, an attractive but not particularly spectacular waterfall.

Ol Doinyo Sabuk (or Sapuk) and Fourteen Falls

Ol Doinyo Sabuk is the whale-backed mountain near Thika which can readily be seen from Nairobi and from the Mombasa Road. Its Masai name means the Big Mountain but in Swahili it is Kilima Mbogo or Buffalo Mountain. The hill is covered with thick forest and is a good place for bird watching. There are buffalo, waterbuck, bushbuck, impala and a few leopards and rhino on Ol Doinyo Sabuk although all are difficult to see. Most people go to the mountain because of its magnificent view and its many pleasant picnic spots.

The mountain is reached by leaving the east side of Thika along the Garissa Road. Almost eight miles past Thika Station is a fork. Take the right branch. After a further five miles or so there is a bridge over the Athi River. Above this bridge are the Fourteen Falls, an attractive sequence of rapids rich in bird life. The Falls are a favourite weekend picnic place for Thika residents. Just after the bridge, the track up Ol Doinyo Sabuk goes off to the right. Because the mountain is now a National Park the track has recently been much improved and it is possible to get right up to the top. There are many attractive picnic sites along the way. About three quarters of the way up the mountain are the graves of Sir Northrup and Lady McMillan and their faithful servant Louise Decker who was with Lady McMillan for seventy five years. Lady McMillan founded the McMillan Library in memory of her husband.

Aberdare Ridges and Valleys

The ridges and valleys of the Aberdares running eastwards from the main range are densely populated, heavily cultivated and both interesting and beautiful. Because the valleys are so steep and their bottoms so rocky, settlements, roads and other contacts tend to be along the ridges. It is the rivers rather than the ridges which separate population groups from one another. Typical scenery may be seen from almost any of the roads which run westwards and upwards into the Aberdares from the main road between Nairobi and Fort Hall. The following three are particularly recommended.

    1. Take the Kiambu Road from Nairobi. From Kiambu take the Upper Limuru Road to Gachocho, Kamondo and Limuru. Return to Nairobi either via Tigoni and Banana Hill or via the main Nakuru-Nairobi Road.

    2. Take the Thika Road to about three miles after Ruiru. There turn left along the tarmac road to Gatundu where President Kenyatta has his private home.

    3. Take the main road to Thika. After crossing the Chania River but before going over the Thika River at the bottom of the hill near the Blue Posts Hotel, take a road on the left to Gatanga and Gatura Market. The road is clearly marked to Kimakia Forest Station. The Forest Station is high on the Aberdares and it is possible to drive right over to South Kinangop and the main Nairobi-Nakuru Road.

    Each of these trips makes a pleasant half day excursion. A full day should be allowed for the drive right over the Aberdares via the Kimakia Forest Station.

Nyeri

Nyeri is just over ninety miles from Nairobi. To reach it continue past Thika on the main road northwards. Throughout the route travels through intensely cultivated Kikuyu country with its steep hills and rushing rivers. If you are lucky the view on the northward trip will be dominated by Mount Kenya but all too often this is hidden by cloud. On the way one passes two important population centres, Fort Hall and Sagana. Fort Hall is the place where the Kikuyu first settled after their wanderings and a roadside sign directs you to 'The Garden of Eden of the Kikuyu'. At Fort Hall there is a church decorated with striking murals showing the work of a black Christ in African surroundings.

They were done by an African artist, Elimo Njau. Sagana has a colourful market and is at an important road junction. Here the main road northwards divides into two, one going west around Mount Kenya via Nyeri and Nanyuki and the other going east via Embu and Meru.

Nyeri itself is a pleasant little town in the Aberdare foothills. It receives regular rainfall and is also well watered by streams and rivers so that it is a lush green all the year round. It is noted for its magnificent eucalyptus trees. There are two good hotels, the White Rhino on the main street and the famous Outspan which is the base for Treetops. The Outspan has a superb view of Mount Kenya from its main public rooms and gardens. In the grounds of the Outspan can be seen the little bungalow where Baden-Powell, the founder of scouting, spent the last few years of his life.

The Aberdare National Park

It is a hard but worthwhile day trip from Nairobi to drive to Nyeri, over the Aberdares through the National Park to Naivasha and back again to the capital. The journey is described under the Aberdare Park in chapter 7.

Nanyuki and the North Side of Mount Kenya

In order to reach Nanyuki one can either go through Nyeri or take the short cut which leads off to the right just before the bridge over the Chania River and about seven miles short of Nyeri itself. Almost immediately north of Nyeri the whole character of the country changes. The road goes across a huge plateau stretching between Mount Kenya and the Aberdares. This clearly receives much less rain than the country through which one has just been passing. Instead of small shambas, this is a land primarily occupied by huge farms which have cattle ranching or wheat as their main source of livelihood. On the Plateau is situated the little township of Naro Moru, an important base for climbing Mount Kenya and the start of the Naro Moru route. Going north from Naro Moru you cross the Equator just before entering Nanyuki, once an important European settler town but now rapidly returning to African ownership. Nanyuki has several good hotels and two safari firms which specialise in the journey up Mount Kenya either on foot or on horseback. The Sportsman's Arms Hotel is the base for Secret Valley, the only place in East Africa where you are virtually guaranteed to see leopards. The Silverbeck Hotel has a famous bar through which the line of the Equator runs. The Mount Kenya Safari Lodge is a luxurious American owned hotel just out of Nanyuki on the slopes of Mount Kenya.

To the west and north of the Naro Moru-Nanyuki road is the vast ranching plateau of Laikipia where the estates may be as large as 100,000 acres. It may be reached by taking the Mweiga Road north from Nyeri or the Ngobit Road west from Naro Moru. The two join about thirteen miles west of Naro Moru. About two miles past Ngobit where there is a trout hatchery and fishing lodge, the road divides, going either north to Rumuruti or west to Thomson's Falls.

Beyond Nanyuki the main road turns towards the east to go around the north side of the mountain. At the time of writing the tarmac is like the curate's egg and eventually peters out altogether but the situation should rapidly improve as a new round-the-mountain road is being constructed. Almost due north of Mount Kenya is another important road junction: here the Ethiopian Highway goes north from Mount Kenya to Isiolo and beyond while the mountain road goes eastwards towards Meru. Scenically this is a splendid part of the world with superb views northwards down to the desert and to the peaks rising from it. Isiolo itself is a fascinating and rapidly growing town, the meeting place of many different ideas and peoples and cultures, of highland and desert, of cattle and camels, and of Bantu, Nilo-Hamite and Hamite. It is well worth a visit.

Embu, Meru and Eastern Mount Kenya

These places are reached by turning east at the Sagana road junction instead of west. Embu (eighty two miles from Nairobi) is a pleasant tree-shaded little town with beautiful rivers nearby and a famous fishing and shooting hotel known appropriately enough as the Izaak Walton. On the plains below Embu is a large irrigation scheme where rice is grown.

Eleven miles past Embu is a road junction where old and new roads diverge. The old road goes to the left and passes Runyenje's, Chuka and Nkubu before joining the new road again just before Meru. It is exceedingly tortuous and four wheel drive vehicles are required if there has been any rain at all. Strong nerves are necessary and the driver is unlikely to see much of the scenery because he dare not take his eyes off the road. The new road which goes lower down the mountain is a little longer, but much faster, much straighter, and much safer but not nearly so interesting or beautiful. Meru on the north east side of the mountain is the capital of the tribe of the same name. It has an informal little hotel and some beautiful gardens flanking a rushing river. The main entrance to Meru National Park is a little over fifty miles away (see chapter 7).

Nakuru

Nakuru is ninety seven miles from Nairobi along a good road and can easily be reached in a day trip. However it is an important centre in its own right and will be described in a chapter of its own.

K

❧ 10 ❧

Nakuru

Nakuru is often known as the farming capital of Kenya. It lies in the heart of some of the country's richest farming areas and is well-equipped to provide all the services which farmers need. Ninety seven miles from Nairobi by rail or by a good tarmac road, Nakuru is the third largest town in Kenya. Like Nairobi, the modern town is of very recent vintage. But quite unlike Nairobi the Nakuru area seems to have been an important population centre for tens of thousands of years and many important prehistoric sites have been located in the vicinity.

The town itself is attractive and distinguished primarily by its wide streets and splendid flowering shrubs and trees, particularly those along the road side as one enters Nakuru from the Nairobi direction. It has a couple of good hotels and shops catering for most tastes. There are two local specialities which may appeal to the visitor. First there are very reasonable yet first class items made from sheepskin and zebra skin which can be obtained from the Nakuru Tanners. Second, there are brilliantly conceived and beautifully made artificial flowers made from flamingo feathers: these are available from the Bethany Bookshop. No flamingos are killed in order that their plumage may be used. All the feathers are discarded ones collected from the lake shore. Nakuru is also a good place to buy Kisii carvings made from soapstone.

The feature of Nakuru which has made it world-famous, however, is its alkaline lake. This receives the River Njoro and a few other small streams but has no outlet. It thus has a high salt content because of the evaporation, making it ideal for the growth of the minute plants known as algae. It is the algae which attract to Nakuru the almost incredible numbers of flamingos which make the lake edge such an awe-inspiring sight. The lake may be seen from the National Park or from the Baharini Wildlife Sanctuary which is currently being developed. The Sanctuary comprises a lodge, strategically placed hides along the lake shore, an educational centre and a research centre. It should be open in the very near future and promises to be a mecca for visiting ornithologists from all over the world as well as being a centre for informing Kenya's own citizens about their unique heritage. Research will also be carried out at the Sanctuary on the problem of Lake Nakuru's future. Many modern chemicals enter the lake in the water running off the surrounding farms. These could affect the algal growth and also enter the flamingos via the algae, possibly interfering with the birds' breeding potential. Work done at the Sanctuary could thus be important in preserving this magnificent place for the enjoyment of future generations.

EXCURSIONS FROM NAKURU

Nakuru is a good centre for the motorist and every road leading from the town is full of delight. All run initially through some of the finest rolling farmland in the world. Particularly worthy of note are the main roads north to Mau Summit and south to Gilgil and Naivasha, the attractive scenery of Turi and of Molo where there is a comfortable and informal country hotel, the road north east to Thomson's Falls, the roads into the high country around Mau Narok, and the road along the Subukia Valley, one of the most idyllic in all Kenya. Specific places of interest include the following:

1. Hyrax Hill Prehistoric Site. The track to this is clearly marked and leaves the east side of the main road just on the Nairobi side of Nakuru. Hyrax Hill is a pleasant grass-covered mound commanding good views of Lake Nakuru and the surrounding countryside. At one time the lake probably lapped the foot of the hill and the mound is full of evidence of what were probably shore settlements including villages, burial sites, and holes in the rock which were used for the very ancient African game of mbau. The whole place has a dreamy atmosphere and it is easy to laze away the whole of a sunny day. There is a small museum on the site and a guide is always ready to take people around.

2. Kariandusi. This is another prehistoric site, this time on the roadside just on the Nakuru side of Gilgil. It too was probably on the shore of what must have been a huge Rift Valley lake. It is open for visitors and there is a small museum.

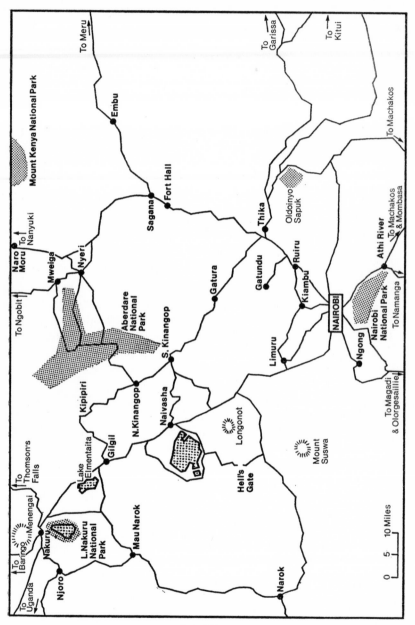

Central Kenya.

3. Gamble's Cave and Njoro River Caves. These prehistoric sites which are not far from Nakuru are not normally open to the public. Those wishing to visit them should enquire at the National Museum in Nairobi.

4. Gilgil. This small farming town between Naivasha and Nakuru was once famous as the headquarters of 'The Happy Valley Crowd'. This was a group of people, mainly of British origin and mostly with more money than sense who settled as 'farmers' in one of the valleys running east from Gilgil. They were famous for their wild orgies and were responsible for the saying, current in Britain at one time, of 'Are you married or do you live in Kenya?'. But all that has now changed. The last of the Crowd left years ago and all the farms have now reverted to African ownership.

5. Elmentaita. This is yet another of the alkaline lakes of the Rift which are haunted by flamingos and myriads of other water birds. It lies west of the road between Gilgil and Nakuru. It is surrounded by farmland and the visitor who wishes to see it at close quarters should enquire locally at the farms or ask the advice of the ornithologists at the National Museum in Nairobi or the Baharini Wildlife Sanctuary in Nakuru.

6. Menengai Crater. Nakuru is built on the outer slopes of this huge mountain whose inner caldera is about seven miles across, thirty five square miles in area and two thousand feet deep. A picnic point on the crater rim is only about six miles from the centre of Nakuru. The well-marked road leaves the main road on the Nairobi side of the town. The picnic point is marked by a crazy signpost which gives the distances to some local landmarks and also to further places such as London, New York and Tokyo. There are magnificent views over the cliffs and it is fascinating to sit and imagine the scene over a hundred years ago. Then in a famous battle the Laikipia clan of the Masai were decimated as their moran were driven by other Masai to their death over these forbidding walls.

7. Thomson's Falls and Rumuruti. Both these are farming townships which were mainly developed during the days of European domination. The farms around Thomson's Falls have now largely reverted to African ownership and few Europeans are to be seen. As its name implies, the town has a splendid waterfall named after one of the early European travellers. There is an attractive Lodge near the waterfall which is in the process of being renovated and enlarged. Unlike Thomson's Falls, Rumuruti remains largely a European centre. The farms there are mainly vast ranches now for the most part owned and operated by Europeans who have thrown in their lot with the new independent Kenya and become citizens. Thomson's Falls is thirty six miles from Nakuru while Rumuruti is twenty one miles further on. *8. Lakes Hannington and Baringo.* These two alkaline lakes lie north of Nakuru in the floor of the Rift Valley. They are both frequented by flamingos but the concentrations to be seen on Hannington are particularly spectacular. Baringo is much the larger and supports an active fishing industry with a small fish processing plant. It has a camping site and a luxury lodge near Kampi ya Samaki. Apart from the flamingos the outstanding features at Hannington are the very hot springs. The road to both lakes leaves Nakuru from the west end of the town on the north side of the railway. It goes to Mogotio and Maragat on its way to Kampi ya Samaki on the Baringo shore. Campers at Baringo should beware of hippos and crocodiles. Just before reaching Mogotio there is a T junction. The main road is the left one to Baringo but the right one is a much rougher though now reasonably well-sign-posted track to Hannington. There is also an extremely rough road between Hannington and Baringo. This should not be attempted by those who do not possess the relevant 1/250,000 map.

❧ 11 ❧

The Kenya Coast

The Kenya Coast is potentially one of the greatest holiday areas in the whole world. Even today it has everything except the most sophisticated varieties of night club entertainment and restaurants. It has a climate which is pleasant and sunny the whole year round, it has mile upon mile upon mile of virtually empty beaches, it has magnificent coral reefs, it has superb deep sea fishing, it has a colourful local culture and finally something which makes it quite unique, within easy reach are some of the greatest big game areas in Africa. In recent years many new hotels with the highest standards have been built and the individual who leaves this coast dissatisfied with his or her holiday must have very unusual tastes indeed.

THE CORAL COAST

The Kenya Coast is sometimes known as the coral coast because of the continuous stretch of coral reef which guards it. The only major breaks in the reef and at the deep water inlets of Mombasa, Mtwapa and Kilifi and the wide sweep of Malindi Bay.

Corals are fascinating creatures which can survive only in waters which are warm all the year round, which are less than about 150 feet deep and which are relatively free from mud and silt. A living coral consists of a vast colony of myriads of minute animals, each of which has built itself a tiny skeleton, usually rich in lime. As old colonies die, new ones are built on top of them outwards and upwards into the sea so that eventually the coast is protected by a mass of dead coral, sometimes over a mile wide. The seaward side of the coral forms a steep cliff and it is a frightening experience for the first time to swim out over the reef.

On the reef itself, even at high tide, the water is only a few feet deep and
the bottom can easily be seen: but suddenly without any warning the
bottom falls away to fifty, a hundred feet or more and one has a sensation almost of vertigo at this sudden vast chasm.

For the most part the living corals are on the seaward side of the reef.
Each tiny coral is a carnivore which feeds on the even more minute
free-swimming animals in the sea. As these food animals are brought
to the coral by currents they are captured by tiny tentacles and
poisoned by tiny stings before being engulfed and devoured. The vast
majority of coral stings are quite unable to penetrate human skin, but
one or two species are capable of stinging like a nettle. The corals
themselves are preyed upon by a large variety of brightly coloured fish
which usually possess special pointed mouths for getting into the crevices.

Even the dead coral is by no means a lifeless mass for it provides
home and shelter for myriads of other creatures which live in its holes
and crevices. Crabs, starfish, sea urchins, fish and many other types
of obscure little animals are all found in profusion. Most are quite
harmless but sea urchins and some of the fish which live in the sand
have sharp spines which may be poisonous and which can cause a
painful and troublesome wound. Therefore, although the risk is slight,
it is sensible to wear light canvas shoes when walking or swimming in
the vicinity of coral reefs.

There are three ways to see the coral. One may walk out on to the
exposed dead reef at low tide, one may travel over the reef in a glass-
bottomed boat and perhaps best of all, one may swim oneself, either
with simple goggles or with underwater breathing apparatus. All the
hotels along the coast will arrange trips in glass-bottomed boats and
give advice about goggling.

THE COUNTRY AND THE PEOPLE

The coast has a warm and sunny climate all the year round. Rain also
occurs all the year round but it is most unusual for it to last for very
long on any particular day. The warmest weather is between December
and March and the coolest between June and September. April, May
and November are the wettest months.

As a result of the warmth and the reliable rainfall, the vegetation is
lush and typically tropical. Many crops, flowers and trees grow in

profusion. The most obvious and best known plant is the coconut palm. This is useful in many ways. First the nuts when green yield a delicious drink which may be served either straight from the nut or with gin, brandy or other form of alcohol: this milk of green coconuts is pure and so close to human plasma (the watery part of human blood) in composition that it makes an excellent fluid to give as a transfusion to seriously ill patients if blood or other more conventional types of fluid replacement are not available. Second, white nutty material inside makes excellent eating, either fresh or grated and dried. Third, the sun-dried white material known as copra is used for making coconut oil. Fourth, the juice of the coconut can be fermented to make potent palm wine. Last of all, the leaves of the coconut tree can be plaited and used for makuti roofing. This is used almost universally for village houses and even for many of the homes of the wealthy. It is cheap, durable, waterproof and, above all, very cool.

The staple foods on the coast are maize, bananas and cassava, the last being a root which is not unlike arrowroot in taste. Bananas were introduced by the Indonesians and maize and cassava by the Portuguese. As far as cash income is concerned, the main crops are coconuts cashew nuts, fruits of many kinds (especially mangoes and paw paws) cotton in the region of Malindi and sisal between Mombasa and Malindi. In some areas, particularly in the north, the coast is fringed by mangrove swamps. Mangroves are a group of plants with tough, waterproof and shiny leaves which have become adapted to a life in sea water, giving the odd picture of a bay full of evergreens growing from the sea. As might be expected, mangrove wood is extremely tough and resistant to rotting. Mangrove poles are widely used for scaffolding and for building the framework of houses. These poles are very much in demand in South Arabia with its severe shortage of wood and they form a major item of cargo for the homeward going dhows. For the same reason, charcoal is an important coastal export.

Many coastal people live by fishing but because of the coral the fish must be caught on hand lines, in small nets or by trapping. Large nets dragged from boats too easily get caught and torn. Some of the small fish caught around the reef are dried in the sun and form a local delicacy. With the development of the holiday trade, new opportunities for fishermen have been opening up. Prawns and lobsters are excellent and are much in demand, while shells, coral and starfish make popular souvenirs. Some of the shells are magnificent but they are not dirt cheap and anything from five to twenty shillings may be asked for a first class large specimen.

Today, as has been true for the past three thousand years or more, trade is the life blood of the coastal town population. Part of this trade is still carried on by the dhows, wooden vessels whose design has not changed significantly for hundreds of years. Each year in late November and December they come to Mombasa from South Arabia, from the Persian Gulf, from Pakistan and from India. They are to be seen in large numbers in the old Dhow Harbour at Mombasa for several months and they return when in May the monsoon winds swing round and start blowing from the south east instead of the north east. Slaves and large amounts of gold are no longer carried but in many respects the trade has not changed a great deal from that of five hundred years ago. Ivory and wood still leave East Africa in exchange for carpets and cloth, fine chests and jewellery. Apart from the dhows the coastal trade has of course changed radically within the past hundred years. Mombasa with its fine deep water berths is the main port for both Kenya and Uganda and most of the exports from and imports to both countries leave or enter via Mombasa.

The people of the coast are more varied than in any other area of Africa. In the area immediately behind the coastal strip itself live the Nyika Bantu tribes of which the Giriama are probably the most numerous and conspicuous. They are famous for their graceful women who perform surprising feats of balance as they carry all sorts of unusual items on their heads. Many of them wear under their skirts and over their bottoms a mass of cloth which gives the impression of an enormous backside: the effect is similar to that of the Victorian bustle. Dancers from the Giriama tribe are well known for their verve and rhythm and they put on regular displays at many of the hotels. Their houses are interesting and well built. There are two main sorts, the basis of both being a framework of mangrove poles. One sort is rather like an upturned boat and is roofed and walled with grass. In the other sort of interstices between the poles are filled with mud or a mixture of mud and coral blocks. The coastal fishermen are also basically Bantu but down the centuries they have hybridised with all the people who have come to the coast to trade.

It is in the towns that the greatest variety of people is seen. There are Africans and Europeans, Swahili and Arabs, and many different peoples from the Indian sub-continent. Some of these Indians have been established on the East African coast for many centuries. For example, when Captain Smee went to Zanzibar in 1811 on behalf of the Government of British India he found that Indian traders were even then the dominant merchant and commercial class in the town. But the Indian population undoubtedly received a great boost in the early days of British rule when so many were brought to work on the railways and in other large commercial enterprises.

The dominant religion on the coast is that of Islam. Arabs and Swahili are Muslims virtually exclusively but the religion also has adherents among most of the other racial groups. Most of the towns and villages still have an active mosque but it is probable that far more are in ruins than are in use, testifying to the fact that the absolute dominance of Islam is a thing of the past. Muslim men typically wear long white robes and a small embroidered or beaded cap. Many women still go outside their homes only in the black veiled garment known here as a buibui. Other garments which originated here have recently become fashionable in other parts of the world. A kikoi is a length of material worn by men: it is wrapped around the waist giving the appearance of a long skirt. Khangas are very colourful pieces of printed material: they wrap around underneath the armpits and fall to mid-calf length. At all the coastal resorts there are shops with wide selections of these colourful materials, now cut and made up into many different garments. They have proved extremely popular with visitors.

MARINE NATIONAL PARKS

These are a unique experiment in conservation, the attempt to preserve for the future some of the very finest stretches of coral in the world. From Vasco da Gama Pillar at Malindi to just south of Mida Creek about twelve miles down the coast is a Marine National Reserve in which it is an offence to spear fish or to collect shells, wildlife or coral from the reef. The Reserve includes Mida Creek, a vast area of mudflats and mangrove swamps which is one of the best places to watch shore birds during the migration season.

Within the Reserve, two of the most beautiful stretches where living coral can be easily seen in sheltered waters have been designated as National Parks. One is at Casuarina Point, three miles south of Malindi, and the other is at Watamu near the southern end of the Reserve. Within the Parks walking along the beach is free but in order to help pay for the experiment those who go out to the reef in glass-bottomed boats or who use goggling equipment have to pay a small fee. This is well worth while for the privilege of gazing at the splendour of the coral with its myriad multi-coloured fish.

SPORT AT THE COAST

The most important sports are undoubtedly swimming, goggling and deep sea fishing. There are two good golf courses in Mombasa and a nine hole one in Malindi. Sailing is available, espeically in Mombasa. A Malindi speciality is riding along the sands which can be arranged by many of the hotels.

MOMBASA

It is the opinion of some that Mombasa is the most interesting town in the whole of East Africa. It certainly has one of the bloodiest histories and much of the tale has been told in chapter 5. Mombasa is an island opposite a break in the coral reef and for the most part surrounded by deep water. Its position made it an ideal site for a trading post, readily accessible by sea and easily defensible from attack by land. As in the past, its life blood today is trade. The traditional dhows still come but now much more important in volume and value are the major exports and imports of Kenya and Uganda. The main items of interest for the visitor are outlined in the following pages. Perhaps the first call should be made to Information Bureau run by the Mombasa and Coast Tourist Association. The Bureau is ready to help with any query or problem and is very easy to find. It is on the Kilindini Road about a hundred yards on the harbour side of the giant elephant tusks which straddle the highway forming the traditional Gateway to East Africa on the main route from the docks to Mombasa Town.

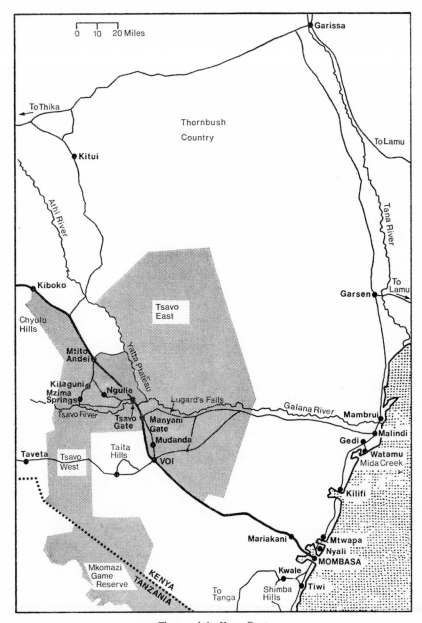

Tsavo and the Kenya Coast.

The Old Town

Situated on the north east corner of the island, this is the original town
of the Arabs and Swahili who have lived in Mombasa for over a thousand
years. Many of the buildings are very old and the narrow streets and
twisting alleys could easily be somewhere in North Africa or the Middle
East. You will undoubtedly be much entertained if you engage one of
the numerous unofficial guides who will offer to take you round but
it is wiser to agree on the cost of his services before the trip rather than
afterwards. There are a number of motor roads through the town but
they are extremely narrow and if you go by car you will undoubtedly
fail to catch the atmosphere of the place. The only way really to see it
is to walk, leaving your car or taxi near Fort Jesus and entering the old
quarter by the street known as Mbarak Hinawy. The Old Town is
very hot in the middle of the day and most of its inhabitants, being
sensible people, are inactive at that time. It is therefore pleasanter and
more interesting to visit the place either early in the morning before
about 10.30 or late in the afternoon after about 4 p.m. Undoubtedly
the best time to see it is between late November and April. Then the
north east monsoon has brought the dhows in laden with chests, carpets
jewellery and other exotic goods. The place really springs to life and the
streets swarm with colourful sailors, coffee sellers and street traders.

Specific places to be seen in the Old Town are the oldest mosque
on Mbarak Hinawy and the warehouses near the Customs House where
carpets and chests may be bought. If you do happen to be in Mombasa
when the dhows are in, moored side by side across the channel, you
should not fail to pay a visit to one. You will have no trouble in finding
someone to take you out to one and you need have no fears about being
robbed or kidnapped. Often the dhow captain, the Nahada, will
welcome you aboard and offer you bitter black coffee while he shows
the wares he has brought. Do not however, imagine that you will be
able to obtain ridiculously cheap carpets or chests and do not under-
estimate the Captain's bargaining ability. Also do not forget to find out
whether the price includes Customs Duty or not and, if it does, whether
you as a visitor may be able to avoid paying it. Whether or not you make
a dream purchase, the visit is something you are unlikely to forget.
During the dhow season you should also ask to be shown the dhow dry
dock at the western end of the Old Harbour. Here these superb boats
may be careened and repaired for their long and hazardous journey home.

FORT JESUS

This massive, obviously ancient, and yet equally obviously European structure is one of Africa's surprises for those who forget how old is the story of contact between Africa and the rest of the world. It lies at the end of Nkrumah Road, just opposite the entrance to the Old Town which it was so clearly built to dominate. Even today it looks virtually impregnable and it is not surprising that during its long history it was taken only when the odds were utterly overwhelming or after dissension and treachery on the part of the defenders within. The Fort was started in 1593. It was part of a determined Portuguese attempt to assert their supremacy following two Turkish raids down the coast which seemed to be potentially threatening. Its architect was Joao Batista Cairato, an Italian. He employed labour from Mombasa's chief rival, Malindi and brought masons from Goa in India. In structure the Fort is basically a rectangle with four protruding bastions at the corners so constructed that every part of the base of the Fort could be swept by defending fire from protected positions. The main entrance is angled behind the north east bastion. At various times three subsidiary entry passages were constructed so that the Fort could be reached via outworks from the seaward side. Fort Jesus is today in a remarkable state of preservation and from the ramparts there are superb views over the sea and the Old Town. Most visitors will probably want just to wander, drinking in the atmosphere and imagining the scenes of long ago. For those who are indefatigable in identifying every stone and room, an excellent little guide book is available at the gate.

The first time the Fort changed hands was in 1631. The Portuguese-educated Sultan Yusuf proved that he was no puppet by personally killing the Captain and organizing a massacre of almost all the Portuguese. However, because of dissension within the Arab ranks the Fort was abandoned and reoccupied without trouble by the Portuguese in 1632. It was held by the Europeans without much difficulty until 13 March 1696 when the rising power of Oman laid siege to it. At the start of the siege there were in Fort Jesus about 50 Portuguese soldiers and about 1,500 loyal Swahili and others. On Christmas day 1696, the defenders were overjoyed to receive reinforcements from Goa. But the relievers brought a kiss of death and doomed the Fort more effectively than any Omani attackers ever could. They carried the germs of plague and within a few months most of the defenders were dead. By the 20 July 1697, there were only four Portuguese and seventy-one Arabs and Swahili left inside, over two thirds of the latter group being women. The Omanis felt that the time was ripe and tried to take it by storm. It speaks much for the design of the Fort that the paltry defending forces were able to hold out successfully against a determined attack. In December 1697, a new garrison of a hundred men arrived to assist the weary defenders. But disastrously the plague had not been eliminated and by the following December only nine Portuguese, three Indians, two African women and an African boy were left. On December 12 1698, thirty-three months after the beginning of the siege, the Fort fell. It was temporarily reoccupied by the Portuguese in 1728 as the result of an inter-Arab quarrel but they capitulated and left again without a struggle in 1729.

In 1741, the Mazrui Governor of Mombasa felt strong enough to declare himself independent of Oman. Five years later he paid the price of his rebellion, being murdered in the Fort by assassins sent by the Sultan. After doing the deed, the assassins, few in number, foolishly sealed off the Fort. The Governor's brother, Ali, who escaped over the wall organised a scaling of the Fort and the assassins were forced to barricade themselves in one of the bastions. Ali could not take this until an English Captain named Cook, came to his aid. Cook, whose ship happened to be taking on provisions and water in the harbour, landed a cannon and obligingly blew a hole in the bastion. The assassins surrendered and were, of course, promply executed. In 1828 the Fort was again occupied by the forces of the Omani Sultan, this time without much resistance. A few months later, the new Governor whom the Omanis left behind was forced to surrender because the Mazrui-dominated town would not supply him with food. He too was conveniently murdered. Finally, again without fighting the Sultan took control in 1837. The last military action was in 1875 when the Commander of the Sultan's forces in the Fort revolted. By this time the Sultan was closely allied to the British who were using their 'friendship' to force him to suppress the slave trade. When two British naval ships bombarded the Fort the rebellion soon collapsed and the bloody episodes of the story of Fort Jesus were at last over.

One of the most interesting features of the Fort as it stands today is the museum, established in 1958 with the aid of a grant from the

Gulbenkian Foundation. It contains an excellent collection of exhibits illustrating the history of Mombasa including some fine Chinese porcelain and many Arab and Indian articles. There are excellent examples of the carved and bossed Arab doors for which the coast is famous and some beautiful models of dhows. There are also three carved wooden Giriama grave memorials.

The walk around the outside of Fort Jesus is well worth doing. The seaward side is especially attractive with its lawns and cannon and frangipanni trees beneath the towering walls.

Religious Buildings

Mombasa abounds in religious buildings of many different varieties, the oldest probably being a small mosque in Mbarak Hinawy Road in the Old Town. Another old mosque, the Wailing Mosque is down Archbishop Makarios Drive. The new Sheikh Jundani Mosque is off Salim Road. There is a new Hindu Temple with a gold top in Jeevanjee Road just off Nkrumah Road, and a new Jain Temple off Salim Road. The Roman Catholic Cathedral is at the corner of Nkrumah Road and Nyerere Avenue while the Anglican Cathedral with its striking silvery dome and gold cross is half way along Nkrumah Road.

The Ivory Room

This lies off Treasury Square behind the National & Grindlays Bank building which is in Mvita Road. Here ivory is collected from all over Kenya and put on display. Fascinating auctions are held in May and December which are obviously the best times to see the room.

Shopping

Mombasa abounds in curio shops where one can buy an abundance of fascinating articles, not only from Africa but also from the Middle East, Persia, Pakistan and India. Perhaps the greatest concentration is to be found at the town end of Kilindini Road and on Salim Road. The stalls in the middle of Salim Road contain an enormous variety of carvings and African goods. The Bazaar in the Old Town is also a good shopping area and is situated east of Salim Road opposite the end of Jomo Kenyatta Avenue. A quite different atmosphere is found in the African Market of Mwembe Tayari a couple of hundred yards down Jomo

L

Kenyatta Avenue from Salim Road: it is an excellent place to buy fruit, vegetables, carvings, kikois and khangas.

Other Places of Interest

Mombasa abounds in fascinating corners just waiting to be discovered by the curious. Apart from those already mentioned, three favourites are the deep water harbour of Kilindini with its many ships of all nations, the residential suburb of Tudor on the north-west coast of the island with its superb houses, colourful gardens and numerous grotesque baobab trees, and Mama Ngina Drive. The last of these has magnificent views over the Indian Ocean and over the narrow channel into Kilindini Harbour where the great ships come and go.

EXCURSIONS FROM MOMBASA ISLAND

The whole of the Kenya coast south of Mombasa and north to Malindi, the Shimba Hills Game Reserve near Kwale and Tsavo National Park, the world's greatest elephant sanctuary, can all be seen in day trips from Mombasa. Several tour organisations specialise in day tours especially to Tsavo. However these attractions are described elsewhere in the book and this section covers a few places of interest which are off Mombasa Island but relatively close to it. There are four dry surface routes off the island. Two, the road and railway to Nairobi, cross the shallow water at the western end. Northwards is the floating toll bridge of Nyali and southwards is the Likoni Ferry where a new fast boat of large capacity has recently come into use.

Freretown

This was founded in the last century by Sir Bartle Frere as a colony for freed slaves and it is still largely occupied by their descendants. It has one of the oldest Christian churches in East Africa built at the end of the nineteenth century. It is reached by going over Nyali Bridge and taking the first turning left (the Malindi Road). After a few hundred yards a track off to the left points to the church.

English Point

This is reached by going over Nyali Bridge and taking the first turning right. It is now dominated by an enormous cement silo but it has

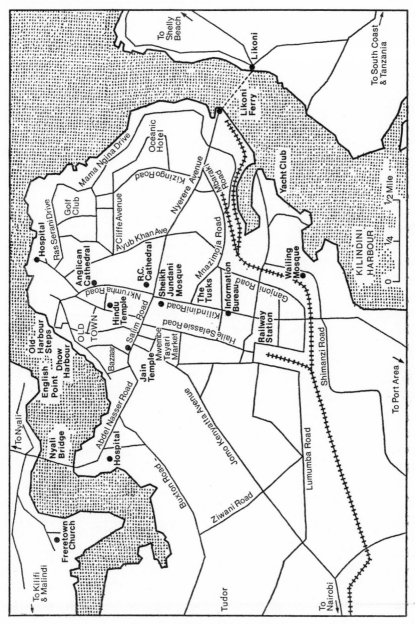

Street map of part of Mombasa Island.

splendid views across to the Old Town, Fort Jesus and the Old Dhow Harbour. On the point is a memorial to Ludwig Krapf, the first Christian missionary to Kenya, the first European to see Mount Kenya and to report its existence to the outside world and the translator of the New Testament into Swahili. Within a few weeks of his arrival both his wife and small daughter died of malaria and their graves are to be found on the Point.

Nyali Estate

This is reached by going across Nyali Bridge and continuing straight on. It is worth driving around simply to look at the magnificent private house and gardens. There is a splendid beach with which the visitor can most easily reach via the two hotels, the Nyali Beach and the Mombasa Beach.

Wakamba Wood Carvers

This association of carvers produces many of the animals for which Kenya is famous. Their workshop may be reached by leaving Mombasa Island along the Nairobi Road and entering Changamwe Township. Turn left along the road to Port Reitz Airport and the Carvers will be found about a hundred yards along on the right hand side.

Mazeras Municipal Gardens and Nurseries

These beautiful gardens are about twelve miles from Mombasa along the Nairobi Road. They supply the flowers and shrubs which make the streets and open spaces of Mombasa so attractive. They are an excellent place to see at close quarters many of the vast number of flowers, shrubs and trees which flourish in Kenya.

The Kaya of the Giriama

Kayas are described at the end of chapter 4. This is perhaps the most accessible but is nevertheless not easy to find. It is reached by driving along the Nairobi Road to Mariakani, twenty-two miles from Mombasa. The Kaya lies along dirt tracks about seven miles north-east of Mariakani. It is advisable to go with one of the local tour organisers and to specify in advance what you want for this is not a routine trip.

MALINDI

Malindi is the perfect place for an away-from-it-all holiday with everything the visitor could conceivably want except for noise, crowds and extreme sophistication. Sunshine, blue skies, warm water, coral reefs, big fish and mile after mile of clean and empty sand are here for everyone's enjoyment.

Unlike many of the other ancient towns along the coast, Malindi has no deep water harbour. It probably owes its foundation to a long break in the coral reef which allows boats to approach close to the shore without danger of being wrecked. Malindi probably had its first small beginnings about 1500 years ago. It increased rapidly in importance between A.D. 1000 and A.D. 1500 and by the time the Portuguese arrived in 1498 it was the major rival to Mombasa. The people of Malindi were the only ones on the coast who truly welcomed the Portuguese for they saw in these Westerners with the highly manoeuvrable boats and powerful cannon a possible ally in their struggle to dominate. But for Malindi and its ruling family, the kiss of Portuguese friendship was in the long term to prove the kiss of death. Initially Malindi and its Sultan did very well. In 1505 the Portuguese defeated Mombasa and although its citizens repeatedly felt strong enough to revolt, for the next ninety years or so Malindi was the most important place on the coast with a thriving commercial life, many mosques and a large number of important buildings. In 1589, the Portuguese, helped by the cannibal Zimba (chapter 5) finally broke Mombasa. The Zimba moved up the coast and were about to fall upon Malindi which unlike Mombasa had no natural defences when quite fortuitously the town was saved: the Zimba cannibals were wiped out by the Bantu Segeju moving down from the north. In 1593 the Portuguese and the Sultan left vulnerable Malindi and made their headquarters at Mombasa with its much better harbour. This effectively ended Malindi's commercial life for most of the trade moved south with the Portuguese. The Sultan did not long survive the move. After protesting against the injustices of Portuguese rule and receiving no satisfactory answer, he fled into the interior and was murdered by tribesmen who had been bribed by the Europeans. The Sultan's son, Yusuf, despite a Portuguese education, also revolted 23 years later. He succeeded in killing virtually all the Portuguese and his revolt was temporarily successful. But he was defeated by dissension within his own ranks and a year later he sailed away to become a rather unsuccessful pirate. Thus ended any direct or indirect connection of Malindi with important events at the coast.

Malindi then seems to have fallen into a profound decay with almost all its fine houses and public buildings vanishing as though they had never been. No doubt their foundations and some of the things which the rulers of Malindi owned are still in the earth awaiting the archaeologist's spade. But now only two obvious structures dating from the period of Malindi's prosperity remain. These are the pillar tombs outside the rebuilt mosque and the Vasco da Gama Pillar on the coral headland which forms the southern border of Malindi Bay. The origins of the pillars are unknown. They have been associated by different workers with the typical obelisks found at Axum, the Ethiopian Empire which flourished 1500 years ago and, perhaps a little more plausibly with the pillars found on the island of Madagascar. They are however decorated with pottery which is indubitably fifteenth century and so the most likely date for their construction is probably around 1400. But their origin is still a mystery which awaits solution. We know much more about the Vasco da Gama Pillar. It is surmounted by a cross made from limestone of a type which can be found near Lisbon. It was originally set up by da Gama outside the Palace of the Sultan but later in the sixteenth century was set on the cone-shaped pillar in the dominating position where it stands today.

In the latter part of the last century Malindi became re-established as a fishing village and since then its importance has again steadily grown. Between the two world wars it began to be visited as a holiday resort and this trade rapidly grew after the second war. Today one suspects, half unhappily, that its natural advantages ensure that it is on the verge of a period of explosive growth.

Malindi Today

Modern Malindi's most important feature is the vast five mile stretch of wide sand which gently curves from the da Gama Pillar to the mouth of the Galana (Sabaki) river in the north. The bay is completely coral free, probably because any that attempts to become established is promptly killed by the very fine sand that is brought down by the Galana River during its periods of heavy flood. This allows the huge Indian Ocean swells to come rolling in with no barrier and forms an ideal beach for surfing, sun-bathing or digging sand castles. The southernmost part of the bay is very sheltered and serves as a harbour for the local fishing boats and also for the modern cruisers which serve the deep sea fishing enthusiast. This is a good place to examine at low tide the construction of the dug out canoes, outriggers, and small dhows. As the tide comes in fishermen may be seen operating in the shallows. The lone ones are probably casting their nets for prawns. Those in groups of three are after fish: two hold out the net while a third tries to drive the fish into it by beating the water with a stick.

Also at the south end of the bay on the roadside away from the sea are the sad and dilapidated ruins of a little church which was probably founded by the Portuguese, thereby becoming the first Christian church in East Africa. All the readable tombstones refer to this century, however and some tell tales which are pathetic in the extreme. Moving north along the sea front one comes to the jetty and the fish market where the monster fish are landed and weighed. On the opposite side of the road to the jetty are the Headquarters of the Marine National Parks and the Malindi Sea Fishing Club. The latter has a magnificent pair of bossed and polished Arab doors. The beach by the jetty is a favourite site for local evening football matches. Also near the jetty in a commanding position on a little hill is the gleaming white rebuilt mosque with the old pillar tombs just in front of it.

In the centre of Malindi, facing the sea and protected by cannon, is a large old house which was the colonial headquarters in the area. It now holds the offices of the Malindi and Mambrui District Council. North of here the coast is largely occupied for a mile or so by hotels and private houses. These back on to Harambee Road which runs parallel to the beach. On Harambee Road are all the more modern shops, safari organisations and curio stores. As well as patronising these, many visitors will enjoy wandering in the narrow streets of the older Arab, Asian and African parts of the town. The African market in particular is full of attractive and exotic local produce and vibrates with life. The people are extremely friendly and seem to enjoy bantering and bargaining with visitors.

Around Vasco da Gama Point the coral starts again and to the south one might almost be in a different world, so different is the coast. The outer reef is about half a mile off shore. It is exposed at low tide and it is well worth paddling out to see the crabs, starfish, fish and other creatures in the pools in the clefts of the coral. The sand here is glistening white – silver on moonlit nights – and the stretch is appropriately enough called Silversands Bay. This area is hardly developed at all commercially and at present most of the buildings facing the sea are private houses. The only places catering specifically for visitors are a delightful tree-shaded camping site and an informal beach club. The silver sand continues in a glorious sweep round to Leopard and Casuarina Points, the latter being the site of one of the new Marine National Parks. Casuarina Point may be reached by going along the coast road from Malindi: the tarmac ends almost immediately the road leaves Malindi Bay.

Things to do in Malindi

The obvious things which almost everyone does are swimming and sunbathing. Malindi Bay itself is enormous fun for surfing and for bathing in the huge breakers. For actual swimming as distinct from playing in the waves, the more sheltered waters of Silversands Bay are better. Horse riding along the Malindi sands can be organised by any of the hotels or touring companies. Low tide, especially when the rise and fall of water is great at the spring tides, is the time to go to Vasco da Gama Point and walk out on to the outer part of the reef. Children of all ages will enjoy messing around in the pools.

No visitor to Malindi should miss seeing the living coral from a glass-bottomed boat. The boat usually goes out to a particularly fine stretch of reef where it anchors. Those who wish to can then go over the side to swim and to observe the fish at even closer quarters. Goggles are usually provided by the boat operator but it is advisable to be sure about this point before you leave.

Deep sea fishing, at its best from October to April is also something that should be tried. No previous experience is needed and paradoxically some of the biggest fish have been taken by total novices. This activity is certainly not cheap and the absolute minimum cost for half a day's fishing is about five pounds per person. Non-residents of Kenya require a five shilling licence. Children (and their parents) can have plenty of fun fishing for smaller fry from the jetty or from the rocks around Vasca da Gama Point. Those with the right equipment may find surf casting rewarding, especially near the estuary of the Galana but local advice should be sought.

Excursions from Malindi

All the coast southwards to Mombasa can be comfortably reached in a single day by car. Perhaps the favourite places are Gedi with its mysterious ruins and Watamu with its white sands and first class coral. To the north the road is not tarmac surfaced. Crossing the River Galana (Sabaki) five miles north of Malindi by the new suspension bridge, one is very much in rural Giriama country with its attractive villages and houses. The village of Mambrui, the beach at Ngomeni, the gorge at Marafa and the town of Garsen can all be reached within the day. It is just possible to visit Lamu by road and return within the day but this is a very tiring trip of three hundred miles or so over not very good roads and is not really recommended. Visitors to Lamu should either go by air, or if they go overland, should spend at least one night on the island

Inland from Malindi there is first of all lush cultivated country and then the dense Arabuko-Sokoke Forest, an excellent place for observing some of Kenya's rarer birds. Only a few years ago an entirely new species, the diminutive Morden's Owlet was discovered here. An interesting circular drive of about thirteen or fourteen miles can be made around some of the Giriama villages the largest of which is Ganda. Still further inland the thick forest gives way to the dry thorn-bush big game country of the Galana Game Scheme and the Tsavo National Park. The Park entrance is only seventy miles away. While Tsavo can relatively easily be visited within the day this is again not particularly recommended as the visitor is then not in the park in the early morning and the evening, the best times for seeing animals. A stay of at least one night at one of the Park camps or lodges is likely to produce a much more satisfactory trip.

Within recent years the air charter firms operating from the excellent modern airstrip at Malindi have opened up vast new areas for the one or two day tripper. Tsavo, Amboseli and Lamu are perhaps the three favourite ones and all provide unforgettable experiences.

THE COAST SOUTH OF MOMBASA

This is reached by the Likoni Ferry from Mombasa. From Likoni a narrow tarmac road runs for about forty miles to Ramisi. The last few miles to Shimoni, the end of the road, are murram. This section of the coast is very heavily populated but the friendly and colourful people only add to and do not detract from the attractiveness of the region. Most live in small villages and cultivate small plots, although there are a few large sugar and coconut plantations. The coastal villages are all very small and very sleepy: most have a few ruins dating from the period of Arab domination but none is in the least bit organised to cater for tourists. Holidays on this part of the coast are very informal and particularly suitable for children. The beaches are very white and all along the coast behind the reef are beautiful sheltered lagoons offering absolutely safe bathing: they are ideal for teaching youngsters to swim. Most of the accommodation available at present is of the self-service or camping variety although there are a few excellent hotels and clubs.

Possible activities are much the same as those described for Malindi. Mombasa is within very easy reach. The beautiful green and rolling Shimba Hills, behind the coastal strip, form one of the most attractive small game areas in Kenya. They are the home of sable and roan antelopes, elephants and a few lions and leopard.

THE COAST BETWEEN MOMBASA AND KILIFI

As on the south coast, tourism is as yet very informal here and there are no resorts as such although there are more hotels. These are mainly concentrated in the fifteen miles or so north of Mombasa on the beaches of Nyali, Bamburi, Paradise, Shanzu and Kikambala. At all the story is the same, a relaxed informal atmosphere, an empty beach of silver sand, beautiful coral, a warm sea and almost constant sunshine.

The country behind the coast in this section is all highly cultivated, mostly in large units. There are many dairy farms and citrus groves and some huge sisal plantations where the cutting operation may easily be seen.

The coral coast is broken at two points, Mtwapa Creek eleven miles from Mombasa and Kilifi Creek, thirty-seven miles from Mombasa. Both are deep water inlets opposite breaks in the coral and form first rate harbours for small boats. Many large houses have been built along their banks. The creeks offer opportunities for every conceivable form of water sport including water skiing and sailing. There is a famous club on the south side of Kilifi Creek which specialises in deep sea fishing. On the west side of the road, immediately south of Kilifi Ferry is a small Snake Park.

KILIFI TO MALINDI

The main road crosses Kilifi Creek by means of a free ferry: Malindi is thirty eight miles away. Except at Watamu and at Malindi itself, the beaches along this section are totally undeveloped. Behind the coast too, there is much less cultivation and between Kilifi and Gedi the population is rather sparse. In this area is the last remnant of the vast forest which presumably at one time covered the whole of the coastal region.

Watamu is a beautiful spot reached by a three mile tarmac road which leaves the main road at Gedi (or Gede). Watamu Bay and Blue Lagoon, the bay immediately south of Watamu are small jewels. Each has a stretch of brilliant white sand, a few hundred yards long, bounded by coral headlands. South of Blue Lagoon is the much larger Turtle Bay which because of its magnificent living coral has been declared a Marine National Park. The fish here are very tame and some groupers are exceptionally large. Trips in boats to the best coral areas are organised by all three Watamu hotels.

Mida Creek whose entry is just south of Turtle Bay is more likely to appeal to the naturalist and to the ornithologist than to other visitors. Nevertheless a boat journey to it is a fascinating experience for anyone. Entering from the sea via a narrow channel one reaches a vast area of mangrove swamps, mud flats and narrow twisting passages where the leaves brush the boat sides and all sorts of mysterious and sinister noises can be heard. The bird life in the Creek, especially during the periods of migration, is incomparable. The fishing is also quite good although naturally those caught are relatively small. Again visits can be arranged through the Watamu hotels. The Creek cannot effectively be seen from the shore.

GEDI

The modern village of Gedi (or Gede) is nine miles south of Malindi at the turn off to Watamu. Looking at its bustling little market and its modern school one would not dream of the mystery which lies hidden in the forest so close by. For some unknown reason about seven hundred years ago a large city was founded on this unlikely site, well inland from the sea and in an indefensible position. Why it was founded and the sources of its prosperity are both unknown. It may have been a satellite of Malindi, a sort of resort city with no natural commercial life of its own, but this is mere speculation because there is nothing about it in the writings of any of the travellers who visited Malindi itself. But whatever its origins it must have had access to substantial wealth because forty-five acres of land were covered with stone buildings with a large palace, several mosques and many prosperous private houses. Gedi lived for three hundred years and then equally mysteriously died. Whether it was destroyed by the cannibal Zimba, faded away when power shifted from Malindi to Mombasa or sank into oblivion when its many wells dried up is unknown. A relatively peaceful end seems more likely since most of the houses seem to have been carefully evacuated. But whatever the cause its ruin was total. Galla tribesmen may have lived there for a while but they soon left and the forest moved in. Trees grew in and around and over the roofless mosques and palaces and animals and birds made it their home. Snakes glide noiselessly as spirits through the leaves and a dense and heavy silence settles, a silence more disturbing and profound than the silence of the desert or of snowy wastes for here man lived and is no more.

The silence of Gedi was not really broken until the early part of this century when the trees and roots and creepers were cleared from a small part of the ruined city where the most impressive buildings were to be found. In the course of the investigations many interesting items were discovered including trinkets from Persia and India, many Arabic inscriptions and much pottery, including some fine Ming ware, from China. But apart from the numerous dry wells there was no clue as to the cause of the decay. Even today most of the city remains uncleared and it gives one a strange sensation to wander around the eerily silent ruins, so impressive and once so prosperous, yet with a history of which we are utterly and totally ignorant. It is not surprising that most local people regard Gedi as haunted and refuse to spend a night anywhere near the ruins. Apart from the ruins there is a good practical reason for this: Gedi abounds in snakes and those with sharp eyes should be able to see several of them festooned in the trees.

Gedi is now a National Park and there is a small entrance fee. There is also a little museum in which are to be seen some of the objects found during the excavations.

NORTH OF MALINDI TO LAMU

The tarmac road ends just north of Malindi town and those who travel further may well feel that they are explorers entering the unknown for few visitors come this way. The first place of note is Mambrui, a small village about ten miles from Malindi. There is an enormous mosque which utterly dominates the small fishing village. A mile or so after the Mambrui turn off which is to the right, another small road leads off to the left. This after about twenty miles reaches Marafa where there is a gorge with some fine rock pinnacles. The road is rough and it is not easy to find the right route as there are several other turn offs and no sign posts.

On the main road northwards, a little over two miles after the Mambrui turn off, is a tiny unmarked track going off to the right. This leads to the promontory of Ngomeni which can easily be seen ahead so that once you are on the track you cannot lose your way. The road continues for about ten miles along the promontory getting considerably worse after going through the village of Ngomeni itself. If you are the sort of person who finds the beaches of Malindi crowded then Ngomeni is the place to visit. There is a splendid beach with a beautiful reef and many shells.

Six or seven miles north of Mambrui on the main road is the long and quite large village of Gongoni where there is a salt works. Beyond Gongoni there is virtually nothing and the road travels through mile after mile of deserted bush country until Garsen is reached, seventy-one miles from Malindi. Garsen is in the valley of the Tana, Kenya's largest river. In going to it one leaves the country of the Giriama and enters that of the Galla who seem very fond of brilliant blue clothes. The country around Garsen is very green and often flooded. Even during the dry season there are many small lakes and this is one of the best areas in Kenya for bird watching. Near Garsen there is a huge heronry where not only herons but many other types of birds make their nexts. Immediately after passing through the town the road crosses the Tana by means of a free ferry. It then goes through fairly open country interspersed with palm trees and thicker areas of forest where elephant may be seen. Witu, twenty-six miles from Garsen is the next place of interest. It was once the site of a proud and independent sultanate but is now an attractive, if rather sleepy, village, After Witu the country is again very sparsely inhabited until one arrives at Makowe where two types of petrol are available. Go through Makowe and after a few hundred yards you will reach an unsignposted fork. The left one takes you to the Lamu ferry about 145 miles from Malindi.

LAMU

Lamu Island is one of the most remarkable places left in the modern world because on it not only cars but even bicycles are outlawed. Walking on the island in the cool of the day is therefore a rare and unmitigated pleasure. James Kirkman, the archaeologist who has done so much to work out the history of the Kenya coast once wrote of Lamu 'It is refreshing to find one place in the world that does not pretend to believe in progress or indeed in motion at all.'

Lamu is one of a group of three large and many small islands at the far northern end of the Kenya coast. The three large islands, Lamu, Manda and Pate, were all once sites of semi-independent sultanates, each with the turbulent history so characteristic of this part of the world. Lamu last entered the world scene when, during the reign of the Mazrui, Mombasa made a bid to dominate the whole coast. Pate acknowledged Mombasa's supremacy and a joint Mombasa-Pate army crossed the narrow strait to invade Lamu Island. To the astonishment of the invaders and perhaps even more to the astonishment of themselves, Lamu's minute army put the Mombasans to rout at the battle of Shela. Immediately after this resounding victory and frightened by its success, Lamu sent emissaries to Oman, asking the Sultan to protect Lamu and to subdue the Mazrui. Having won a famous victory, Lamu then subsided into a delightful sleep from which it has not yet been roused.

All visitors must come to Lamu by sea. They arrive by ferry either from the roadhead at Makowe on the mainland (about 30 minutes) or from the airstrip on Manda Island (about 10 minutes). As one approaches one sees a group of quite large houses (now mostly Government offices) fronted by the harbour wall with its impressive row of ancient cannon. Behind and dominating the town, are the towers of the ancient fort of the sultan which is now a prison. Along the harbour front can be seen boats of all kinds ranging from the smart District Commissioner's launch to dugout canoes and from ocean-going dhows to a speedboat from the only large hotel on the island at Shela, two miles from Lamu itself.

Lamu Town is a maize of narrow twisting streets which genuinely can have changed little for a hundred years or more. The population is very obviously of primarily Arab extraction and equally obviously follows the religion of Islam. The fascinating shops cater for local trade. The one or two which do have tourist goods such as Arab chests and daggers and Persian and Indian jewellery are so pleasantly sleepy that you can nose around and examine the wares without anyone pressing you to buy. The two most interesting walks are the one along the harbour itself, watching fishermen, sailors and boat builders at work and the one along the street which runs parallel to and behind the harbour and where most of the shops are.

Lamu is a place in which it is good just to wander and to drink in the atmosphere without having to rush around and see the sights. The carved doors, the tall narrow buildings, the cool mosques and the glimpses of secret courtyards all fascinate. By far the most impressive building in the town is the huge fort with its white washed façade and one black cannon. The fort dominates the little tree-shaded square which lies behind the Customs House and the main landing stage. Its thick walls and dark barred windows encourage the imagination to make up stories of ancient wrongs and the shrieks of helpless prisoners. Lamu is an island on which to dream.

The coasts of Lamu present two very different aspects. Facing the land is mangrove swamp from which are cut the poles which form the main Lamu export for the homeward going dhows. Facing the sea is a magnificent beach, completely empty and perfect for swimming. The one first class hotel on the island is at Shela and can be readily reached from Lamu or from Manda airstrip by launch. Most visitors to Lamu travel by air and stay only a few hours. The fortunate ones stay and refresh themselves in one of the most restful places on earth.

❧ 12 ❧

The Thornbush Country

This is the vast tract of sparsely inhabited, arid land lying between the fertile coastal strip in the east and the highlands bordering the Rift Valley in the west. To the north it is bounded by the desert. It has been virtually untouched by twentieth century farming or industry. For the visitor its main interest lies in the huge game population it still supports. Tsavo and Meru National Parks and Amboseli Game Reserve lie within this tract.

The easiest way to see the bush country is to drive from Mombasa to Nairobi along the tarmac road. The train follows much the same route but it usually – and very sensibly – passes through at night. For mile after mile after mile the thorn bush continues, broken here and there by the sight of a charcoal burner's camp, a large baobab tree or an elephant or two. On the way there are three main oases, at Voi, at Mtito Andei and at Kiboko.

Four main groups of people live in the region although everywhere it is very sparsely inhabited and large tracts are completely unpopulated. Near the coast are the Nyika Bantu. South of the road and west of Tsavo are the Nilo-Hamitic Masai. North of the road and west of Tsavo are the Bantu Kamba. North and north east of Tsavo are the Hamitic Galla.

VOI

This little town at the eastern edge of the jagged Taita Hills exists because of its railway and road junctions, because of its sisal estates and because it is one of the main entrances to Tsavo and the headquarters of the eastern part of the National Park At Voi the Mombasa-Nairobi railways and roads both link up by means of routes which cross the border at Taveta, with the Tanzanian road and rail systems. There are two excellent hotels which offer facilities for a pleasant transit stop or overnight stay. The visitor who is not in too much of a hurry and who is not totally preoccupied with game should take a day off to drive up into the very beautiful Taita Hills. The hills are the home of the Taita people one of the smaller tribes in the central group of Bantu. After Mombasa, Taita was one of the earliest centres of activity for Christian missions in Kenya and Rebmann and Krapf made several journey's to it. It was from Taita that Rebmann had his first glimpse of the snow of Kilimanjaro which was so to startle the outside world. The hills are lush and well-cultivated and offer spectacular views of the surrounding countryside. They may be explored by car by taking the main road to Taveta and then turning right on to a minor road about one mile past Bura. About eight miles from the main road is a cross roads at a col between the two highest peaks Vuria to the left and Yale to the right. It is relatively easy to walk up either of them.

MTITO ANDEI

This is little more than a rest stop with a good hotel, several petrol stations and a snack bar. It lies almost exactly half way between Mombasa and Nairobi and is the main entrance to Tsavo West National Park.

Kiboko and Makindu

Makindu is the site of what is perhaps the most interesting and unusual building on the whole road, the Sikh Temple. As in all Sikh Temples, weary and homeless travellers can here find water, food and rest.

A few miles further west at Kiboko is Hunter's Lodge, another oasis in the wilderness. Here there is a small stream which has been dammed to give quite a substantial lake. It is possible to fish here for Tilapia and Barbus or simply to have fun by throwing bread into the water and watching it boil as the fish struggle to grab the pieces. There are here many large and beautiful acacias which offer pleasant shade from the hot sun while one sips a cool drink.

Other Roads

The tarmac strip in some ways shields the traveller from appreciating fully the harshness of the terrain through which he is passing. In order

M

fully to understand what the journey was like not so many years ago one has to take one of the other roads. Of these the main one which crosses the bush country is the one which leaves the tarmac at Thika and which passing through ever more inhospitable country reaches the Tana River at Garissa. Garissa is the site of one of Kenya's most interesting agricultural experiments. At Garissa Boys' Town, two priests have started using the Tana water to irrigate the apparently desert-like terrain along the river bank. The results have been astonishing with both fruit and vegetables growing in quite unexpected abundance. The produce is of such quality that it is now in great demand in the luxury hotels of Nairobi.

Another road leaves the Garissa road about forty miles from Thika, travels south to the town of Kitui, and eventually after a hundred miles or so links up with the Mombasa-Nairobi tarmac at Kibwezi, about twenty miles east of Kiboko. Two other roads of great interest because of the Galla and Pokomo country through which they run and because they are virtually unknown to most visitors (or to most Kenyans for that matter) are the ones which go down the Tana valley. The one on the west side goes to Garsen and the one on the east goes to Mokowe, the little port from which the ferry goes to Lamu.

❧ 13 ❧

Kenya West of the Rift

This part of Kenya contains some of the most beautiful areas of all. As yet, however, with the exception of the Masai Mara Game Reserve in the south it has not been greatly developed for tourism. Nevertheless Western Kenya contains several places which are favourites with local residents and the foreign visitor who would like to see parts of the country which are off the beaten track is recommended to travel in this region.

KERICHO, SOTIK AND KISII

After climbing up slowly from the floor of the Rift, the main road which heads north west from Nakuru reaches a major junction at Mau Summit (Londiani). Straight ahead is the trunk road to Uganda. To the left is the fine new road to Kericho and Kisumu. This delightful route first passes rich farmland and then runs through the great tea estates with their brilliant green bushes and their colourfully clothed tea pickers. The Kericho district receives a very reliable and evenly spaced rainfall (it rains virtually every evening) which together with the year round warmth makes it ideal for the growth of tea. Kericho itself is a lush, flower-filled town with an excellent hotel. It is the head-quarters of the Kenya tea industry and has factories for processing the leaf.

Kericho is in the country of the Kipsigis, the tribe who fifty years ago were primarily pastoral but who have now brought about a complete revolution in their way of life. Instead of wandering with their cattle they now keep animals and grow crops on enclosed farms. The Kipsigis farming country can be well seen from the road between Kericho and Sotik which is also tarmac but of a rather indifferent quality. From

Sotik to Kisii the scenery continues to consist predominantly of small farms. The road is no longer hard-surfaced and is very hilly and tortuous. Kisii is the capital of the Kisii tribe and soapstone carvings and beaded stools can be bought there.

From near Sotik two beautiful but as yet relatively unused routes run southwards to the Masai Mara Game Reserve. About two miles on the Kericho side of Sotik is a place called Kaplong with a market, school and hospital. From here a road marked Narok wanders south to Bomet, Amala Bridge and Ngare Ngare where there is a Game Department control barrier. A few hundred yards after passing the barrier, the track leaves the main Narok road turning very sharply to the right and then going on to Mara via Aitong where there is a Tsetse Survey Post. The second route turns south about a mile and a half after passing through Sotik. It goes first to Gorgor where it turns left along a road marked Kabosen, After Kabosen it joins the other route near Aitong Tsetse Survey Post. Keekorok Lodge is about one hundred and ten miles from Sotik.

KISUMU AND LAKE VICTORIA

Kisumu, the capital of the Luo tribe, has one very well developed tourist attraction. It is the starting point for the round-the-lake steamer cruises operated by East African Railways. It was the original railhead and goods used to be transferred from Kisumu to Uganda by boat. Today it can be reached by train or by air although most people probably travel from Nairobi via the good tarmac road via Nakuru and Kericho. A number of murram roads also connect Kisumu with various points on the main Nairobi–Uganda highway. Not surprisingly, Kisumu has a good harbour. Like most harbours it is very colourful and is the home of a fascinating fishing fleet. Boat races are sometimes held on special occasions and are a splendid spectacle. Just outside the town is Hippo Point where there is a bar and cafe and where visitors can relax while watching the great river horses in the lake waters.

Kisumu is at the head of the Kavirondo Gulf, an eastward stretching arm of Lake Victoria which is a waterfilled side branch of the Rift Valley. It is one of the deeper parts of the lake and its entrance is guarded by Rusinga Island, famous because of the fossils that have been found there and also because it was the birthplace of Tom

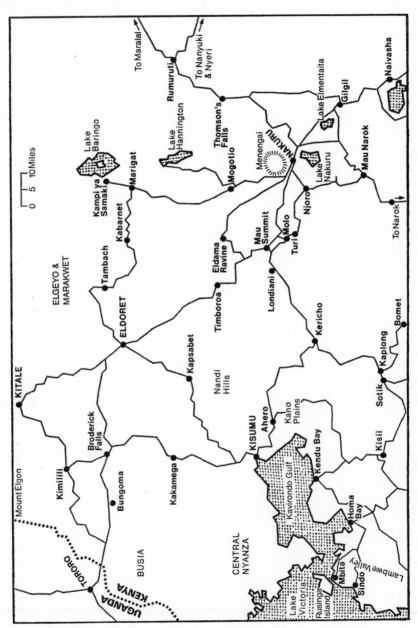

Part of western Kenya.

Mboya. The shores of the lake both north and south of Kisumu are rich and beautiful but are hardly visited even by residents of other parts of Kenya, let alone visitors from overseas. North of Kisumu the lake region is largely occupied by the Bantu Luhya tribe while southwards it is a Luo stronghold. Immediately south and east of Kisumu is a vast flat area known as the Kano Plains, very lush but unfortunately very frequently disastrously flooded. It is hoped that irrigation schemes will soon control the worst of the excess water.

The whole of the shore of Lake Victoria is a paradise for the naturalist and especially for the ornithologist. Interesting birds can be seen almost anywhere but of particular note for waterfowl is a small crater lake known as Simbi, a couple of miles south west of Kendu Bay. Lambwe Valley, west of Homa Bay, is one of Kenya's newer game reserves, created primarily for the preservation of the rare roan antelope and Jackson's Hartebeest.

All of the region south of the Kavirondo Gulf is of outstanding natural beauty. There is one tarmac road running from Kisumu through Kisii to the Tanzania border but accommodation is non-existent. However, for the person with a tent, a reliable vehicle and a 1/250,000 map, this is one of the most friendly and rewarding areas of Kenya to visit.

KAKAMEGA

This is thirty-three miles north of Kisumu and is the centre of one of the most densely populated rural areas in East Africa. The people are mainly Luhya Bantu. Almost fifty years ago it was the scene of an old-fashioned gold rush but although small quantities of the precious metal were found, they were too insignificant for successful commercial operation. Some mining operations struggled on for a time but they have all now completely closed down. The Kakamega Forest, not far from the town, is famous both for its bird life and its snakes.

MAU SUMMIT, ELDORET AND KITALE

The road from Mau Summit to Kitale runs through beautiful farmland with rolling hills and vast vistas. The northern parts are dominated by the cone of Mount Elgon an extinct volcano over 14,000 feet high. Eldoret and Kitale are the two most important towns in the area. Both are rather similar, being pleasant, open, farming centres with reasonable hotels at which to stay.

To the south and west of Eldoret are the Nandi Hills, a delightful region provided that one can cope with its appalling roads. To the north and east are the steep-sided valleys which are the homes of the Elgeyo and Marakwet peoples. Both these areas should be explored only by those with the 1/250,000 map and tough four wheel drive vehicles.

Kitale is almost at the foot of Mount Elgon and is a good base for exploring the mountain or for fishing in its streams. It is also the jumping off place for overland trips to the desert Turkana country west of Lake Rudolf. Not far from Kitale is the excellent little museum founded by the late Colonel Stoneham and now part of the National Museum: it is hoped to move it into Kitale itself in the near future. The museum is particularly noted for its superb collections of East African butterflies and moths.

MOUNT ELGON

This is described in the section on National Parks and Game Reserves.

❦ 14 ❦

The Northern Desert

This is the dry desert and semi-desert region which roughly speaking lies north of a line drawn from Kitale to Isiolo to Garsen. For those who love the genuinely wild, the remote and the unspoilt this is one of the most marvellous areas in the world. Once visited it acquires a hold which draws one back again and again and again. Its wide open spaces, its jagged and spectacular mountains, its unusual wild life, its great lake and its proud and independent peoples are all attractions for those who do not rate personal comfort the most important item on a holiday.

The great majority of the people in this northern area are nomadic pastoralists, wandering from place to place in search of water and grazing for their animals. Towards the south and west cattle tend to be most important but towards the north and east camels come into their own. In their tough way these hardy people utilise the desert more efficiently than anyone else could ever do. It might be possible to irrigate small areas by pumping from deep bore holes but over many years and especially if done on a large scale, this might well be self-defeating. More water might well be pumped out than fell as rain or came in by underground seepage. The water table in the ground would be reduced and what is now sparse scrub might be turned into total desert. It might also be possible to bring in water over vast distances by pipe lines from the great lakes but the cost of such schemes would be so high that no conceivable crop (apart possibly from oil or uranium!) could make them pay. This means that except in very small areas which are close to existing water supplies, a crop form of agriculture is unlikely ever to make sense. After thousands of years of adaptation the pastoralists have found the best way to exploit this remote and tortured land.

Northern Kenya is dominated by a relatively small number of tribes.

TOP *Two male lions at Lobo.*

BOTTOM *A young male lion. Note how the mane is not fully grown. Lions can live anything up to 15-25 years.*

TOP LEFT *Young lion devouring a reedbuck.*

BOTTOM *Hungry lions on the prowl.*

TOP RIGHT *A sleepy mother and her cub at Seronera in the Serengeti.*

The frailty of a female bushbuck in Nairobi National Park provides a stark contrast to the lion's unquestion-ble strength.

A gerenuk poised motionless on a slope near Lake Natron. The slightest warning will set it into headlong flight. The gerenuk is perhaps the most unusual and graceful of all East African antelopes.

TOP *One of the famous earless black rhinos of Amboseli. Note the oxpeckers (tick birds) perched on its back. The grey colour is caused by rolling in the fine Amboseli dust.*

BOTTOM *A black rhino in Ngorongoro.*

ɔP *Elephants in the Samburu-Isiolo Game Reserve. Note that they are grey, the colour of the earth in this reserve.*

ɔTTOM *Red-coloured Tsavo elephants drinking at the Kilaguni Lodge water hole.*

TOP *A giraffe in Nairobi National Park.*
Note the very rich brown of this animal.

BOTTOM *Male Thomson's gazelles. Note the dark*
black stripe and the warm brown colour.

TOP *A giraffe in Tsavo East. Note the mainly*
lighter colour.

BOTTOM *Male and female Grant's gazelles. The*
male has no side stripe.

West and south of Rudolf the Turkana are dominant although they continually have to face the pressure of Merille coming down from Ethiopia. South of the Turkana and bordering on the cultivated areas around Kitale are the Suk or Pokot. South and south east of Rudolf are the Samburu. The east side of Rudolf is very sparsely populated with Samburu and a small group of El Molo in the south and Gabra and Boran coming down from Ethiopia in the north. Between Marsabit and the lake are the Rendille. North, east and south east of Marsabit are the Boran and east of the Boran are the Somali in the north and Galla in the south. Tribal loyalties still run very deep and many of the traditions of stock thieving die hard. It is one of the major tasks of government in this area to keep the peace between the warring factions but in recent years the situation has improved remarkably. Soon after Kenya's independence there arose a dispute between Somalia and Kenya about the border areas, Somalia claiming a large area of northern Kenya. Some of the Somalis who became known as 'shifta' took the law into their own hands and attempted to force the issue by attacking officials and anyone who seemed to be collaborating with the Kenyan authorities. For some time the situation was very tense and for their own safety travellers were barred from the area. But now the border dispute has been settled and permits are no longer needed to enter any part of the area. All that one has to do is to sign the book at the various barriers one comes to. However this is very much in one's own interest in this barren land.

ROADS IN THE NORTH

In recent years Northern Kenya has been increasingly opened up by air charter travel and the majority of non-Kenya residents who visit the area probably fly in from Nairobi to the fishing resorts on Lake Rudolf. But as always, those who go by land can better appreciate the feel of the country and the hardships of those who live there.

There are four main routes of penetration by road. On the west side of Rudolf, a road from Kitale goes a short way into Uganda and the back into Kenya, reaching up to Lodwar opposite the middle of the lake and to Lokitaung in the far north. From Lodwar a branch road goes to Ferguson's Gulf on the lake where there is a famous fishing and bird watching resort. About fifty five miles north of Kitale a very rough track to the east goes along the dramatic and little explored Turkwel Gorge.

South of Rudolf, the second route starts from Thomson's Falls and passes through the ranching country of Rumuruti before climbing up to the plateau around Maralal with its abundant game. Sixteen miles north of Maralal there is a pine plantation on the right of the road. Opposite this a rough track leads in six miles or so to the Rift Valley escarpment near Losiolo peak. Here is one of the very finest views in the whole of Africa with the Valley wall falling away in a series of steps. The main (!) road goes due north getting worse all the time. After passing through Baragoi and the narrow South Horr Valley it reaches the east side of the south end of Rudolf.

The two other routes start from Isiolo, immediately north of Mount Kenya. Going due north is a new high class all weather murram road which is the first section of the proposed Ethiopian Highway which will link Nairobi and Addis Ababa. So far it has reached Marsabit but at the moment beyond there there is little more than a rough track. However the completed Isiolo-Marsabit section is a very interesting piece of road. Starting in Samburu country, it crosses the Uaso Nyiro River at Archer's Post on the edge of the Samburu-Isiolo Game Reserve. It then passes the splendid jagged peaks of the Mathews Range and crosses a fine stretch of true desert before climbing on to the fertile green slopes of Marsabit Mountain.

About fifteen miles past Archer's Post a road goes off to the left, signposted Wamba. This is a superb scenic route through the foothills of the Mathews Range. After Wamba one can either fork left to Maralal or fork right to join the road to Rudolf a few miles before Baragoi.

The fourth road treks north east from Isiolo and heads for Wajir. This is a Beau Geste white painted, battlemented outpost in the middle of the part of the desert country occupied by the Somali. On the way one passes the edge of the Lorian Swamp, a favourite haunt of elephants and other game, especially during the dry season. From Wajir further tracks go north to Ethiopia and east into Somalia.

When travelling by road in northern Kenya it is essential to remember that fuel and water points are exceedingly few and far between, the only reasonably sure supply bases being Lodwar, Marsabit and Wajir. If one breaks down it may be many hours or even days before another vehicle comes that way. It is therefore imperative to travel in a party of at least two cars, preferably both four wheel drive, and to carry an extensive spares kit. April and November when rain is most likely are times to avoid although unfortunately the weather is extremely erratic and wildcat storms can occur at almost any time. In short, an expedition to the north by road should be attempted only after much thought and preparation and preferably in the company of someone who has been there before. It is imperative to leave a detailed itinerary with some responsible person who can take appropriate action if your return is unduly delayed.

LAKE RUDOLF

This is a remarkable desert lake over one hundred and fifty miles long and over twenty miles wide for most of its length. First described to the outside world by Count Teleki following his journey in 1887–88, until a few years ago it had been seen from the ground by only a handful of Europeans. The difficulties and hardships of reaching it put off everyone but a few determined scientists and wanderers in far away places. In one of these early explorations, Vivian Fuchs, conqueror of Antartica went to South Island. In the course of the expedition some of the party were drowned in one of the vicious squalls that can so easily arise.

Today three groups of people form the majority of those who make 'The Journey to the Jade Sea'. Most numerous are those who come after the giant Nile and Golden Perch, Tiger Fish and Tilapia which swarm in the almost virgin waters. Many lake and river resorts all over the world claim that their fishing is superb but few of them live up to the promises made in their extravagant publicity material. Lake Rudolf is one of those very few and I know no one who has come away from the lake disappointed.

At present two luxury fishing resorts are operating, one at Ferguson's Gulf on the west side and one at Eliye Springs near the south end. Both are normally reached by air. There used to be a third resort at the oasis of Loyengelani near the El Molo village but this was closed down during the shifta troubles. The bandas have now been reopened by a group of Italian priests but everything is on a self help basis and no service at all is provided. The old boats are however still available and are in good condition: they may be hired for fishing or for trips to South Island.

Bird watchers form the second group of visitors for the bird life, as on so many of Kenya's lakes, is superb and has so far been little studied. Finally anthropologists come in moderate numbers to study the various tribes whose life so far has been affected remarkably little by twentieth century events in the world outside.

OTHER PLACES OF INTEREST

Apart from Lake Rudolf, the main attractions in Northern Kenya are the Samburu-Isiolo and Mount Marsabit Game Reserves. Marsabit has superb volcanic scenery with a very beautiful crater lake, appropriately enough known as Paradise. It is famed for its greater kudu and its giant elephants although unfortunately the latter seem to have been reduced in number in recent years possibly because of poaching. Samburu-Isiolo Reserve is well equipped to cater for the visitor with a luxury lodge, self service bandas and several camping sites. Marsabit has as yet only a camping site and a self service lodge. There are many other fine hunting and photographic areas in the north but for the visitor it is feasible to visit these only in the company of professional safari organisers.

Of specialised but special interest are the many mountains of the north, many of them virtually unexplored from both the mountaineering and the biological points of view. It is probable that many new animal and plant species are awaiting discovery here. Perhaps the most interesting are the Turkana group, including the Turkwel Gorge north of Kitale, the Mathews Range north of Isiolo, and Kulal, just east of the south end of Rudolf.

On the south side of Kulal, the Africa Inland Mission have established a post. The road up to it is magnificent but hair-raising and recommended only for those with very strong nerves. It is possible to camp near the post which serves the Samburu who pasture their cattle on the mountain. From the camp a track goes up to the South Summit from which one can see the as yet uncrossed knife edge which links it to the North Summit. This is one of the most remote and beautiful spots in East Africa.

There are many other mountains in the north, all interesting. Instructions on how to reach and climb them are given in the Mountain Club of Kenya's Guide *Mountains of Kenya*. Details of this book, and of many others about both Kenya and Northern Tanzania are given in Chapter 34 entitled 'Useful Information' (see page 284).

❧ 15 ❧

Northern Tanzania

It has been said that Northern Tanzania is a microcosm of the whole of East Africa. This, unlike many such sweeping generalisations, is remarkably true. By northern Tanzania I mean the region east of Lake Victoria and north of the 4° parallel of latitude. With the exception of a coastline, it has almost everything, vast open game-filled plains, hot thornbush country, large ranches and sisal estates, coffee plantations, pastoral people, agricultural people, high snow-covered mountains and two important towns, Arusha and Moshi. It has within its narrow confines more beautiful and interesting areas than any other region of comparable size in the world. At the moment it tends to be visited primarily by tourists based in Kenya as it is much closer to Nairobi than to Dar es Salaam. But with the development of the new international airport between Arusha and Moshi and with the growth of Arusha as the capital of the East African Community, it is likely that more and more visitors will start and end their journeys in Tanzania itself. There is certainly enough here to satisfy the most demanding and discriminating of people.

The seven important game parks and reserves in Northern Tanzania, Arusha, Kilimanjaro, Lake Manyara, Mkomazi, Ngorongoro, Serengeti and Tarangire, are described in a separate chapter. This section of the guide is concerned with describing areas of interest which are outside the parks and reserves.

Travel within the area is relatively easy. Even at present there are daily flights from the airports at Arusha and Moshi to Dar es Salaam and Nairobi. The roads on the whole are excellent. The whole road from Dar es Salaam to Arusha via Moshi is hard surfaced. At Arusha it links with the other major tarmac road, the Great North Road which in Tanzania starts at Namanga on the Kenya border and leaves this northern region just south of Lake Manyara. Arusha is also the terminus of the railway line from Dar es Salaam and from the port of Tanga. The railway links with the Kenyan system via the line which goes from Moshi to Voi.

ARUSHA

Arusha is a pretty little town attractively sited at the foot of Mount Meru (or Socialist Peak as it is now officially known). For many years it was the thriving centre of the local farming community (a community which included many Greeks) but its long-term future has now been transformed, first by the establishment since independence of several manufacturing plants and more recently by the decision to establish it as the headquarters of the East African Community. At the moment it is very much a boom town with new offices, hotels, houses and service industries being developed at a great rate.

Arusha is also the headquarters of the Arusha tribe, close relatives of the Masai as can be seen by appearance, language and many customs. Their way of life is however a complete contrast to that of the Masai. They are primarily settled agriculturists growing several crops but particularly maize: the cobs are characteristically stored in bundles hanging on trees or from the tops of posts. Arusha is of course important to the Masai as well for they graze their cattle over the dry country nearby, particularly towards the west and south. The third group of indigenous people are the Meru, a Bantu tribe who live on the slopes of Meru Mountain.

MOSHI

As Arusha is dominated by Meru, so Moshi is overshadowed by the magnificence of snow-capped Kilimanjaro. Moshi too is a pleasant town with good places to stay. It is the headquarters of the Chagga people and is the main centre for both the coffee and the sugar industries of Tanzania.

Because of its delightful climate and situation, many educational establishments have been set up here, including several teacher training colleges. Perhaps the most interesting of these institutions is the

College of Wildlife Management which offers one and two year courses.
Its training for those who will man the national parks and reserves of
East Africa is unique and it attracts visitors and students from all over
the world. The equable climate, so favourable for Europeans, probably
also accounts for the large number of missions which have flourished
in the region. The Lutheran Church is particularly strong and has
recently embarked on an ambitious programme which should enormously strengthen the medical services available in Northern Tanzania.
This is the Kilimanjaro Christian Medical Centre which is a 420-bed
hospital with many advanced facilities and a nursing school. It is hoped
that a full medical school may be established at some time in the future.

Those interested in seeing what can be done by African farmers
working on a co-operative basis should visit the Kilimanjaro Native
Co-operative Union (KNCU) building in Moshi. They may well be
surprised. This splendid complex, financed out of the profits of agriculture, contains offices, a library, a restaurant, a hotel and a printing
press. It is a striking demonstration of the great things which can be
achieved when small farmers band together.

MARANGU

This village is on the slopes of Kilimanjaro, about twenty miles from
Moshi. It may be reached by taking the main road towards Dar es
Salaam and turning north up the mountain at Himo. Marangu is a
favourite resort full of lush vegetation, cheery Chagga people and
myriads of flowers. It is the usual base for climbing Kilimanjaro.
Its two comfortable hotels both organise climbing parties and arrange
hut bookings.

MONDULI

After leaving Arusha, the Great North Road goes almost due west
for a time before turning southwards. Twenty-four miles from Arusha,
just north of the main road, is Monduli, the headquarters of Tanzania's Masai district. The town is at the foot of Monduli Mountain, a
thickly forested eminence which is the haunt of many varieties of game,
notably buffalo.

LAKE DULUTI

Eight miles from Arusha on the south side of the Moshi Road is this well-known picnic spot. It is a water-filled extinct volcanic crater which is over five hundred feet deep. During the week it is a good place for bird watching. At weekends the water fowl and lakeside birds are less in evidence as the lake is used for water skiing, swimming, sailing and fishing. There is a camping site, a small guest house and the club house and bar of the Aqua Sports Club.

LAKES JIBE AND CHALA

These two very different and little visited lakes near the Kenya border are thriving haunts of bird and animal life. Lake Chala is a crater lake about thirty-four miles from Moshi. It may be reached by taking a northward turning just short of Taveta and driving for about nine miles. Lake Jibe is about thirty-six miles from Moshi and is reached by driving south from Taveta. It is much bigger than Chala being ten miles long and three miles wide. Visitors to both lakes are advised to ensure that they are in possession of reasonably large scale maps of the area.

MOUNT MERU GAME SANCTUARY

This is a private zoo and animal sanctuary on the Arusha-Moshi Road at Usa River, about thirteen miles from Arusha. Here many of East Africa's wild animals and birds may be seen at close quarters and under ideal conditions. The whole atmosphere of the place is delightful and it is clearly run by people who care. There is a large paddock with a lake where the animals and birds are fed at 4.30 each afternoon. There is a small but very high class hotel in the Sanctuary which is a favourite with East African residents. Many who have been there once return again and again and again.

ENGARUKA

This interesting historic site in Masailand may be reached by taking a track which leads northwards from the village of Mto wa Mbu which is at the entrance to the Lake Manyara National Park. On a hill side

N

are the remains of what was evidently at one time a large and stable settlement. The origins of the settlement are unknown but it was certainly not built by the Masai. It is possible but by no means certain that it was established by the Iraqw (Mbulu) people who now live on the plateau between Manyara and Ngorongoro.

LAKE NATRON AND OL DOINYO LENGAI

Both these areas are more easily visited from Kenya via Magadi and the approach is described in chapter 9. It is possible to reach Lengai from Tanzania by means of a very rough track which goes northwards from Engaruka. 1/50,000 maps are more or less essential for this journey which is impossible in anything other than a four-wheel drive vehicle.

NABERERA AND NGASUMET

These two villages lie in the centre of the great dry thornbush covered Masai Steppe which lies south of the Monduli-Meru-Kilimanjaro group of mountains. They may be approached by going from Arusha along the Great North Road to the Monduli turn off and then instead of going north to Monduli turning south to Naberera. The road is a rough one and runs through very dry land, much of it covered with dense thornbush but with some more open areas of savannah. Game is fairly plentiful and gerenuk, lesser kudu and oryx may be seen. The importance of Naberera and Ngasumet lies in the fact that they are two of the rare sources of water in this barren land. To them the Masai drive their cattle from many, many miles away. At each place, deeply carved out of the rock and many feet below the surface of the surrounding country are freshwater wells. Huge stepped open tunnels have been excavated so that the water level can be approached. The origin of these impressive excavations is unknown. They have certainly been deepened and extended by Bantu labourers employed by the Masai but it seems that the original wells antedate the coming of the Masai into the region. Whatever their origin they are a fascinating sight. During the dry season they can be located from many miles away by the great column of dust kicked up by the thousands upon thousands of cattle which come to them.

✤ 16 ✤

The Common Animals

Over 140 species of mammal may be found in the area covered by this guide. Most of them are small, nocturnal, elusive creatures rarely seen by the visitor except in the briefest of glimpses. Most have been little studied by naturalists and not much is known about them. They are of more interest to the professional zoologist than to the ordinary visitor. This section of the guide describes all the mammals which all tourists are reasonably likely to see. Most of them present no problems of identification and more emphasis will be placed on their interesting habits than on details of their anatomical structure. The weights given are only approximate and are those of well-developed adult males. Lifespans are also only very approximate.

THE BIG CATS

There are four small species of wild cat here, the serval, the caracal, the golden cat and the African wild cat, but all are rarely seen. It is the big cats, the lion, the cheetah and the leopard which particularly attract attention.

The Lion Lifespan, 15–25. Weight 400 lbs. Gestation 4 months.

This is perhaps the one animal which *every* tourist knows about and wants to see. Lion can be observed in almost all the game parks and reserves but they are largest and most numerous around Keekerok Lodge in Mara, Seronera in the Serengeti and on the floor of the Ngorongoro Crater.

The teeth of the lion are not particularly big in relation to the size of the skull and the claws are more important in killing. The claws are large and withdrawn into a sheath when not in use in order to preserve the sharpness of the points. The mature lion usually kills by very carefully and incredibly slowly stalking up to the prey and then making a violent rush over the last few yards. This is why one cannot be sure that lions are not about even when plains game appear to be grazing peacefully. At the end of the rush the lion leaps upon the back of its victim, puts its paws around the head and jerks the neck backwards, breaking it and killing instantly. Normally only immature and old animals will attempt to kill by using their teeth. Because the teeth are relatively small, this method of slaughter is often not very effective and the unfortunate victim may take a long time to die.

Except when actually stalking, lions give the impression of being extraordinarily lazy as most people who have seen them during the day in Nairobi Park will testify. Once they are gorged they often lounge around for several days before killing again. Most of the killing seems to be done by immature animals of both sexes and by mature females. Early hunters often told of the way in which an old male would stay on one side of a herd of plains game while the rest of the pride slowly worked round to the other side. The male would then roar, driving the panicking herd towards the waiting lionesses. More recent naturalists have thrown doubt on this method of killing but a few months ago I was fortunate enough to observe myself such a kill in the Nairobi Park.

Lions mature at the age of four or five. They are often spotted when young. Once mature the females regularly have litters of cubs. They may come into heat at any time of the year and will mate several times during one day. Mating does not normally seem to be for life. A lion is old at ten and it is doubtful if any in the wild survive beyond the age of fifteen.

Lion cubs are attractive and frolicsome little creatures and when food is plentiful they are treated with great indulgence by their elders. But this does not apply to the time of a kill. The males eat first, then the females, then the immature animals and finally the cubs. If food is scarce, the mature animals will take all that is available and the cubs will quickly starve to death. This apparently cruel practice is in fact essential for the health and survival of the species. It ensures that the numbers do not outgrow their food supply.

The Leopard   Lifespan 10–20. Weight 150 lbs. Gestation 3½ months.
This is probably not uncommon but because it lives in trees or rocks
and is nocturnal and lurking in habit it is not often seen. It usually
hunts at night, frequently dropping on to its prey from a tree branch
above a game trail. Compared to the lion it has very well developed
teeth and both teeth and sharp claws are used in killing. Beginners
often confuse leopards and cheetahs. Apart from differences in habit
and shape, the most obvious distinction lies in the spots. The spots of
the cheetah are a uniform black while those of the leopard are more like
rosettes, each big spot consisting in fact of three or four smaller ones.

Like other carnivores the leopard does not seem very particular
about its choice of meat and it does not mind feeding on animals which
it finds dead. It has the remarkable habit of hauling up into trees the
uneaten part of the bodies of its victims. Some of the victims are as large
or larger than the leopard itself and it must be incredibly strong in
order to drag them up to such a height. It is said that baboons are its
favourite food but in the vicinity of villages it seems to be particularly
fond of dogs. Its willingness to eat dead meat often leads it into trouble
as it will readily come for a dead goat or other bait put out by a hunter.
Many tales are told of its unprovoked attacks upon humans and it is
probably the animal which is most feared by Africans.

Although leopards are found in all the game parks, in most of them
they are difficult to spot and it is just good luck if a visitor manages to
get a glimpse of one. However in the Seronera Valley in the Serengeti
leopards are plentiful and the guides can usually locate one resting in
the branches of a tree. At Secret Valley on Mount Kenya, visitors who
stay the night are virtually certain to see leopards and the proprietor
is prepared to give a money back guarantee if they do not. Secret
Valley Lodge is run by the Sportsman's Arms Hotel in Nanyuki.

The Cheetah   Lifespan 10–15. Weight 130 lbs. Gestation 3 months.
This is seen far more frequently than the leopard but rather less often
than the lion. It is an animal of open country where it can use its speed
to the full and it is most likely to be seen in Amboseli, Nairobi, Mara and
the Serengeti, although again it can be encountered almost anywhere.
In distinction to the leopard's, the cheetah's spots are a uniform black.
It has an incongruously small head superbly equipped with teeth, a
long body and very long legs. It does not use its claws for killing and as
there is little need for them to be razor sharp they are not sheathed like

those of the lion and leopard. It can run at over sixty miles an hour and is probably the fastest animal on earth. However, despite its speed, it does not always catch its prey. It cannot turn quickly whereas most of the creatures it chases can. It also has limited endurance and if a gazelle by a sudden turn can escape the first fantastic rush, its superior endurance will probably carry it away. The cheetah kills by knocking its victim over and then ripping open the great vessels in the throat with its teeth. It is a relatively small animal and usually kills small gazelles although it will sometimes attack the larger plains game such as zebra or wildebeest.

OTHER PREDATORS AND SCAVENGERS

There are many smaller carnivores in East Africa but most are nocturnal and rarely seen. Only the most important will be described.

Hunting Dogs   Lifespan 10. Weight 40 lbs. Gestation 3 months.

This is not a common animal and it is not often seen but I have included it because of its remarkable habits. It is a medium sized dog with large rounded ears and a blotchy brown, black and white colour pattern. It goes around in packs and by the other animals seems to be the most feared of all predators. All animals flee when the dogs first appear but flight will not greatly help the chosen victim, even if it is the fleetest of animals. Once an animal has been picked out by the pack it is followed utterly ruthlessly, first one dog and then another taking the lead in the chase. The endurance of these animals seems phenomenal. Once the pack is running alongside, mouthfuls are snatched from the living victim so that it soon weakens and falls. No attempt is made to kill the prey which is usually eaten alive. It is perhaps fortunate that the multiplication of hunting dogs seems to be strictly limited by a form of distemper which always breaks out and kills them when their numbers increase. But for this there would seem to be little to prevent them from totally dominating the African wild life scene.

Jackals   Lifespan 10–15. Weight 25 lbs. Gestation $2\frac{1}{2}$ months.

These are attractive fox-like little animals which often go around in pairs. There are three species, the golden, the striped and the silver-backed. The last is also known as the black-backed and is by far the commonest of the three in the area covered by the guide. Jackals eat large insects and small animals and also get much of their food by scavenging on the kills made by the big cats.

Hyaenas   Lifespan 10–20. Weight 150 lbs. Gestation 4 months.
There are two varieties, the common spotted and the much rarer striped type with its prominent mane. Both have sloping backs and a most peculiar shambling run which once seen is never forgotten nor mistaken for the gait of any other animal. Like jackals they scavenge on the kills of the big cats and on the carcases of animals which have died because of disease. They are by no means cowardly and will often try to snatch food while lions are still in the vicinity. When hungry they will also kill living animals, even ones as large as wildebeest. But like the hunting dogs they do not kill the animal before eating it and the poor victim has a miserable death.

Hyaenas always seem to look scruffy and filthy. They are heavily infested with skin parasites and their habit of lying in muddy pools may be an attempt to relieve the irritation. During the rainy season hyaenas often lie in the water in the wheel ruts on roads and they are very frequently disturbed by motorists.

Finally perhaps the thing which most people always remember about hyaenas is their extraordinary wailing, cackling cry which splitting the African night stirs the imagination to think of lost and desperate souls.

ANIMALS OF OPEN COUNTRY

There is inevitably some overlapping between this group and the next, the animals of bush and woodland. However in general the animals described in this section will be seen only where there are large stretches of open grassland. Many of these plains animals look thin, even at times of the year when food is obviously plentiful, a fact which often causes visitors some concern. But there is usually no need to worry because most of these species, all dwellers in hot climates, deposit their fat not beneath their skin but internally around the gut and especially in a great mass around the heart. If they did have thick fat layers under the skin they would have difficulty in losing heat and keeping cool. Unlike cattle and pigs, antelopes and gazelles do not even deposit fat between the muscles: this is why their meat is often described as dry.

The animals in this group, with the exception of the massive eland, all very commonly fall prey to lions.

Wildebeest or Gnu   Lifespan 10–15. Weight 450 lbs. Gestation 8 months.
This ungainly looking creature is about the size of a small cow. It has a prominent beard hanging from its neck, very high shoulders and a steeply sloping back which causes an amusing and curious gallop. The wildebeest very commonly associates with zebras. It is by far the commonest of all the East African antelopes and the vast herds seen in the Serengeti and Mara are legendary. Wildebeest are famous for their migrations when herds of over a hundred thousand strong may be seen trekking across the Tanzanian plains, followed by numerous lions, hyaenas and jackals ready to pounce on the unwary, the young or the weak. This phenomenon is described more fully in the section on the Serengeti Park. The wildebeest can be seen in most of the parks but Nairobi, Mara and the Serengeti are probably the best areas.

Kongoni or Coke's Hartebeest   Lifespan 10–15. Weight 400 lbs. Gestation 8 months.
This too is a curious animal often found with wildebeest. It is about four feet high at the shoulder, is brown in colour, has a very long face and a steeply sloping back. Its horns are unique in that they both spring from a single common base on top of the skull. It can be seen in most of the parks but the Nairobi Park is particularly good for them.

Topi   Lifespan 10–15. Weight 450 lbs. Gestation 8 months.
This is a close relative of the kongoni but is altogether a much more beautiful creature. It has an outstandingly sleek reddish-brown coat with dark areas on the upper legs which in the right light appear indigo. As with the wildebeest and kongoni both sexes have horns. The topi is common in the Mara and the Serengeti but is otherwise rare in the region covered by this book. It is very common in Western Uganda.

Eland   Lifespan 15. Weight 2,000 lbs. Gestation 10 months.
The eland is an enormous antelope, about six feet high at the shoulder. It is very heavily built with stout spiralled horns and a well-developed dewlap. It is usually seen in small herds. For an animal of its size it is a phenomenal jumper and can clear high fences and wide ditches with

TOP LEFT *A sable antelope in the Shimba Hills.*   TOP RIGHT *A male impala in Mara Game Reserve.*

BOTTOM *A young dik dik – one of the smallest members of the antelope family.*

TOP LEFT *A family group of Kongoni. Note the two horns arising from a single pedicle.*

TOP RIGHT *A large eland.*

BOTTOM *A male and female waterbuck face the camera.*

Buffalo at Amboseli. In spite of their appearance these animals have finely attuned senses and are extremely dangerous. Many hunters regard them as the most treacherous of all animals to pursue.

Wildebeest are the commonest of all East African antelopes. Their migrations, when they cross the
Tanzanian plains in huge herds, are famous.

TOP LEFT *A rock hyrax on Mount Kenya.*

TOP RIGHT *The head of a hunting dog.*

BOTTOM *A silver-backed jackal in Nairobi National Park.*

1 fine female cheetah in the Nairobi National Park.

TOP *The head of a cheetah. Note the black tear-drops coming down from the eyes: a leopard does not have these.*

BOTTOM *The tree is the leopard's favourite habitat. This one is in a large thorn tree.*

TOP *Young cheetahs devouring a gazelle.*

BOTTOM *A young leopard lying in an acacia tree.*

ease. It is a splendid sight to see these huge animals in full flight taking all sorts of obstacles in their stride. Eland are relatively docile animals and some recent efforts at domesticating them have proved encouraging. If such domestication could be achieved on a large scale it might have important consequences for the whole of Africa. This is because the eland shows an astonishing ability to devour all sorts of tough woody and thorned plants which cattle and other animals will not touch. Thus they could be kept in places which would not support other domestic animals. This powerful digestive ability enables eland to keep in good condition even during long periods of drought when the only surviving plants are those which are tough and drought resistant. It is widespread but yet again is probably most easily seen in the Nairobi Park.

Gazelles Lifespan 10. Weight, Thomson's 100 lbs., Grant's 150 lbs. Gestation 8 months.

These are perhaps the most attractive and graceful of all the animals of the plains. There are two types which are often confused but which can easily be distinguished if a few points are remembered. The smaller one, the Thomson's gazelle or Tommy, is a little over two feet high with a jet black stripe along its side which is present in both sexes: it is mainly chestnut brown in colour and has a black tail which perpetually goes round and round and round. Grant's gazelle is a larger animal, a little under three feet in height. Its basic colour is a beige brown, the difference between this and the Tommy's colour being easily seen when the two are side by side. The male Grant's either has no dark stripe at all or one which is very pale. The female usually has a well-defined or dark grey stripe but it is not an intense black like that of the Tommy. Grant's gazelle has a white tail with a black tip, while Thomson's has an all black tail. In both species both sexes have horns but those of the male are much larger. The Tommy is virtually confined to really open grassland country which is moderately well watered. The Grant's has a much wider distribution being not infrequent in dry thornbush regions. Both are especially easy to observe in the Serengeti, Mara and the Nairobi Park.

These gazelles, and especially the Thomson's, are a delight to watch because they seem so full of life. In order to signal danger they bounce along all four feet hitting the ground together. When frightened they can run surprisingly quickly for such small creatures but their speed cannot always save them from the cheetah of which they are the favourite prey. The gazelles are particularly pleasant to see when they have young. These are usually born at the end of the dry season in early March so that when they are weaned from their mothers there will be plenty of juicy grass available.

Zebras Lifespan 15–20. Weight, Common 600 lbs., Grevy's 750 lbs. Gestation 7½ months.

These are clearly quite different animals from the antelopes and gazelles described earlier in this section. There can be no doubt that they are close relatives of the horse although they have never been domesticated on a large scale. Occasional settlers trained one to pull a dog cart but although zebras are very fast off the mark they do not appear to have the endurance of the horse. There are two distinct species in East Africa. The common or Burchell's zebra is about four feet high, has broad stripes and is familiar to everyone. Those from southern Kenya and Tanzania usually have a faint dark shadow stripe in the centre of each white stripe but those from the north have pure white stripes and therefore are more striking and prized for their skin. The other species, the Grevy's zebra is found only in the north of Kenya and adjacent areas of Uganda and is less familiar. It is about five feet high at the shoulder, a foot taller than Burchell's zebra. It is also much more heavily built with a well-developed mane and very large round ears with a prominent fringe of hair. The stripes of Grevy's zebra are very narrow and one does not have to be very far away before they merge giving the animal a pale grey appearance which often blends well with the arid background. Both types of zebra look much fatter than the antelopes and gazelles. This is because unlike the others the zebras deposit their fat beneath their skin. This must create considerable problems for them in the elimination of heat and it is not yet known how these are overcome.

One characteristic of most wild animals which is particularly evident in the zebra is that their guts are often swarming with parasitic worms. In the case of the zebra there may be several million in the intestines of a single animal. People are usually horrified at this but much of the evidence suggests that these worms are actually beneficial to their host. They and bacterial parasites probably digest tough plant material with which their host alone cannot cope. When the worms die, they themselves are easily digested and utilised so enabling the zebra, through this intermediary, to make use of foods which otherwise it could not digest. Antelopes, gazelles and zebras born and reared in captivity are rarely as healthy as those seen in the wild. It has been suggested that this is because in captivity they do not acquire their usual complement of parasites and bacteria.

ANIMALS OF WOODLAND AND BUSH

These are a group many of which may be seen in open country but which are not often very far from trees. They are a very varied collection ranging from the imperious giraffe to the splendidly ugly warthog.

Giraffes   Lifespan 15–25. Weight 2,000 lbs. Gestation 15 months.

This is one of those African animals which almost all children throughout the world can readily identify because of its popularity with those who produce children's picture books. There are two distinct species. The reticulated giraffe, 15 to 17 feet high, lives in northern Kenya and can be seen in the Samburu-Isiolo, Marsabit and Meru Game Reserves. It is dark chestnut with a crazy paving sort of pattern: the chestnut patches are separated by narrow but very clearly defined cream lines. The common giraffe is found over most of the rest of Kenya and Tanzania. It is a lighter brown with spots which are much less clearly defined and which have highly irregular edges. It is slightly taller than the reticulated, large males being sometimes 19 feet high. The common giraffe has two varieties, the Masai found in the southern part of the range which has two or rarely three horns, and the Rothschild's, found in central Kenya which has three to five stubby horns.

The long neck of the giraffe is very useful as it enables the animal to browse easily on the leaves of tall trees. It also enables the giraffe to spot predators: this and the vigour of its kick probably account for the rarity with which giraffe are caught by lion. The main problem caused by the neck is the difficulty of drinking easily. The animal can get down to the water only by splaying its front legs wide. It is then in a relatively vulnerable position and judging by the way it scans the landscape before drinking it is fully aware of its danger. The neck is probably important in sexual display and it is not uncommon to see pairs of giraffe with their necks entwined together. The giraffe is one of those unusual animals whose males know that a female is ready for mating not by her smell but by the taste of her urine which they savour and then spit out without drinking.

Superficially, the stationary giraffe looks one of the most ill-designed and ungainly creatures on earth. Hence most people are surprised at the imperial grace with which the animal walks. Those fortunate enough to see a giraffe at full gallop cannot fail to be electrified by this thrilling sight. However one unkind friend of mine once said, 'The poor giraffe just has to be graceful: if it were not it would spend all its time falling flat on its face!'

Impala   Lifespan 10–15. Weight 150 lbs. Gestation 6 months.

This beautiful antelope is widespread and common in Kenya and Tanzania. It is often the first wild creature to be seen by visitors to East Africa as there is almost always a herd to be seen by the roadside near the main entrance to the Nairobi National Park. It is about three feet high and a relatively uniform rich chestnut colour. Its white rump is flanked by two black stripes. The tail, which is dark on top but white underneath, is normally well tucked in between the buttocks. During sexual display the tail is lifted and then the whiteness of its underside can be quite startling. The male impala has graceful horns usually said to be lyre-shaped but the female has no horns at all. Both sexes make fantastic leaps in order to clear obstacles: as they jump their tails fly upwards, showing a white flash which may possibly be a warning to other animals of danger. Impala usually breed just before or at the beginning of the rains in March. The males compete with one another to achieve dominance and the fortunate few bucks may gather together harems of twenty, thirty, forty or more. Younger and less successful males often hang around in the vicinity and may attempt to dislodge the dominant buck. Fierce fights may ensue and occasionally the horns of the two become locked together so rendering both animals helpless.

Gerenuk   Lifespan 10. Weight 150 lbs. Gestation 6 months.

This is of the same general colour and size as an impala but is even more graceful, if that is possible. This is because it has exceptionally thin legs and a very long, very thin neck which it uses for browsing off bushes. In order to gain additional height it not infrequently stands up against a bush on its hind legs. Only the males have horns which slope first backwards and then forward again at the tips. The gerenuk is an inhabitant of dry thornbush country. It is most common in the Samburu-Isiolo Reserve but can also be seen in Marsabit, Amboseli, Meru, Tsavo and Tarangire. Gerenuk rarely if ever drink water, getting most of their fluid requirement from the leaves on which they browse.

Oryx   Lifespan 10–15. Weight 400 lbs. Gestation 9 months.

This is another animal of dry country. It likes trees and in the heat of the day may often be seen standing beneath the shade of a large acacia but on the whole it prefers more open country than the gerenuk. Apart from their preference for dry places, however, there could hardly be a much greater contrast between the two antelopes. The oryx is something over four feet high at the shoulder and heavily built. It is basically a pale beige-grey with striking black and white markings on the face and upper part of the forelegs and thin black lines along the ridge of the back and on the flanks. Both sexes have absolutely straight very long horns. The young oryx is much browner in colour and from a distance its shape and run can sometimes be mistaken for that of the lion. Oryx are very commonly seen in pairs, often after the rains accompanied by a single youngster. There are the two varieties, the Beisa and the Fringe-eared, the latter being distinguished by a tuft of hair at the tips of its ears. The Beisa oryx is found in the north of Kenya: it is most easily seen in the Samburu-Isiolo Reserve but can also be spotted in Meru and Marsabit. The Fringe-eared oryx is found in southern Kenya and Tanzania: it may be seen in Amboseli and Tarangire Reserves and particularly on the rough road which runs between Lakes Magadi and Natron.

Kudus   Lifespan 10–15. Weight, lesser 170 lbs. Gestation 7 months.

These too like dry thornbush areas. There are two species, the greater about five feet high at the shoulder and the lesser about three feet high. Both are greyish in colour with superb long spiral horns and vertical white stripes on their sides. Neither is very easily seen. In Kenya the greater kudu is virtually confined to the Marsabit area and to other wooded hilltops in the arid north: it becomes commoner on moving south through Tanzania. The lesser kudu is widely distributed in the east and north of Kenya and is most likely to be seen in Tsavo, Meru, Amboseli or Samburu. In Tanzania it is fairly common in Tarangire.

Waterbucks   Lifespan 10–15. Weight 400 lbs. Gestation 8 months.

The waterbuck is widespread and common in wooded areas which are not too far from water. It is a heavily built animal about four feet high at the shoulder. Only males have the heavily ringed, powerful and gently curved horns. The hair is greyish-brown and remarkably thick. I always feel that waterbucks must be permanently overheated and that they would be much happier in some cooler northern climate. There are two species, closely related but nevertheless easily distinguished. The only difference is to be seen in their bottoms. The common waterbuck has a whitish ring around its rump with a dark centre. In the Defassa waterbuck the dark centre is absent and the whole rump is whitish. The Defassa species tends to be more common west of the Rift Valley with the common one more frequent on the east. But the two ranges overlap and there is a probability that they interbreed. Waterbuck are usually found in small family groups, often resting in the shade of trees.

Bushbuck   Lifespan 10–15. Weight 150 lbs. Gestation 7 months.

This is a small antelope about 2.5 to 3 feet high at the shoulder. It is rather shy but is again very commonly seen in the woodland near the main entrance to the Nairobi Park. The females are reddish-brown, the certain distinguishing mark being a white crescent on the front of the neck. The males are very much darker, with spiralled horns, but they too have the tell-tale white crescent. The males also have on their bodies a variable number of white spots and vertical white stripes.

Dik-diks

These are the smallest of antelopes, not much more than a foot high. They are common and widespread but tend to prefer dry country. They have tiny straight horns, much used for the making of jewellery. They are very agile and may frequently be seen dashing across the road in front of a car. There are two species, the common one, Kirk's, being seen in central and southern Kenya and in Tanzania and the Gruenther's, with its elongated snout, being found in the north.

Sable and Roan Antelopes

These handsome antelopes with their long, curved, sweeping back horns are uncommon in Kenya and Northern Tanzania. The roan has rather shorter horns than the sable and its ears have very long tufts of hair on them. Both roans and female sables are a lightish brown but male sables are a very dark brown. The only place in the region where sables may be found is the Shimba Hills Reserve south of Mombasa. The roan may be seen in Mara and the Serengeti. A small herd used to be found near Thika but it seemed unlikely that they could survive there long and so in 1970 they were trapped and transferred to the safety of the Shimba Hills.

Warthogs and Bush Pigs Lifespan 10–15. Weight 200 lbs. Gestation 6 months.

The warthog is the clown of East Africa. It is very common in almost every environment from thick mountain forest to open plains. It is grey and has the most extraordinarily ugly face with tusks which it uses to grub in the earth. The face is covered in bumps, especially below the eyes and some believe that these protect the eyes when the animal is grubbing in the ground with its tusks. When a warthog runs it holds its tail straight up in the air and a whole family trotting along in this way can be an especially amusing sight. But despite its comical appearance the warthog is not to be underestimated. It can be vicious and formidable when cornered and probably inflicts more wounds on human beings than any other animal.

The bush pig is related to the warthog but its tusks are much less well-developed even in the male. It is a rich brown in colour and has a pale grey mane. Although common it is not often seen because of its nocturnal habits. Both bush pigs and warthogs live in shallow burrows which they excavate themselves.

Hyraxes

A hyrax is about the size of a rabbit but much more like a guinea pig in appearance. Despite its size, its anatomy reveals that it is more closely related to the elephant than to any other animal. It is perhaps because of this relationship that the hyrax has for its size an astonishingly long gestation period: it carries its young for about seven months. There are two species, both brown and very similar to one another, known as the tree hyrax and the rock hyrax. The tree hyrax is distinguished by its much longer and softer hair. In practice in the field the two are very difficult to tell apart: it is usually simply assumed that a hyrax which is in a tree is a tree hyrax while one that is among rocks on the ground is a rock hyrax. The tree hyrax has a call which has terrified many an unsuspecting visitor lying awake on his first night in Africa. It has a wide repertoire of creaks and groans and finishes up with a quite unearthly scream which conjures up all sorts of half-conscious European fears of witchcraft and murder in the heart of darkest Africa. It must be admitted that some East African residents deliberately do not tell their visitors what to expect, just to have the fun of a little teasing at breakfast time.

Baboons Lifespan 10. Weight 60 lbs. Gestation 6 months.

Baboons are particularly common in areas where woodland and open plain meet. They go around in troops, often of thirty or forty, but sometimes of more than a hundred. They seem to vary considerably in size. Very big old males may be almost five feet tall, but in any troop animals of all sizes are to be seen. There are usually three or four big dominant males which control the troop and which appear to be particularly responsible for looking out for danger: in the case of the baboons this usually means leopard. Baboons are said to be a favourite food of leopard and this is borne out by the fact that if the leopards in an area are killed the baboon population seems to increase rapidly. After the old males come the females who almost always seem to be nursing or pregnant, and the young males. For the most part the troop leaders do not seem to be particularly sexually jealous and they allow the young males to mate with the females. The mothers often carry their young either riding on their backs or hanging on to the fur under their bellies. Finally in the troop there are the young animals, weaned but not yet sexually mature. There is a rigid social order but this seems to be maintained by mutual understanding rather than by brute force. It probably depends on the younger males and the females recognising the mailed fist behind the velvet glove treatment which they receive. Baboons are very curious animals and frequently approach cars and hotels. Visitors are usually asked not to feed them. Baboons which are fed soon become at best a nuisance as they try to steal anything and everything. At worst they are a real danger as a bad-tempered one can inflict quite a serious bite which can transmit some very unpleasant diseases.

Black-faced Vervet Monkeys

These are the monkeys most frequently seen by visitors. They especially frequent acacia trees in the vicinity of water but they too often like to come to hotels where food may be available. While they are fascinating and cheeky like the baboons they can become dangerous, not because of the severity of their bite but because of the diseases they can transmit. Apart from infections of the wound most animals which are not primates (monkeys, baboons, chimpanzees, etc.) do not transfer very serious diseases to humans with the exception of rabies. This is probably because humans are so different from, say, antelopes, that a bacterium or virus which is adapted to living in them cannot also easily thrive in human beings. But primates are so closely related to us that many of their diseases, notably some very unpleasant viral diseases of the brain, can be handed on to human beings. On the whole, the vervets are unremarkable in appearance apart from the bright red and blue genitals of the males which always attract a certain amount of embarrassed attention.

ANIMALS OF THE FOREST

With the exceptions of the giant forest hog, the bongo and the colobus monkey, the animals described in this section may also be found in bush and open woodland. However they all seem to be more at home in fairly thick forest.

Elephants   Lifespan 50–80. Weight 5–6 tons. Gestation 22 months.

Many who have spent a whole life time watching game have come to the conclusion that their favourite animal is the elephant. It is not difficult to see why: their immense size, their great age, the affection they show to their young and the sense of humour which they often seem to have are all appealing. Elephants are widely distributed throughout East Africa. As far as Kenya and Northern Tanzania are concerned, the best place to see them in large numbers is undoubtedly Tsavo Park, where there are approximately 20,000 elephants. They are also almost certain to be seen by visitors to Amboseli, Mara, Samburu-Isiolo, the hotels in the Aberdares, Marsabit, the Ngorongoro Crater and Manyara. Marsabit has the biggest elephants with the largest tusks.

Adult elephants are nine to twelve feet high, males being larger than females and having larger tusks. The brain of an elephant is much smaller than might be expected from the size of its skull. A major

o

purpose of the skull is to act as a point of attachment for the tusks and great muscles: the bone must be as light as possible and so it is full of empty air cells. There is an excellent specimen in the National Museum in Nairobi which shows this clearly. This explains why so many inexperienced hunters have been surprised when their shot into the head has had no effect on a charging elephant. The most obvious way in which the African elephant differs from the Indian elephant is in its possession of enormous ears which are important in cooling the body. Large amounts of warm arterial blood are pumped into the ears and this blood is then cooled as the enormous flaps wave in the breeze.

Elephants normally live until they are about sixty years old. As with most wild mammals, the age at which they die probably depends primarily on how long their teeth last. An animal which has lost its teeth and which therefore cannot chew its food will soon perish. The elephant is very unusual in that each side of the upper and lower jaws can carry only one large molar tooth at a time. The elephant during its long life can produce three of these teeth for each part of the jaw. When the first four are worn out, the second four grow forwards to replace them and so on. When the third group of four are finished then the animal can no longer eat its normal food. Very old elephants usually travel to swamps where they can devour the soft vegetation without having to chew it. When they die, they sink into the mud and this may explain why elephant skeletons are so rarely found, leading to the legend that elephants go to a secret place to die and that somewhere there must be a vast graveyard.

Female elephants carry their young for two years before birth. Their first one is usually born when they are between the ages of ten and twelve and thereafter they produce one every three to five years until they die. Elephants usually go around in large family groups containing animals of all sizes from tiny babies to the largest tuskers. The young may be born at any time of the year but December seems to be the favourite month.

It cannot be stressed too much that although elephants may appear amiable they are potentially dangerous even to people inside cars and they should not be provoked. Male elephants are not particularly easy to rouse and usually make one or two mock charges, stopping after just a few steps, in an effort to frighten the supposed enemy away. It is often possible to tell whether an elephant is serious or not by the position of its tusks. If they are pointing downwards it is not likely to be angry but if they are almost horizontal, then it is time to move away quickly. Female elephants with young are much more treacherous and will often charge seriously without any warning at all. There is only one safe rule when watching from a car a herd of elephant with young: that is to keep the car engine running and always try to point the vehicle away from the herd so that a quick get-away can be achieved if the worst happens.

For the most part, however, elephants do not use their tusks as weapons of offence. Their main employment seems to be in digging in the ground for water and salt. The right tusk seems to be more often employed and it is frequently partially worn away or even broken.

Perhaps the most fortunate people who watch elephants are those who have the chance to see them descending a muddy slope. They slither around on their feet and then give up the struggle, sit on their backsides and slide straight down, carrying all before them. One can almost see them smile, they so obviously enjoy it. They also obviously enjoy wallowing in mud and giving themselves dust baths although the purpose of these activities is not known. In consequence elephants are always the same colour as the earth in the area where they live and at a distance are frequently mistaken for termite mounds.

Rhinos Lifespan, 50–60. Gestation, 16–18 months.

Rhinos are animals which look as though they should have become extinct thousands of years ago. In fact all species of rhino are now in danger of just that, primarily because of the lunatic demand in the Far East for powdered rhino horn as an aphrodisiac. Two species can be found in East Africa. The white rhino is rare and is found only in Meru Game Reserve where it has recently been re-introduced and in a few localised areas in Uganda. The black rhino is the common one. It is found in all the major parks and reserves although Amboseli and Treetops in the Aberdares are the places where they are virtually certain to be seen in good conditions.

Both rhinos are massive creatures. The black is ten to eleven feet long and a little over five feet high: a big specimen may weigh two and a half tons. The white rhino is even bigger. It may be fourteen feet long, six feet tall and weigh three and a half tons. The other main difference between the two is in the shape of the mouth. The white one has a pointed and very mobile upper lip which it uses for browsing off bushes and trees. The white one has an enormous square mouth and primarily feeds by grazing on the ground. Despite the name, the white rhino is not pale in colour. The word 'white' is a corruption of the Afrikaans 'weit' which means wide and refers to the shape of its mouth. Both rhinos have horns which are different in structure from the horns of other animals. They consist of a mass of hard material known as keratin with no bony core or attachment to the skull.

Rhinos are reputed to be bad-tempered and to charge without warning. This may be true of occasional individuals but most rhinos seem to be relatively lethargic, especially in the day time, and charge only when repeatedly disturbed and provoked. A serious rhino charge is a frightening sight as the animal puts its head down and accelerates to thirty miles per hour within a few paces. Perhaps fortunately the rhino does not seem to be able to turn very quickly and in theory it is possible to escape by dodging at the last minute.

Lions have been known to attack and kill rhinos but this must be a very rare event. In reality the predators which trouble these vast tanks most are not the large ones but the minute ones, the ticks and other insects. Rhinos seem to welcome the attentions of oxpeckers which presumably help to keep down the population of these parasites. Another insect irritant is the rhino bot fly, a huge dark brown inset with a wing span of over two inches. This fly lays its eggs beneath the rhino's skin. When the eggs hatch, in an unknown way the maggots make their way to the rhino's gut where they live for some time before being passed out in the droppings. The maggots then pupate and eventually emerge as the adult flies.

Buffaloes   Lifespan, 25. Weight 1,700 lbs. Gestation, 11 months.

Most hunters and game wardens have no hesitation in saying that the buffalo is the most formidable animal with which they have to deal. It is the size of a very large cow, it has a large pair of very tough horns and it appears to be particularly intelligent and wary. One well-known trick is that an animal which has been disturbed will often seem to move away from the man who has disturbed it. But when out of sight it cautiously travels round in a large circle and then suddenly attacks from the least expected region, the back of the man. Most buffaloes are found in large herds and in the Mara and the Serengeti these may number over one thousand animals. These large herds behave more like cows than vicious wild animals and rarely seem to cause any trouble. But a number of bull buffaloes live a solitary existence and it is these which seem to attack humans. They will carefully watch an approaching human and if not seen they may make a sudden unprovoked frontal charge. If they are observed they may then circle round to attack at the back. Surprisingly little is known about the habits of what is after all quite a common animal. Again they are found in most of the parks. They are very rare in the Nairobi Park itself but quite a large herd is resident just outside the park on the nearby Ngong Hills and buffaloes not uncommonly confront those out on the Hills for a quiet walk. Buffalo love to wallow in deep mud and this behaviour can be ideally watched from Treetops in the Aberdares.

Giant Forest Hogs Lifespan, 10–15. Weight, 300lbs. Gestation, 4½ months.

This close relative of the warthog is strictly a forest species and it is never seen in bush or open country. It is likely to be observed only by those who visit Treetops or the Ark where numbers of them are often at the water-holes at night. It has black hair and a large hairless bump below its eyes which may help to protect the eyes when the animal is grubbing in the earth. The most surprising thing about it however is its sheer bulk, large males approaching three feet in height and being over four feet long. It is strictly nocturnal in habit.

Bongos

This too is a strictly forest animal. It sometimes comes to the waterhole at Treetops and more often to the one at the Ark, but even at these places visitors should count themselves very lucky to see one. It is a very beautiful large antelope, bright chestnut in colour and with vertical cream stripes on its flanks. Both sexes have spiralled horns. The male is over four feet high at the shoulder but the female is considerably smaller. Because of their relative rarity and extreme shyness virtually nothing is known about their habits.

Black and White Colobus Monkeys

This is the most beautiful of all the monkeys with its enormously long black and white coat. Because of its beauty it has been much killed and there are now some fears for its survival. It occurs in thick forest anywhere but it is most likely to be seen easily in the high bamboo forest of the Aberdares, Mount Kenya, Mount Elgon, Mount Meru and Kilimanjaro. It seems to use its long coat as a sort of parachute or gliding device and makes enormous leaps from branch to branch.

Sykes' Monkey

This is the other common forest monkey. It is greyish-brown, with a dark face and limbs, a white chest patch and a little white beard. It has a characteristic hoarse bark which it uses whenever alarmed or disturbed.

ANIMALS OF LAKES AND RIVERS

Only two mammals are truly adapted to this type of habitat in East Africa. These are the otter, which is not uncommon but which is unobtrusive and rarely seen, and the hippopotamus, which when present could hardly be missed. The Hippo is widely distributed and is found in all the parks where there is any reasonable amount of permanent water. One of the surprising things about it is that it is often found in small areas of water which are very far from any major river or lake. It is interesting to speculate, for example, on the ways in which the hippos got to the pools in the Athi River in Nairobi Park or to those at the bottom of the Ngorongoro Crater.

The hippo is a vast creature, twelve to fifteen feet long and almost five feet high. It may be over two tons in weight and lives for about 40 years. Its upper parts and flanks are blackish brown but its underparts are pink. It has an enormous mouth with very large teeth which are sometimes used for carvings or for personal decoration. During the day it spends most of its time submerged beneath the water with only its nostrils and perhaps its eyes and ears to be seen. Occasionally it will emerge for a moment and open its mouth in a cavernous yawn. The hippo does not however feed in the water. Every night it emerges on to the land and grazes on the surrounding grass, sometimes travelling many miles during the hours of darkness. But with the approach of dawn it returns to the water. The reason for the hippo's behaviour is unknown but it is probable that it is not able to lose heat easily, nor can it allow its body temperature to fluctuate. The rhino in contrast, during the heat of the day, allows its body temperature to rise to quite high levels without suffering any obvious harm. But the hippo, like human beings, must regulate its body temperature much more precisely if it is to survive and hence it cannot emerge from the water for long periods during the tropical day time. Despite its apparent toughness, the hippo's hide seems to be relatively delicate and easily damaged. When on land, special glands in the skin secrete an oily material containing a red pigment which appears to offer some protection against drying of the skin and the action of the sun. The secretion of this red pigment has given rise to the myth that the hippo sweats blood.

The lakes and rivers of Uganda are undoubtedly the places where hippos may be observed in the largest numbers. In Kenya and Northern Tanzania probably the best place to see them is Mzima Springs in Tsavo Park. A herd of hippo live in the fantastically clear water of the springs and can often be observed in the daytime from the unique underwater observation chamber.

Finally, it should be remembered that hippos, despite their apparent lethargy are dangerous animals. Their jaws can crush a man without trouble and it is foolish to provoke them. They not infrequently fight among themselves, especially when they are present in large numbers, and many animals may be seen with large gashes which have been inflicted by other hippos. This sort of behaviour does not seem to occur in areas which are not over-populated and this may be a warning to humans.

❧ 17 ❧

Snakes and Other Reptiles

The main reptiles likely to be encountered by the visitor to East Africa are the crocodiles, the lizards, the snakes and the tortoises and their relatives.

CROCODILES

Crocodiles are familiar to everyone. They differ from the alligators of America in two main respects. The biggest tooth in the lower jaw in alligators fits into a socket in the upper jaw, while in crocodiles it lies outside the lower jaw when the mouth is closed and can therefore be readily seen. The head of an alligator is much shorter and broader than that of a crocodile whose head is relatively long and tapered. Crocodiles grow to a length of eighteen feet or so but most of the ones seen are much smaller than this.

Crocodiles live in most freshwater lakes and rivers in East Africa, but undoubtedly the Nile, the lakes of Uganda and Lake Rudolf are the best places to see them. It is unwise to be misled by the sluggish appearance of a crocodile resting on land for they can move remarkably quickly. It is essential never to come within reach of the animal's powerful tail, one sweep of which can knock over even a large animal. The crocodile hunts in four main ways. It may catch waterfowl from the surface by coming up underneath them, it may swim after fish, it may disable an animal on land with a blow from its tail and then drag its victim into the water or it may lie in wait beneath the water in a place where animals come down to drink and drag some unsuspecting creature in by the nose. Crocodiles are definitely dangerous to humans and at regular intervals foolish people who ignore local warnings about

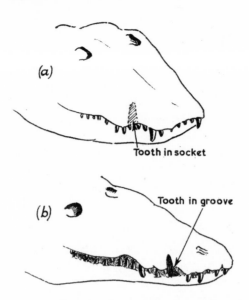

Jaws of alligator (a) and crocodile (b) compared. (*Courtesy Evans Bros. Ltd.*)

swimming are eaten. Crocodiles, although they can digest fresh meat, appear to have difficulty in tearing it into small enough pieces to swallow. It is therefore believed that they store many of the victims in underwater caves, leaving them until decomposition has gone far enough to allow them to be easily torn apart.

The teeth of the crocodile are quite different from those of mammals in that when one set is worn out it is replaced by another. The process apparently goes on indefinitely although no one can be sure. This form of replacement may allow the animal to live to an age of several hundred years although again no one can be certain. Crocodiles often bask with their mouths open and when this happens a bird, usually an Egyptian plover, may peck around the teeth removing bits of rotting flesh and the frequently numerous leeches. The crocodile does not seem to mind these attentions. This habit must be one of the earliest recorded facts about natural history because it is accurately described by Herodotus.

Crocodiles lay eggs in holes in the sand, usually about thirty to sixty at a time. They are then covered and allowed to hatch by the heat of the sun. The young crocodiles hatching are very vulnerable and many are eaten by lizards and by Marabou storks. Initially the young ones eat insects, then they graduate to fish and finally to mammals and birds.

The numbers of crocodiles in most of the river systems of the world are rapidly decreasing. This is almost entirely due to the activities of poachers who kill them because of the value of their hides for the manufacture of handbags, wallets and shoes.

LIZARDS

There are innumerable species of lizards in Africa but only three groups are likely to attract attention. All African lizards are quite harmless to humans.

The lizard most likely to be encountered is the little house gecko which lives in most East African buildings. It is in fact a very useful guest because it lives almost entirely on insects. The gecko is mainly nocturnal and like cats has a slit pupil which can open to an enormous extent. The way the gecko can run over walls and ceilings is fascinating. It can probably do this partly because of a suction mechanism and partly because of myriads of microscopic hooks which can hang on to the most minute projections on a wall. Geckos are the only lizards which can make a noise apart from hissing and this is what has given them their name. They click their tongue against the roof of the mouth and to the imaginative ear this makes a noise which sounds like geck-ko.

Agama lizards are common in the drier areas, often being seen around buildings though usually on the outsides. The males, which may be over a foot long, can have quite remarkable colours, being blue, brown and reddish orange. The intensity of colour seems to depend on the current degree of sexual success. The males compete with one another for a harem of females by fighting with one another using sideways blows of their tails. Successful males are startlingly bright, but defeated ones are a rather dull grey.

The third type of lizard not infrequently seen is the chameleon which is hated and feared by most Africans. It certainly has a quite extra-ordinarily horrible appearance but in spite of this is completely harmless. In fact it is helpful to man as it feeds exclusively on insects. Perhaps the chameleon's strangest features are the large protruberant eyes which can move entirely independently of one another. By using both of them to scan different places the animal can keep watch over a wide area for possible prey. When an insect is seen, the head is turned towards it and both eyes are brought to bear upon the victim, presumably to utilise the advantages of stereoscopic vision in assessing distances. The extremely long and sticky tongue which is normally folded in the front of the mouth then flashes out, captures the unfortunate insect and drags it back into the chameleon's jaws.

There are a number of species of chameleon most of which have a horny plate on their head which adds to their fearsome appearance. Some species have three frightening horns and it is easy to see how they got their evil reputation.

SNAKES

Because a few snakes are very poisonous and because a bite from one of these may kill within hours, these reptiles are almost universally feared. With some species, notably the mambas, cobras and puff adders, this fear is undoubtedly justified but the vast majority of snakes are harmless. Even with those snakes which are harmful, it is relatively rare for them to inject enough venom to kill an adult. The main problem with snakes is that only experts can tell the difference between the few poisonous snakes and the many harmless ones which often resemble the dangerous species closely. A policy of extreme caution should therefore be followed and for the non-expert the only safe snake is a dead snake.

All snakes are carnivorous and feed mostly on frogs, lizards and small mammals. Some eat eggs. They all have extraordinarily loosely hinged jaws which enable them to swallow victims whose bodies are greater in diameter than the snake itself. Most harmless snakes eat small creatures which they swallow whole and alive without trouble. Those which eat larger creatures must in some way kill their victim either before or during swallowing. The pythons and constrictors do this by crushing while the poisonous snakes do it by injecting venom.

According to the anatomy of their teeth and jaws, snakes can be divided into four groups, one harmless and three poisonous. The harmless snakes have many small teeth, all pointing backwards and relatively uniform in size. The three groups of poisonous ones all have one pair of teeth in the upper jaw which is much longer than the others.

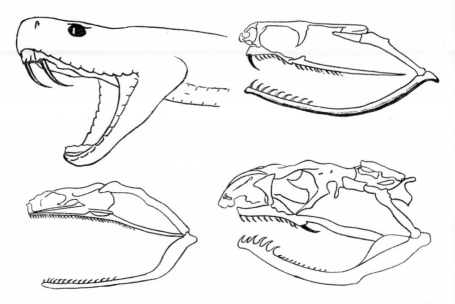

The jaws of a harmless snake (bottom left) and the three types of poisonous ones (Courtesy Evans Bros. Ltd.)

Each tooth in this pair has a fine hole down the middle rather like the needle of a hypodermic syringe. Above the tooth is a bag of venom which can be rapidly squeezed out when the snake seizes hold of its victim. The three types of fang are:

1. At the back of the mouth and fixed. The fangs are the last teeth in the upper jaw, well-placed to inject poison into a victim which has already been half-swallowed but not very effective for injecting venom into newly grasped prey. These snakes are therefore unlikely to be dangerous to human beings because unless by some remote ill chance a finger happens to go down the snake's throat or the limb of a very small child is bitten, the snake cannot effectively inject its poison.

2. At the front of the mouth and fixed. The cobras and the mambas come into this group. The two are closely related, the main difference being that cobras when roused erect a hood around the neck. Cobras and mambas are very alert and move like lightning. Almost invariably they flash off at the approach of human beings, the main exception to this rule being the Indian Hamadryad or king cobra which can be very aggressive. Cobras live primarily in the ground while mambas

live primarily among trees and vegetation and are very common in the coastal forests and also in makuti roofs. The venom of these snakes is extremely dangerous and a large dose can kill within the hour, although several hours is more usual. Because the fangs are fixed and relatively short, even thin loose clothing offers quite good protection as the jaws cannot then get a grip of the underlying skin. Some of the cobra family primarily inject their venom by spitting rather than biting. They direct their fangs at any bright object and are remarkably accurate over a distance of several feet. In most cases, the brightest objects on an animal or human are the eyes: venom which enters the eyes is almost as quickly absorbed into the blood as if it were injected.

3. At the front of the mouth and hinged. The vipers and adders have fangs of this type and in some ways are the most dangerous snakes of all. This is because their fangs are very much longer than those of the other groups and are kept folded back along the upper jaw. When the snake is aroused they are erected in a flash and because of their length and forward position it is relatively easy for the snake to get a good grip even through clothing. The vipers and adders can be fairly easily recognised because they have a flat triangular-shaped head, a definite neck and a very heavy thick body. They are sluggish and paradoxically this greatly increases their danger to human beings because they do not quickly get away as humans approach. The sluggishness does not apply to their striking speed and hence puff adders are probably the commonest causes of snake bite death. The puff adder lives mainly in relatively dry country and likes to lie on rocks or on patches of sand such as are found on pathways. The Gaboon viper is closely related but lives mainly in forests.

Snakes produce two main types of venom. One type acts primarily on the nervous system causing paralysis and affecting the normal function of the heart. The other acts primarily on the blood, destroying red blood cells, preventing clotting and causing bleeding into the lungs, skin and internal organs. The cobras produce the former, the vipers the latter, although the Gaboon viper may produce both types.

Only a very large dose of venom from a large snake will kill within an hour or so. More usually if death is going to occur it happens after several hours or even one or two days. The principles of first aid treatment are outlined in chapter 24. Treatment with anti-venom should not usually begin until definite symptoms are noticed. Most bites even from dangerous species do not inject enough venom to cause trouble. The anti-venom itself can be toxic and so it is unwise to inject it unless absolutely necessary. Preferably the treatment should be given by a qualified doctor.

Anti-venoms are prepared by using the venoms themselves. The snakes are 'milked' by making them strike at a cup covered with a rubber diaphragm. The venom then drips into the cup below. The process can be seen at the Nairobi Snake Park on Wednesday afternoons at 5.30. The anti-venom is prepared by injecting the venom into a horse, starting with a very small dose and then gradually increasing. The horse becomes immune to the venom because it produces antibodies which can neutralise the poison. The horse is then bled at intervals and the antibodies are extracted from its blood.

TORTOISES AND THEIR RELATIVES

Several species of tortoise are found in East Africa. The largest are the leopard tortoises with their high domed shells: they may reach sixty or seventy pounds in weight. Some of the species of tortoise here are interesting in that their shells are hinged about a third of the way from the rear end. This enables the back end to be more effectively closed to protect the soft parts when danger threatens.

Terrapins are similar to tortoises but they spend much of their time in water and have partially flattened legs which act as paddles. They are primarily carnivorous, eating worms, small fish and other creatures.

Turtles are completely adapted to life in water and their paddle limbs are very clumsy on land. They leave water only during the breeding season in order to lay their eggs in sand. One type, the soft-shelled river turtle lives in fresh water. It has an extremely long snout which enables it to breathe when otherwise totally submerged. It grows to about three feet long and can inflict a very nasty bite. Three turtles are found in East African seas. The leathery turtle is quite different from its relatives in that instead of hard horny plates it is entirely covered by a leathery type of material with marked longitudinal ridges. The green turtle is the one which is used for making soup. The hawk's bill is remarkable for its overlapping plates, used as 'tortoiseshell', and its beak-like jaws, the upper one curving over the lower.

Bird Life and Where to Find It

East Africa is an ornithologist's paradise. Well over one thousand species have been recorded here and in the remoter areas of the north and in the dense forests there may well be entirely new species waiting to be discovered. This abundance compares very favourably with the below eight hundred species which have been seen in North America and the under five hundred recorded in the British Isles.

But more important for the ordinary traveller is the fact that not only is there a large number of species but many of them are large, brilliantly coloured, easily observed and have fascinating habits. Even the visitor who knows absolutely nothing about birds and has no interest in learning their names can find pleasure in looking at their beautiful plumage and in watching their amusing antics.

Birds can be found in abundance in all the parks and reserves, on farmland and in gardens. Excellent places in the parks are the water courses and the lodges to which birds are attracted by the supplies of food. Perhaps the most easily accessible places where anyone can see a vast amount of interesting bird life are Lakes Nakuru, Naivasha and Magadi in the Rift Valley. At the coast, Mida Creek near Gedi provides spectacular concentrations of shore birds, especially in March, April and early May when there are almost incredible numbers of migrants on their way to Northern Europe and Asia. Other good localities for the bird specialist are listed at the end of this chapter. The person who is interested in making bird watching the main purpose of his trip to East Africa is strongly advised to seek advice from the National Museum in Nairobi at an early stage in planning. On arrival in East Africa a couple of hours spent in studying the superb collection of mounted birds in the Gandhi Room in the National Museum in Nairobi will pay dividends in the field.

Birds can be seen at any time of the year, but most of them breed and are therefore in their most beautiful plumage during and immediately after the long rains in March, April and May. At this time supplies of food for the young nestlings are most abundant. This rule does not apply to many of the birds of prey which have difficulty in seeing and catching their victims in the long grass which springs up so quickly when the rains come. They therefore tend to breed during the dry season when the grass is withered and small creatures on the ground can be more easily spotted and caught.

The remainder of this chapter is devoted to describing briefly those birds which the non-ornithologist can hardly fail to notice in his travels around the country.

Starlings

To a European the word starling conjures up a vision of a rather scruffy, dull bird with noisy habits. He will therefore be astonished when he sees the East African starlings which are of quite a different sort, as far as feathers are concerned, but which nevertheless have the same noisy and gregarious habits. Over thirty species are found here, but three are particularly common around game lodges and in the parks. Two of these, the blue-eared glossy starling with dark blue and green iridescent plumage and the superb starling, bright blue and green on top and on the upper part of its chest with a rich chestnut belly, are seen almost everywhere. Around Kilaguni Lodge in Tsavo Park, the golden-breasted starling, one of the world's most graceful and beautifully coloured birds is common. It has a very long tail, a blue back and a brilliant yellow belly. All these starlings are valuable to man because of the vast numbers of grubs and insects which they consume.

Sunbirds

As a group these are the most beautiful birds of all, comparable only to the humming birds of the Americas. They are small, brilliantly coloured, and have very fine curved bills which they use to extract nectar from flowers and to catch the tiny insects on which they feed. There are over fifty species and while it is easy to say that a bird is a sunbird, even experienced bird watchers often have difficulty in telling one type from another. Sunbirds can be found in almost every type of country from the hot and dry thorn bush plains to the alpine moorlands of the high mountains. They are perhaps most easily seen in gardens around Nairobi and in the Highlands and also feeding on the giant plants of the Mount Kenya Moorland.

Weaver Birds

Wherever you go in the parks and reserves where there is thorn bush or savannah country you will see trees with many birds' nests hanging from them. These are made by weaver birds and are very firmly and finely woven to provide a secure structure hanging from a twig. The apparently fragile nests are remarkably tough and are rarely displaced even by high winds. Moreover because they are hanging free and are roofed, it is very difficult for predators whether snakes, lizards, animals or larger birds to get into the nests to steal the eggs or nestlings. These nests are built by a group of birds known as the weavers, which are closely related to sparrows. Their thick tough beaks show that they are primarily seed eaters although they are not averse to devouring almost anything. The true weavers which make the best nests are all black and yellow and there are over forty species here. Some are colonial and build many nests together in a single tree while others build singly.

Related to the true weavers but having many other colours in their plumage and building much scruffier nests, is a vast army of other birds all of them obviously sparrow-like in build. Perhaps the most important of these is the red-billed quelea, an almost incredibly prolific species which starts breeding at the age of six months and nests in huge colonies. Outside the breeding season the flocks of queleas which can be large enough to darken the sky like locusts range far and wide in search of food. If they descend on a farm where rice or wheat or some other palatable crop is being grown, the devastation can be almost total. In consequence much thought is being devoted to ways in which the red-billed quelea may be controlled.

Whydahs

Whydahs are also basically sparrow-like birds but ones which are distinguished by the fantastically long tails which the males develop during the breeding season. They particularly favour grassland country. The Paradise Whydah with its basically black plumage but yellow nape and belly is not at all uncommon. Its tail is heavy and almost three times as long as the birds itself. The males have the habit

P

of struggling in a fluttering flight up from the grass and then dropping
like a stone as if exhausted.

Oxpeckers or Tick Birds

These are brownish birds closely related to the starlings. There are two
varieties, the yellow-billed, more common in Uganda, and the red-
billed, more common in the rest of East Africa. Oxpeckers force themselves on the attention of anyone who watches game animals. They
commonly swarm over game, like so many acrobats searching for ticks
and other parasites in the hair. Apart from killing parasites they also
help the game by giving warning by their shrill cries of approaching
intruders. Hunters in particular do not like oxpeckers as they will often
warn a quarry that it is being stalked. Their activities may not be entirely beneficial as they have the extremely unpleasant habit of pecking
at the surfaces of raw wounds and so preventing healing. Elephants do
not like oxpeckers at all and always try to brush them off with their
trunks.

Shrikes

When driving along almost any road one cannot fail to see perched on
various vantage points, often telegraph poles or wires, black and white
birds which are rather bigger than sparrows. Close observation shows
that these birds have a tiny hooked beak like that of a miniature hawk.
And that in habit is what these birds are. They are known as fiscal
shrikes and they spend most of their time sitting on some suitable wire
or post staring at the ground watching for the slightest movement
which might betray the presence of a lizard, grasshopper or other small
creature. So long as a small animal, even a brightly-coloured one,
stays absolutely still, the shrike appears to take no notice. But with the
slightest movement the bird is on to its prey in a flash, grasping it and
flying back to its vantage point to kill and devour it. In times of plenty,
these shrikes may use a nearby thorn tree as a 'larder'. Such trees are a
gruesome sight with scores of insects and small animals impaled upon
the thorns. The purpose of these larders is uncertain as the shrike never
seems to go back to eat the food stored there.

There are over a score of other shrikes to be seen in East Africa, all of
interest to the keen ornithologist. But only the fiscal is likely to catch
the eye of everyone.

Hornbills

These are large birds with enormous beaks, out of all proportion to the size of the bird. They occur almost everywhere but are often most conspicuous in dry thorn bush country. Although apparently so un-wieldy, their beaks are in fact very light and strong consisting internally of air cells criss-crossed by reinforcing struts. The birds use their beaks primarily for feeding on fruit and berries. On the whole they do not fly very well and one, the ground hornbill, hates to fly at all. This is not surprising since it is about the size of a turkey and very like a turkey in appearance. Unlike the other hornbills, the ground hornbill is largely carnivorous, eating mainly lizards and small snakes.

All the hornbills nest in holes in trees and with the exception again of the ground hornbill, they all have the remarkable habit of walling the female up in the nesting hole while the eggs are laid and hatched. In the case of the casqued hornbill the female stays in her hole for about four months: not surprisingly when she finally emerges she is very weak and may not be able to fly for a few days. At the beginning of the breed-ing season, the female climbs into her hole and mud is brought to her by the male. Using this mud she blocks up the entrance hole leaving only a small slit through which she can be fed. The male hornbills show remarkable devotion to their mates and offspring in feeding them right through this period. It is therefore not surprising that hornbills are probably one of the types of bird which mate for life.

Secretary Birds

This utterly unmistakable bird is most often seen stalking through grassland, carefully searching the ground in front of it. It stands over three feet high and has a bunch of feathers sticking out from behind its head: these give the impression of the quill pens stuck behind the ear of a medieval clerk, hence its name. The upper parts of the bird are grey but the wing tips and feathers at the top of the legs are black. Secretary birds are most reluctant to fly and will in preference run away from a car or an intruder at great speed. However when necessary they are strong fliers although because of their bulk they have trouble in lifting themselves into the air. They spread their wings wide and run into the wind, getting faster and faster rather like an aeroplane rushing down a runway, until eventually they have enough lift to take off.

The secretary bird is looked on with favour by most humans. It hunts on the ground, killing small rodents and lizards and, of course, the snakes for which it is famous. It kills a snake by hitting it with its hard horny feet, protecting itself from being bitten by flapping its huge wings at the reptile.

Vultures

Vultures are generally regarded as the most evil of birds and their name has passed into literature as a term of violent abuse. Certainly they are hardly beautiful when seen on the ground. Their grotesque bare heads are essential, as feathers would become hopelessly soiled in the process of feeding on and in rotting carcases. Vultures are undoubtedly gluttons and there are few more horrible sights in Africa than an animal's body on which a score or more vultures are squabbling and feeding. They gorge themselves to the limit and when absolutely full they stand around looking sick with their wings spread half open. There are six species to be seen here although two, the griffin and the white-backed are particularly common.

But once in the air a vulture is transformed into a thing of grace and beauty, as using the rising currents of hot air it glides and soars for hour after hour, always keenly scanning the ground for signs of carrion. Once a bird spots a dead or dying creature it will then start to glide down. Vultures seem to watch each other as well as the ground and as soon as it appears that one bird has found something it will quickly be joined by others so that soon the sky is full of circling, waiting birds. For the visitor keen on seeing lions, the vultures are good friends because they often enable a fresh kill to be easily located: without the tell-tale sight of circling birds many hours could be spent in fruitlessly searching the bush. For the game warden they are also invaluable for several reasons. First they rapidly clear the flesh from dead animals so that within a very few days the small insects and other scavengers finish the job leaving only a pile of clean white bones instead of a rotting carcase. Second, they point to areas where animals are dying and perhaps may give warning of an outbreak of disease. Third, and perhaps most important in this rapacious modern world, they give warning of where poachers are at work. Many poachers have been caught in remote areas of game parks only because their presence has been betrayed by a circling column of vultures.

Other Birds of Prey

For many people, predators are the most exciting of all birds, partly because of their handsome appearance and partly because of their dramatic modes of flight. In Europe and North America birds of prey are now not very common because intensive farming and the widespread use of pesticides have destroyed the populations of smaller creatures on which the predators feed. But this has not yet happened in Africa and one of the most striking things which will be noticed by the visiting ornithologist is the profusion of birds of prey of many different varieties.

The three that almost everyone will see and take note of are the African black kite, the augur buzzard and the African fish eagle. The black kite is common, especially around villages and towns. It is rather smaller than a crow, has a very graceful hovering, swooping and dipping flight and is readily identified by its dark colour and V-shaped tail. The augur buzzard is a large bird which eats rodents exclusively: it is the one which is frequently seen by the roadside perched on a telegraph pole, sisal plant or other suitable point of vantage. It is dark grey on top and has a chestnut tail. Its underparts come in two varieties, either dark grey or white: the two types belong to the same species and readily interbreed. Fish eagles may be seen on almost any reasonably substantial stretch of water, perhaps most easily at Lake Naivasha where they can usually be observed perching on the dead trees sticking out of the water not far from the Lake Hotel. They are unmistakable with white heads, chests, backs and tails, chestnut coloured bellies and black wings. They have a wild shrieking cry, one of the unforgettable sounds of Africa. Like all eagles they are superb fliers and to see one plunge into the water from a height of thirty or forty feet is a magnificent sight. However, like many birds of prey they are just a little lazy and are by no means above chasing other fish-eating birds such as herons and forcing them to drop their catch.

Storks

Storks are large birds with long beaks and long legs. They fly with their necks extended straight out. They are among the most conspicuous birds on the African scene. Of the several types found here, two, the yellow-billed stork and the Marabou stork are particularly common.

The former is not usually far from water but Marabous can be seen almost everywhere. The Marabou is a grotesque looking creature with a bald head, a repulsive pink pouch of no known function hanging down from its neck, a dejected look and a habit of sitting back on its knees. In behaviour it is closer to the vultures than to the other storks and it feeds on carrion of all varieties, being very commonly seen at the site of a kill. Unlike the vulture, however, it does itself kill and eat living creatures, for the most part frogs, lizards and grasshoppers.

Crested or Crowned Cranes

This is a magnificent bird which has been adopted as the national emblem of Uganda. It stands over three feet high and most obviously differs from the storks in having only a small beak. It is basically greyish in colour but with a striking head which carries a beautiful crest of yellow bristle-like feathers. It is most common in grassland and in marshy areas. The cry of the crested crane is a dramatic trumpeting call, most often uttered in flight and not dissimilar to the call of wild geese. Both male and female birds dance a great deal, often using most complicated forms. Unlike many birds the cranes do not dance only in the breeding season and their performance may be seen all the year round.

Flamingos

There can be few people who have not seen these beautiful pink birds in a zoo or who have not been attracted by photographs of hundreds of thousands of them massed by the side of some African lake. Yet despite their familiarity their habits are still largely either unknown or not understood. There are two varieties, the greater flamingo which stands about five feet high, and has bright red on its wings but is otherwise a very pale pink. The lesser flamingo is three to four feet high and is a much redder bird with a dark carmine beak.

Both types prefer alkaline, mineral-rich lakes as opposed to truly fresh water and they are particularly found on the chain of soda lakes in Kenya and Northern Tanzania, Hannington, Nakuru, Elmentaita, Magadi, Natron, Manyara and Eyasi. They usually occur in vast flocks and often form an incredible band of pink, many yards across, along the lake shore. Flamingos feed on the algae which swarm in these mineral-rich waters and their beaks are especially adapted for the purpose. Inside the beak there is a network of fine but tough bristles through which water is pumped by the tongue. The algae are trapped by the bristles and swallowed. The flight of these masses of flamingos is one of the most striking sights in the world. Often towards evening for no apparent reason the whole flock will take off and slowly circle upwards until they reach a certain height with which they are satisfied when they suddenly fly straight off to another part of the lake or to a different lake.

The factors which govern the breeding of these birds are very obscure. They certainly do not breed every year in East Africa and often several years go by without any breeding record at all. There is also no apparent consistency in the time of year chosen for nesting. The favoured sites appear to be Lakes Magadi and Natron. When the birds do decide to breed they build a pile of mud about a foot high on which the two eggs are laid. The nestlings hatch out about four weeks later.

Game Birds

Game birds, guinea fowl, spurfowl and francolins are common in the grass, savannah and thorn bush areas of East Africa. Guinea fowl are large dark grey birds which usually go around in large flocks. There are three types, the helmeted, the crested and the vulturine, all of which have striking heads and necks. Spurfowl and francolin are small brown partridge-like birds which are very common everywhere. Spurfowl are distinguished by having a patch of bare skin on their throats.

Bustards

Bustards are yet another group of large birds common on open grassland. They walk in an extremely stately manner and appear to go very slowly but in fact although they are usually seen on the ground and are reluctant to fly, one never seems to be able to get close to them while on foot. The giant of all bustards is the Kori bustard, the males of which may be five feet tall. Female bustards tend to be much smaller than males and the female Kori is about three feet tall. The birds have very loose neck feathers giving the impression of an extraordinarily thick neck. They often stand with their beak pointing upwards at an angle of 45°. They eat all types of insects including locusts and grasshoppers and are therefore very useful to farmers.

Ostriches

These huge flightless birds are, of course, utterly unmistakable and are very common throughout East Africa. The males have a striking black and white plumage while the females are a rather dowdy brownish-grey. There are two varieties to be seen in Kenya and Tanzania. In the common one, seen over the greater part of the region, the legs and neck of the male are pink. In the Somali Ostrich, found in Northern Kenya and easily seen in the Samburu-Isiolo Game Reserve, the legs and neck of the males are bluish-grey. The females of the two varieties are indistinguishable from one another.

The ostrich eats only vegetable food and constantly seems to be pecking at something or other on the ground. It is often polygamous with several females laying their eggs in one nest. As a result the number of eggs is enormous, sometimes being as many as sixty. The male usually sits on the nest at night and the females during the day. If the male sat during the day his black and white plumage would make the nest very conspicuous. In fact ostrich nests are not nearly so easy to find as might be expected because the sitting birds extend their necks flat along the ground so that they cannot easily be seen. It is said that ostriches are a favourite food of lion but they are virtually never caught. By virtue of their height they can see any lion approaching and unless caught unawares in the first mad rush they can outpace, outlast and out-dodge most lions.

Pelicans

These too are birds which are unmistakable and known to everyone. They are common on all stretches of water but are most easily seen on Lake Naivasha. There are two varieties, the white which has a white head and back and the pink-backed which has a grey head and pink rump. Pelicans do not easily take off from water but once in the air they are excellent fliers: this especially applies to the larger white variety with its huge wing span of about nine feet. When landing they look just like old-fashioned large flying boats. They use their beak and the enormous pouch hanging from it for catching the fish on which they feed almost exclusively. They seem to be highly intelligent and sometimes fish in groups, gathering in a half circle to drive a shoal of fish into the shallows.

Where to Find the Birds

The most spectacular places for both ornithologists and non-specialists to visit are Mida Creek near Gedi on the coast and the Rift Valley

TOP *A Kori Bustard in Samburu-Isiolo Game Reserve.*

BOTTOM *A male ostrich.*

TOP *A ground hornbill at Amboseli.*

BOTTOM *A secretary bird in the Serengeti.*

TOP *A martial eagle taking off. This bird had been waiting at the entrance to a rodent burrow to catch the animal as it came out.*

BOTTOM LEFT *A superb starling.*

BOTTOM RIGHT *A fiscal shrike in Nairobi National Park.*

A magnificent red billed hornbill at Kilaguni.

TOP *Flamingos taking off from the soda lake in Ngorongoro Crater.*

BOTTOM *Four yellow-billed storks feeding on Lake Magadi.*

The Hammerkop. It is widely believed that anyone who harms the Hammerkop is liable to ill fortune for the rest of his days.

TOP *Vultures waiting for lions to finish their meal.*

BOTTOM *Pelicans at Lake Naivasha sitting on the branches of a dead tree, killed by the rise in the lake's level.*

A heron at Lake Naivasha.

TOP *The typically scruffy nest of a sparrow weaver.*

BOTTOM *A chameleon hanging upside down.*

TOP *A male Agama Lizard in Tsavo.*

BOTTOM *A puff adder. Note the flattened head and thick body.*

Lakes, Baringo, Hannington, Nakuru, Elmentaita, Naivasha, Magadi and Natron. Of these Naivasha and Nakuru are the most easily accessible, Naivasha being fresh and Nakuru soda.

For birds of open country and woodland, the parks and game reserves without exception all have rich bird populations. For the woodland birds to be seen around Nairobi, including sunbirds, the Arboretum is an excellent place. For birds of prey and cliff dwellers, Hell's Gate near Naivasha and Lukenia Hill on the north side of the Mombasa Road about 40 miles from Nairobi are both good locations.

The bird specialist who wants more information on where to find particular species is strongly advised to write to the National Museum, P.O. Box 658, Nairobi.

❦ 19 ❦

Insects and their Allies

To most non-naturalists, anything small and creepy crawly is an insect and this chapter deals with such creatures. In fact the true insects are characterised among other things by having six legs. Spiders and scorpions, for instance, have eight legs and belong to another group but this is hardly something which is likely to bother most people.

In fact East Africa is a far less insect-ridden place than most visitors expect and fear. Holidays in southern Europe, western Scotland or northern North America are likely to be far more disturbed by insect pests than vacations in Kenya or Tanzania. This chapter briefly describes those varieties which the visitor will encounter and some which he may fear but is most unlikely ever to see.

Mosquitoes

Mosquitoes are usually unable to complete their life cycle above about 6,000 feet because of the cold and so it is only in the areas at lower altitude where they are likely to be troublesome. They also require water for breeding and so they are most frequent at the coast, near lakes and rivers, and in swamps. A number of diseases can be transmitted by mosquito bites but most are rare and in practice malaria is the one of overwhelming importance. Malaria is transmitted only by the Anopheles group of mosquitoes which can be identified because they are the only mosquitoes which rest with their tail ends tipped up into the air and their back pair of legs off the ground. All Anopheles mosquitoes do not transmit malaria: it is only the females which do the blood sucking, the males surviving entirely on plant juices. Furthermore, the only females which can transmit the disease are those which have already had a blood meal from someone who has malaria parasites circulating in the blood. The majority of bites even by Anopheles mosquitoes are therefore likely to be quite harmless. However it is foolish not to take the precautions of treatment with a prophylactic drug and of sleeping under a mosquito net in places where they are plentiful.

Tsetse Flies

These are rather like large brown house flies which settle with their wings folded on top of one another. Their bite is painful and so in contrast to the mosquito one almost always knows that one is being attacked. Tsetses are important because they transmit the group of diseases known as the trypanosomiases (sleeping sickness in man). This is primarily a disease of wild animals and is transmitted to man more or less by accident. A policy of elimination of their breeding areas has now ensured that tsetses are much less common than formerly in areas frequented by tourists. Sleeping sickness is now rare even among the local inhabitants and it is not a disease which the visitor need fear.

Butterflies and Moths

This is not the place for an account of East Africa's butterflies and moths which are very beautiful and very numerous. Interestingly enough as far as these insects are concerned, the country is very much divided by the Great Rift Valley, many species found on the west not being found on the east and vice versa. The western butterflies show affinities with those of West Africa while those east of the Rift are more closely connected with those in south and south eastern Africa. Those interested in butterflies should visit the National Museum and in particular its Kitale branch. The latter houses the magnificent collection made by the late Colonel Stoneham and given to the nation.

Ants

Contrary to popular belief, the large mounds seen all over Africa are not built by ants but by termites. Although termites are sometimes called 'white ants' the two groups are quite unrelated. The nests of true ants are much less conspicuous above ground but below may go down a remarkable fifteen to twenty feet. The most spectacular of all the myriad varieties of ants are undoubtedly the safari or driver ants known in Swahili by the special name of siafu. They make only temporary nests and migrate from place to place in huge columns, the workers carrying with them the queen and the young ants. Safari ants are particularly vicious and will attack almost any living thing in their way. They have been known to get up the trunks of elephants, so making the huge beasts extremely bad-tempered and destructive. The ants are notorious for entering chicken runs and devouring all the inhabitants alive. Fortunately they also kill other insects and one of the best ways to rid a house of cockroaches is to persuade a column of safari ants to pass through. The house is quite uninhabitable while they are passing but once they have gone it will be free of cockroaches for many months.

Termites (*'White Ants'*)

These are the creatures responsible for the large mounds of earth, often with fantastic turrets and towers, seen all over tropical Africa. As with ants, there is a well-marked division of labour among termites. At the head and centre of the colony is the queen who, if seen in an isolated state, would not be recognised by most people as an insect. The fore-quarters are typically insect-like but the abdomen is grossly swollen to form a vast egg-laying machine over half-an-inch thick and several inches long. The queen chamber is in the centre of the nest and in it she lays eggs which are carefully taken by workers to places where they can safely hatch out into nymphs. The nymphs will grow and develop into one of three types of adult, soldier, worker or reproductive.

In any colony the workers are in the great majority: they are sterile males and females with no wings. Their first job is to construct the nest with its fantastic network of tunnels and galleries. The second task is to gather the grass and wood which are stored in the galleries: it is this wood gathering which can prove so destructive to the fabric of a house. Third, and perhaps most remarkable, the workers tend the fungus gardens which appear to form the major source of food for termites. The termites probably do not themselves eat much of the wood and vegetable material which they gather. Instead they persuade fungi to grow on the collected material and then they eat the much more digestible fungi. This habit preceded the human development of agriculture by millions of years.

There are much smaller numbers of soldiers, also sterile, blind, wingless males and females but with powerful jaws which can see off most other insect intruders. The only exceptions are safari ants which can quickly destroy a termite colony.

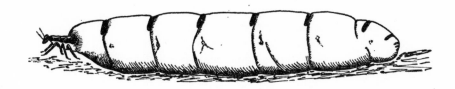

A queen termite, approximately natural size. (*Courtesy Evans Bros. Ltd.*)

Finally there are the reproductives which have wings and eyes and which are much larger than workers and soldiers. At some signal to which they all respond they leave the nest in vast numbers for their nuptial flight. The force which starts them off is unknown but it often seems to be a shower of heavy rain occurring at the right time of the year. Whatever it is applies over a wide area for the reproductives from termite colonies several miles apart often leave their nests at approximately the same time. Their long flimsy wings cannot carry the insects very far and they soon flutter to the ground. There the wings fall off and the reproductives pair up, moving off in a line to a place where they can excavate a hole to start a new colony. For unknown reasons, the king and queen who start the colony will eat no food until the first eggs have developed into workers. Until that time they live on the large stores of fat in the wing muscles and in other parts of the body. This explains why 'flying ants' are regarded as a great delicacy by birds, lizards and even by human beings. If the flight occurs at night as it often does, some peoples set up lights to attract the insects which are then caught, fried and eaten. Certainly the flight of reproductive termites is something never to be forgotten so vast are the numbers involved. But these vast numbers are undoubtedly needed for the slaughter is terrific and only a very small proportion reach their destination.

Dung Beetles

It is an odd fact that the sacred scarab beetle of the ancient Egyptians was a member of a large group of beetles which feeds on dung. Such beetles may often be seen in Africa, rolling along a little ball of dung which they will bury in the ground. The beetles then eat the dung themselves or deposit an egg within the ball so that the newly hatched larva will have plenty to eat.

Scorpions

No visitor to East Africa who does not camp in a dry place is likely to see a scorpion. The risk of being stung, even when camping, is virtually non-existent. When camping it is however wise to take certain elementary precautions such as shaking out one's shoes before putting them on in the morning and exercising caution when turning over stones or logs. The sting of a scorpion is extremely painful and may cause temporary disorders of the nervous system with a more prolonged numbness around the site of the wound. A scorpion sting is unlikely to kill any reasonably healthy adult but children frequently succumb. Anti-venoms are available but they can be dangerous if used wrongly and they should be administered only by a qualified doctor.

Centipedes and Millipedes

These are unpleasant looking creatures with a hard outer shell, many segments and seemingly innumerable legs. Centipedes have only one pair of legs on each segment and can inflict a nasty bite. Millipedes have two pairs of legs on each segment, are vegetarians and are quite harmless. Both centipedes and millipedes are common at the coast.

Ticks

Ticks are flat, hard-backed little creatures which live in vegetation and attach themselves to living animals whose blood they suck. They have remarkable powers of survival and can remain alive in soil or grass for several years if no suitable host presents itself. It is not uncommon to acquire ticks when walking through grass. Their bite is normally painless and they are noticed only on inspection or as the result of itching. They can pass on a disease known as tick fever whose main characteristics are high fever, headache and a general feeling of malaise. The disease responds very rapidly to drugs of the tetracycline group.

20

Flowers and Trees

The first things about Nairobi which impress most people are its colourful flowers and plants. Coming in from the airport along Uhuru Highway no one could fail to be impressed by the bougainvilleas, palms, cacti and other plants which make this major traffic artery and its roundabouts so attractive. This first impression that Kenya is a land of flowers is confirmed almost everywhere one goes. Throughout the country beautiful gardens and colourful flowers are to be seen everywhere.

Clearly in a general guide it is impossible to mention any but a few of the most obvious and striking plants. Many flower all the year round but perhaps two periods are the most favoured. The first is the long rains in April and May when most of the small annuals spring up and bloom, sometimes transforming semi-desert into a mass of colour. The second is October, just before the short rains when many of the flowering trees and shrubs are at their best. It is at this time that the jacarandas transform so many towns and cities with their improbably deep blue flowers. During September, once the cloudy season has passed and the sun has begun to shine, the jacaranda trees steadily shed their leaves. A few pioneer patches of blue appear but not until the branches are almost bare does the true explosion of colour occur. So thick are the flowers that from a distance the trees appear to be covered with blue leaves.

Except when the jacarandas are in flower, the plant which dominates the scene in most of East Africa is the bougainvillea. The bougainvillea developed in the South American Andes and takes its name from a sixteenth-century French explorer. Originally there were probably only two or three colours of the magenta and red types. Also originally the bougainvillea was primarily a climbing plant. But so adaptable is it and so beautiful are the brilliantly coloured petal-like structures which surround the rather diminutive true flowers, that myriads of forms and colours are now known as a result of selective breeding and crossing. Bougainvillea can be grown as a climber, as a bush or as a plant which spreads over the ground. Many of the new varieties originated and were developed in Nairobi under the care of Mr Greensmith who used to be Superintendent of the Nairobi Parks. He is responsible for much of the city's present scenic beauty. Those who are especially interested in bougainvilleas should try to pay a visit to the nurseries in City Park where new varieties are constantly being sought and developed.

Because of East Africa's favourable climate and range of altitude, almost any plant can be persuaded to grow somewhere in the region without too much difficulty. The frangipanni which started its career in Mexico prefers the warmer areas: its strange smooth branches and its creamy white fragrant flowers are unmistakable. The hibiscus, the moonflower and the poinsettia are other South and Central American plants which are now important on the East African scene. Perhaps the most striking of the indigenous flowering trees is the Nandi Flame with its dark green leaves and enormous scarlet flowers. The Nandi flame has been immortalised by Elspeth Huxley in her book '*The Flame Trees of Thika*'.

Like the shrubs and trees, non-woody flowers of all varieties do well in East Africa. This is clearly shown by the colourful stalls of the flower sellers where you can buy an almost unbelievable armful of fragrance and beauty for just a few shillings. Flower growing is an industry which is rapidly developing as the potential of the overnight air freight service to the darkness of the northern European winter is being realised.

Away from the gardens and cultivated areas, the dominant plants tend to be the trees and bushes. In the dry areas the thorn bushes with the occasional massive baobab are the most obvious types of vegetation. These plants often look dead because except during the wet periods they do not carry leaves: this is a device for conserving water which would evaporate very quickly from the sufaces of leaves. In the savannah areas the beautiful acacias especially of the yellow barked variety are very striking. Magnificent examples of these trees may be seen at Naivasha, around Ol Tukai in Amboseli and around Seronera in the Serengeti. The yellow barked acacias used to be called fever trees:

R

they grow along water courses and the old pioneers who took advantage of their shade for camping sites frequently went down with malaria. Only later was the association between the mosquito and malaria discovered, thus freeing the trees from direct guilt.

Finally, those interested in plants will probably want to see the heights of the great mountains with their dense bamboo forests and their high moorlands. The moorland is the home of perhaps the most extraordinary of the indigenous plants, the giant heathers, lobelias and groundsels. These are frequently much taller than a man and are hardly recognisable as cousins of the much humbler European types which bear the same names.

This brief chapter cannot hope to do justice to the abundance of plant life to be seen and enjoyed in East Africa. Those interested are strongly advised to read one of the longer accounts in the books listed in the guide to further reading.

❧ 21 ❧

Sport

If you ask a Kenyan what he regards as the most important sport in his country he is very likely to answer 'Athletics'. And it is certainly athletics which has helped to give Kenyans such confidence in themselves which is one of the things which makes Kenya such a pleasant place to visit. Kenyans have proved that they can beat larger and richer nations at their own games and they feel that it is now only a matter of time before Kenya achieves an equal world importance in many other spheres.

The athletic achievements of Kenya are indeed outstanding. In the track events in Mexico City in 1968, this small country won three golds and four silvers, in the athletic events coming second only to the Soviet Union. The names of Kipchoge Keino, Amos Biwott, Naftali Temu, Wilson Kipragut and others became world famous overnight. There was much carping, of course, by people who said that Kenya's successes occurred only because her athletes normally lived at altitudes above 5,000 feet and athletes who had trained at sea level were at a serious disadvantage. This ignored the fact that in the USA there are more people living above 5,000 feet than there are in Kenya. In any case, in a score of major athletic meetings since Mexico, held at all altitudes, Kenya's athletes have shown that they can win golds and break records.

But most visitors to Kenya are unlikely to be interested in taking part in athletics although if they are lucky they may have the chance of seeing most of Kenya's great runners in action in one afternoon at one of the athletic meetings which are regularly held. Other sports may be divided into two categories, those which are major reasons for attracting visitors to Kenya and those which, while not major attractions, the visitor may nevertheless enjoy. The major attractions which draw people from all

R*

over the world are undoubtedly game photography, hunting, mountain climbing and walking, fishing for big game at the coast and for Lake Rudolf's Nile perch, and swimming and goggling along the coast's magnificent reefs. The minor pleasures which the visitor may enjoy are golf, sailing, fishing on smaller rivers and lakes, tennis and squash. For the spectator, soccer, hockey, cricket and rugby are all popular: because of Kenya's equatorial position, all four are likely to be going on at the same time. Of these four, soccer is undoubtedly the most popular and it is enormous fun to go to one of the important matches at the Nairobi City Stadium. Hockey is primarily an Asian game and rugby a European one, while cricket is played both by Europeans and Asians. All the relevant addresses for these interested in sport are given in the Useful Information section at the end of the book.

GAME PHOTOGRAPHY

This can be carried out in a purely amateur way by snapping shots while on tour and this, of course, is what most people do. Alternatively, the really keen photographer can go on a specialist photographic safari organised by one of the firms which cater for this sort of thing. The first type of photography costs little more than the price of the film on top of the tour costs. The second type may be either reasonably cheap or extremely expensive depending on the degree of luxury demanded and the areas to which you are taken. Amateur photographers need no permits for their activities anywhere in Kenya but professionals must obtain a licence from the Game Department.

A few words of advice for the amateur taking photographs in Africa for the first time may not be inappropriate. The main problems to be considered are the type of camera and focal length of the lens which are to be used and the difficulty of assessing the correct exposure. There can be no doubt that the ideal camera for game photography is a 35mm camera with interchangeable lenses. Even when you are very close to animals (as you very often are in East Africa) photographs taken with an ordinary 50 to 55mm lens are often disappointing: the big game seems much further away than it really was. The ideal lens is probably a zoom with a range of focal length from about 80 to about 200mm. Failing this a telephoto with a 135 or 200mm lens should be able to handle most situations satisfactorily.

Exposure is often a problem because of the strong sunlight: often the best photos are taken before 11 am and after 3 pm because then the shadows are less intense and more interesting. Automatic exposure meters often produce poor results because they are not used wisely. When taking an animal, if the view through the finder contains a lot of sky or open plain, this bright light is likely to overactivate the meter: the result will be that although the sky may be correctly exposed, the animal is likely to be underexposed and dark. The correct exposure can usually be obtained by pointing the camera downwards a little so that the sky is excluded from view. Once the correct exposure setting has been obtained you can then point the camera to obtain the scene you want: do not worry if the meter needle indicates that the picture will then be somewhat overexposed. Similarly, when using a telephoto lens with any type of exposure meter other than a through lens one, the tendency is again to underexpose. In open country in bright light the lens should be opened one stop further than is indicated by the meter reading. In dull light or in enclosed surroundings the lens should be opened one-and-a-half to two stops.

It is worth remembering that at high altitudes the ultra violet light tends to give landscape pictures an unnatural blue colour. The colours will be much toner if you always use an ultra violet filter in front of the lens.

Despite all this it is simple errors rather than technicalities which spoil most photographs. In the excitement of seeing animals many people forget completely about accurate focussing and about exposure setting. They also press the shutter far too vigorously causing the whole camera to shake and the picture to be blurred: at all times the trigger should be pressed very gently. A lens hood should always be used when working in bright sunlight. Care should be taken when loading films to make sure that they engage and advance correctly. The African light is very bright indeed and cameras must always be unloaded in the shade.

Throughout East Africa there are innumerable first class photographic shops which will always be pleased to give advice. The range of equipment available is very wide and high-class makes are very cheap in comparison to prices in many countries. Many shops will offer a 20 to 30 per cent discount and some specialise in tax free sales to visitors who will be taking the equipment out of the country. All types of film are available. Agfacolour films are cheapest because they are processed locally. Other colour films can be processed locally by specialised firms but the cost of this is then over and above the price of the film.

The important thing to remember when taking photographs here is not to get so excited that you forget to think about the simple things. If you do take a few very elementary precautions you will go home with a superb set of pictures.

HUNTING

The expeditions of Theodore Roosevelt did much to publicise the pleasures of hunting in East Africa and ever since a stream of rich men and women has come to this part of the world in search of big game. In recent years the relative importance of big game hunting has dwindled considerably but in absolute terms the demand is almost as great as ever. The sport is now extremely carefully regulated. Outside the game parks, reserves and conservation areas, the country is split up into a number of hunting blocks, only one party being allowed in each block at one time. The blocks must usually be booked far in advance. For each animal shot a fee must be paid which varies with the rarity and the size of the beast. The booking of blocks and the obtaining of licences are services provided by the safari organisers.

A hunting safari is certainly not a cheap affair. A good class one is likely to cost in the region of 2,000 East African pounds per month (about 5,600 U.S. dollars) with one client shooting and about £2,500 with two shooting. However, so superbly are the safaris organised that the number of people who complain about the cost must be very small indeed. The great majority of clients are very well satisfied with what they receive for their money. Most are agreeably surprised by the standard of comfort. None ever forget the thrill of sleeping in the heart of Africa with big game only a canvas thickness away. Those who can afford it return again and again and again to repeat their experience.

The address of the Professional Hunters Association is given in chapter 25.

MOUNTAIN CLIMBING AND WALKING

These sports are at present responsible for attracting only a tiny minority of all the visitors to East Africa but their importance is quickly growing. In recent years climbing and walking clubs from all over America and Europe have sent out pathfinders to investigate the possibilities. Most have gone back with rave reports and tours specifically devoted to visiting the mountains are increasing rapidly in number.

The major attractions are, of course, the two snow-covered peaks, Mount Kenya (17,058 feet high) and Kilimanjaro (19,340 feet above sea level). Both comfortably outstrip anything in Europe or the Rockies. Several firms and hotels specialise in arranging ascents and names and addresses are found in the Useful Information section.

Kilimanjaro

The ascent of Kibo, the main peak of Kilimanjaro, is started normally from one of the hotels at Marangu on the south side of the mountain. The climb normally takes five days but longer or shorter trips can be made by arrangement. The trip may be undertaken in any month but January, July and October often provide the best conditions. Climbers stay in strategically placed huts owned by the Kilimanjaro Mountain Club. Hut bookings are usually made by the hotels.

The first part of the journey goes through the Chagga country and then through the thick forest where black and white colobus monkeys are a common and beautiful sight. The first night is spent at Mandera Hut just at the top of the forest. The second day is an 11-mile trek across open moorland to Horombo Hut, over 11,000 feet above sea level and dominated by the jagged cliffs of Mawenzi, Kilimanjaro's subsidiary peak (16,980 feet high). It is towards the end of this stage that the effect of oxygen lack begins to be apparent with feet feeling like lead and headache not uncommon. The third day is occupied by the nine mile walk across the Saddle between Kibo and Mawenzi to Top Hut, 16,000 feet above the sea and surrounded by vast reddish-brown boulders, scattered at random by some giant hand. Here few sleep well because of the altitude and some have to go down again quickly. The real ordeal starts at 3 am the following morning when a guide with a hurricane lamp and a mug of hot tea rouses you to begin the last awful slog up the ash cone. This is terrain where each step up is followed by a slide of half a step down the ash and it can be demoralising in the extreme. But once the crater rim at Gillman's Point is reached, then all is forgotten especially if one has arrived in time to see the incomparable splendour of sunrise over Mawenzi. Many people stop here only too happy to gaze a while and then to slip and slide easily down the ash which earlier caused so much trouble. But if at all possible the 1–2 hour walk around the rim of the 2 miles wide crater to Uhuru Point, the summit of Africa, is a journey to be made. Compared to the slog up the cone, the going is relative easy and even if the plains below are hidden by cloud, the 200-feet thick glaciers and the inner crater provide spectacular views. Normally one then descends straight back to Horombo Hut to spend the fourth night, arriving back at the hotel for a hot bath on the evening of the fifth day.

The ascent of Kibo requires no mountaineering experience but much determination and endurance. The ascent of Mawenzi is a very different matter: it can be achieved only by those reasonably experienced in climbing on rock and ice. The base for climbing is a small hut at the bottom of the West Face which can be booked through the Kilimanjaro Mountain Club. Ascents should be made only after close consultation with someone who has experience of climbing the mountain. There are many different routes and there are opportunities for the establishment of new ones.

Mount Kenya

Seen from far below Mount Kenya is not so spectacular as Kilimanjaro. However, the peak area itself is much more jagged and impressive: this is a real mountaineer's mountain. There are three main peaks and a myriad subsidiary ones. Batian (17,058 feet) and Nelion (17,022 feet) are extremely jagged and steep and can be conquered only by experienced rock climbers. Point Lenana (16,355 feet) is a tough hike, part of the way over snow, but involves no actual rock climbing. The best season on the mountain is late December to mid-March but July to the end of September is also a satisfactory time.

There are many huts on the mountain, almost all owned by the Mountain Club of Kenya. New ones opening up further areas of the mountain are built regularly. By using the huts an immense variety of different expeditions can be carried out, even by the walker with no interest in rock and ice. Organisations specialising in Mount Kenya journeys are listed in the Useful Information section: they will be pleased to take people on a standard route or on a more extensive journey according to the client's wishes. Those who wish to organise their own journeys should contact the Mountain Club of Kenya for advice and for information about hut bookings.

There are several routes up the mountain. All are fully described in the Mountain Club of Kenya 'Guide to Mount Kenya' and in the book *Mountains of Kenya*. Undoubtedly the two most popular tracks are the Naro Moru and the Sirimon. The Naro Moru Route heads east from the main Nyeri-Nanyuki road at a point exactly opposite the Naro Moru Police Station. The track is clearly signposted, first going through farmland and then forest reserve. The National Park entrance is in the forest zone. The present summit of the track is a little above a rain gauge in a clearing and about 20 minutes walk below the forest edge. However, even in four-wheel drive vehicles it is often impossible to get up the last stretch and depending on the weather it may be necessary to stop up to five miles below the track head. Above the forest the path traverses what is very appropriately called 'The Vertical Bog' and then after a long pull over moorland traverses down into the Teleki Valley where there are two mountain club huts and a tented camp operated by Naro Moru River Lodge. The Teleki Valley is the fastest route to the main peaks and to Top Hut and Firmin Hut, both 15,700 feet above the sea. From Top Hut it is relatively easy to reach Point Lenana.

The Sirimon Track leaves the Nanyuki-Isiolo Road about nine miles after Nanyuki. It is now very clearly marked. This route can be followed by cars right up through the forest and on to the moorland. It is the best track for those who just want to make a day trip to see the moorland and the giant heathers and lobelias. However, the head of the track is a long way from the central peak area and it is not the best route for those who have only a limited time to see the highest parts of the mountain.

Health and Comfort on Kenya and Kilimanjaro

It cannot be stressed too hard that although these mountains are so close to the equator, weather conditions on them can be very unpleasant indeed. Perhaps the worst enemy is cold. Above 12,000 feet, night frost is virtually invariable and rain, snow, hail and strong winds are frequent. Gloves, thick sweaters, a weatherproof anorak and warm headgear are essential. Only those with the 1:25,000 map, a good compass, a tough constitution and plenty of mountain experience should venture up either peak without guide and/or porters. Those who cannot fulfil these conditions should either go in an organised party or hire porters and guides themselves.

Altitude sickness, caused by lack of oxygen due to the low atmospheric pressure high up on the mountains is a very real hazard. Symptoms of the mild disease are loss of appetite, sleeplessness, headache, nausea and vomiting. So long as one stays high up on the mountain there is no cure and the condition will improve only on descending. The mild disease, with the symptoms just described, is miserable but not dangerous to life. Very rarely a much more serious condition occurs which requires urgent action if life is to be saved. This starts with an apparently relatively innocent dry but persistent cough. It progresses to a sensation of severe breathlessness with much fluid entering the mouth and nose, giving the impression of a streaming cold. It ends in death as the function of the lungs fails. Anyone who has previously been well but who starts coughing should get down off the mountain at once.

For the protection of climbers an elaborate safety procedure has been devised. All people going on to the Mountain must sign in at the Naro Moru Police Station and at the National Park Gate, specifying their route and their expected time of return. It is essential that returning climbers should sign out as otherwise investigations will begin 36 hours after the expected time of return. Lone climbers are not allowed on the mountain.

Other Mountains and Hills

Guided parties are not routinely taken up any of the other mountains in Kenya and Northern Tanzania but many of the safari firms will be pleased to organise special trips. After Mount Kenya and Kilimanjaro, the three most climbed of the higher peaks are probably Satima in the Northern Aberdares, Mount Elgon in north west Kenya and Socialist Peak (Mount Meru) in Northern Tanzania. All can relatively easily be ascended by unaccompanied parties and full instructions may be found in '*Mountains of Kenya*'. In this guide may also be found instructions on how to reach and climb many other peaks, a large number of which have been virtually untouched by serious rock climbers.

None of the mountains so far mentioned is likely to be ascended by the casual visitor to East Africa who has not come with climbing specifically in mind. However, two ascents can be made comfortably in half a day from Nairobi, with no equipment apart from a reasonably strong pair of shoes. These are the climbs up Longonot, a relatively recently extinct crater in the floor of the Rift Valley and up the Ngong Hills which so dominate the Nairobi National Park. Both walks offer magnificent views over typical Rift Valley scenery.

Longonot is approached by driving out from Nairobi along the Nakuru Road. It is the mountain which dominates the view when one reaches the Rift Valley Escarpment. Forty one miles from Nairobi, immediately before the Longonot railway crossing, a track goes off to the left. Drive along this as far as possible which may be either three or four miles depending on recent weather and on the state of the track. At the road head the car should be locked and nothing of value left in view. The path is well used and unmistakable. In thirty to sixty minutes, depending on fitness, the crater rim should be reached. The summit is almost directly opposite on the other side of the crater, the track to the right being slightly shorter than the one to the left. A walk right round the crater makes a pleasant excursion and can normally be comfortably completed in about three hours. There are splendid views of the Rift Valley and of Lake Naivasha. The occasional antelope or monkey may be encountered but game is for the most part relatively scarce.

The Ngong Hills usually catch the visitor's eye as he drives from the airport into Nairobi. There are several legends about the way in which this beautiful range was formed. The most picturesque tells how an enormous giant dominated and terrorised the land of the Masai, devouring their cattle and decimating their herds. The Masai themselves could not kill him and so they turned to the animal world for help. None of the great animals, the lion, the buffalo, the elephant or the rhino, could assist, but eventually the humble ant offered aid. When the giant fell asleep, all the ants banded together and covered him with earth. The knuckles of one hand were incompletely hidden and they formed the Ngong Hills. The easiest way to reach the hills is to drive out from Nairobi along the Ngong or Langata Roads to Ngong Village. From the village a rough, steep but clearly signposted track goes up to a car park just below a barrier. The further extension of the road up to the radio station is not open for private vehicles. An obvious path goes along the ridge of the hills to Lamwia, the southernmost of the four and also the highest. This walk is particularly rewarding in the early evening when the deep shadows thrown by the setting sun throw into sharp relief the tangled volcanic structure of the Rift Valley far below. Game is common on this path and it is important to keep an eye open for buffaloes.

FISHING

The two major attractions are undoubtedly Lake Rudolf and the coast. Lake Rudolf is the huge lake, over 150 miles long, which lies in the remoteness of Kenya's northern desert. It swarms with crocodiles, with birds and with fish, notably the enormous Nile Perch. Hundred pounders are frequently caught and the record is over 200 pounds. Also in Rudolf are the much smaller tiger fish which for their size must be classed among the most sporting fish in the world. The fishing is organised at two places, Ferguson's Gulf about half way up the western side, and Eliye Springs, near the southern end. It is usual to fly from Nairobi but those with a taste for adventure will find the tough road journey very rewarding. The accommodation is in the luxury class and fishing can be carried out at any time of the year.

The big game fishing off the Kenya coast is an attraction of rapidly increasing significance. Several All Africa records are held. Although no world records have been obtained as yet most people feel that this is simply because the sea here is as yet very sparsely fished: as the number of boats going out increases so will the likelihood of getting the really big fish. The season begins in September and runs through until March. From Shimoni in the far south of Kenya to Lamu in the far north there are hotels, clubs and firms specialising in big game fishing. Perhaps the best known centres are Shimoni, Mombasa, Kilifi and Malindi. Addresses are given in the Useful Information section.

The visitor to the Highlands who would like to spend a day or two fishing should try the black bass on Lake Naivasha or the trout in any one of many rivers. Lake Naivasha's bass fishing is first rate and the lake itself is extremely beautiful. There are several clubs and hotels on the lake shore which hire out boats. As always the fishermen who starts out early in the morning is likely to have most success and bags of thirty or more are not uncommon.

Because in this equatorial region the water remains warm all the year round and the feeding is rich, Kenya's trout grow very rapidly and fish over five pounds in weight are not uncommon. However, most of the rivers are small, with vegetation right up to the banks and fishing them is not easy. The best times of the year are the dry months: during the rains the rivers are almost all swirling brown masses of water, impossible to fish. Hotels which will advise on fishing are to be found at Kitale, Kericho, Embu, Nyeri, Naro Moru and Ngobit. The last of these is at a trout hatchery and has some open stretches of water where fishing is easy even for novices. Kenya residents who fish for trout often prefer the simple hut accommodation owned by the Fisheries Department and the local Fishing Associations. The huts are often in beautiful surroundings, are operated on a do it yourself basis and are very cheap, the usual fee being five shillings per person per night. Addresses are in the Useful Information section.

OTHER SPORTS

Almost any outdoor sport apart from skiing can be carried out in Kenya and Northern Tanzania. Golf is very popular and there are pleasant courses near all the main centres. The main centres for sailing are Mombasa, the Nairobi Dam near Wilson Airport and Lake Naivasha. Various addresses of sports organisations are given in the Useful Information section.

S

22

The Economy

In East Africa as in most of the economically less-developed parts of the world, the pattern of the way in which people make a living is radically different from that familiar to those from Europe and North America. In the so-called developed nations, the vast majority of people are concerned either in manufacturing goods or in manning the service industries which cater in a thousand and one ways for the needs of a population too specialised to do each of these things for itself. A small proportion of the population is engaged in highly mechanised agriculture. Whatever their work, the overwhelming number of people are in paid employment. The usual age of death is in the sixties or early seventies and the age structure of the population is relatively balanced.

In the developing areas all is different. First of all, until recently the infant mortality rate was very high and the average age of death very low. This situation is now rapidly changing and as a result in most of these countries more than half the population is under the age of fifteen. Of the working population, probably under 5 per cent are in paid employment, the vast majority being engaged in a subsistence form of agriculture which is just sufficient to provide for the needs of their own families. In East Africa of those who are in paid employment almost all come into four basic categories, manufacturing, agriculture, tourism and minerals.

The success of a manufacturing industry depends almost entirely on the availability of a home market of reasonable size. Most manufactured goods familiar in the west in Africa can be purchased by only a minute fraction of the population and the home market is rarely large enough to justify filling this demand by local manufacture rather than by imports. In a few cases, however, such as textiles and soap, the home market is sufficiently large and local industries are doing well.

Agriculture as Europeans know it, the growth of food crops for sale and the production of dairy foods and meat is increasingly important. At present wheat, sugar, vegetables, fruit, dairy produce and meat are primarily sold within East Africa. Kenya in particular has an excellent range of dairy produce and the visitor will find the cheeses among the finest in the world.

In addition there is a range of quite different crops, for which the East African market is small. They are grown here because of the favourable climate. They earn the greater part of East Africa's foreign currency and they include coffee, tea, cotton, pyrethrum, cashew nuts and sisal. Very soon the fruit and vegetable industries will also enter this profitable export category as cheap air freight takes their products overnight to Europe.

Coffee is the most important single agricultural product, growing extremely well in the highlands of Kenya, in many parts of Uganda and in Tanzania, particularly around Kilimanjaro. Before independence, with the exception of the Chagga farms in Tanzania, most of the coffee was grown on large European estates but it is now increasingly being grown on small African farms (or shambas as they are known). The farmers band together in cooperatives which organise the collection, processing and marketing of the beans. Rapidly increasing in importance is tea. The stronghold of this industry is the area around Kericho where rain falls almost every day of the year and the climate is ideal for the growth of high quality leaf. Tea is also grown in other areas and some may be seen as near to Nairobi as Limuru.

Cotton is important in Uganda but it is a minor crop in the areas of Kenya and Northern Tanzania with which this guide primarily deals. Sisal is a crop which used to be of major importance in Tanzania and parts of Kenya (the coast, Voi and Thika) but is now rapidly declining as a result of competition from man-made fibres. However, large estates can still be seen and the sisal plant is common in gardens and as an 'escape' on waste ground. It is a tough succulent with long narrow leaves radiating from a narrow base. Each leaf is tipped by a nasty thorn. From the centre of the mature plant there springs up a long pole-like stem, ten or twelve feet high with hundreds of tiny bulb-like structures growing from it. These 'bulbules' when planted develop into new sisal plants. The sisal fibre comes from the leaves which are steadily harvested from each plant over a number of years. The outsides of the leaves are stripped off by machine and the fibres inside are used for the manufacture of ropes, sacking, carpeting and many other forms of tough cloth.

Pyrethrum is an unusal crop in that it requires virtually no capital investment and can be grown profitably on plots only a few square yards in extent. It is therefore ideal for a peasant farmer who wants to acquire some cash income. It grows well in the Kenya Highlands and the greyish green plants with their tiny white nodding flowers are a familiar sight. The flowers contain the powerful insecticide pyrethrum which is a constituent of many insect-killing sprays. Cashew nuts, macadamia nuts, vegetables and flowers are at present small scale exports but ones with considerable capacity for growth. Cashew nuts grow well at the coast but the main problem is the development of a really effective mechanised method for shelling them.

In many developing countries some valuable mineral material such as copper or oil forms the major source of foreign income. Unfortunately the East African countries have no such single source of mineral wealth. Tanzania has a relatively rich diamond mine, Uganda has large amounts of phosphate and moderate amounts of copper but poor Kenya has virtually nothing. It has gold and other deposits but these are not commercially workable. One unusual 'mineral' is bat guano found in caves not far from Hunter's Lodge and deposited over thousands of years by the vast colonies of bats which live there. This is first rate fertiliser and is exported in small amounts. Although many in Kenya bemoan the lack of mineral riches, it is possible to make a good case for the proposition that this is not entirely a bad thing. Mineral industries are usually highly mechanised and the great wealth tends to find its way into the hands of a relatively tiny part of the population. In proportion to the money earned the number of people actually employed is very small. It is therefore extremely difficult even in socialist countries to ensure that the wealth is at all evenly distributed. Agriculture however employs far more people in relation to its earnings and the money tends to filter down to all the rural areas.

Tourism is an industry which is now overtaking agriculture as the major earner of foreign currency. It is also the business with the fastest rate of growth (in the region of 25 per cent per year) and there seems every reason to expect that within a short time it will prove more profitable as an earner of foreign exchange than all the other industries put together. In the past three factors have limited tourist development here, the relative remoteness of East Africa and the cost of travel, the lack of luxurious hotels, and fears of political instability. Cheap travel and an ambitious hotel building programme are rapidly correcting the first two factors. Despite many protestations of gloom, East African countries have also been remarkably stable since independence. Provided that this stability continues, East Africa's natural advantages should ensure that the number of tourists will spiral rapidly upwards.

❦ 23 ❦

Communications

Communications to and within East Africa have changed radically within the past fifteen years. Then a large number of visitors came by sea and outside the towns tarmac roads were virtually non-existent, being limited to two relatively short stretches going north from Nairobi. A road journey from Nairobi to Mombasa was a major expedition. Since then the coming of the big jets and the closure of Suez have together ensured that the great majority of travellers arrive by air. The amount of tarmac in all three countries has increased enormously thus making travel by road much easier.

EXTERNAL COMMUNICATIONS

Air

Each of the three countries has an airport of international standard. Uganda's is at Entebbe twenty miles from Kampala, Kenya's is just outside Nairobi and Tanzania's is just outside Dar es Salaam. Tanzania is well on the way to completing a new airport between Arusha and Moshi which will bring visitors to the doorstep of the magnificent scenic and big game country of Northern Tanzania. Almost all major airlines fly to East Africa and there are easy connections to anywhere in the world. Return economy class fares to Northern Europe cost roughly £250 East African (very approximately £300 Sterling or 700 US dollars) and to New York about £400 East African. Many airlines operate two to three week excursion fares which may cost considerably less than this. There is a flourishing charter flight trade. The charter flight fares may not be much more than one-third the standard economy class fare. Some organised tours of East Africa, for example, include return fares and two weeks' stay at good hotels for less than the normal scheduled flight economy return.

East African Airways is the national carrier operated jointly by the three Governments. It has a modern fleet of jets with a quite outstanding safety record. It is also one of the few national airlines which consistently makes a substantial profit. Its international flights outside Africa go to Europe, the Middle East, Pakistan, India, Thailand, Hong Kong and the USA.

Sea

With the closure of the Suez Canal, relatively few visitors enter East Africa by sea although, of course, the importance of the sea for freight has hardly changed. Only one passenger line now runs regularly voyages from Europe to the East African ports and that is the Lloyd Triestino, operating from Venice, Trieste, Brindisi and Barcelona and going round the Cape. There is no regular passenger connection with America. The British India Line operates a regular passenger service every eight weeks down the coast to South Africa where connections may be made with the Union Castle and other lines which go to that country. Many primarily cargo-carrying lines going to most of the ports of the world also take small numbers of passengers but sailings tend to be erratic. These lines include Robin Lines, Holland Afrika, Scandinavian East African, Farrell Lines, Royal Interocean and Deutsche-Ost Afrika.

Road

With the possible exception of visitors coming from Zambia via the Great North Road, this is not a method of approach to be followed by the ordinary traveller with a tight time schedule. All the other roads are very rough, delays are frequent and four-wheel drive vehicles travelling in pairs are highly desirable. Roads enter East Africa from the Congo, from Ethiopia, from the Sudan and from Somalia. Fairly rapid progress is being made on the Nairobi-Addis Ababa Highway and this should provide an exciting entry route in the near future.

Nile Steamer

This, entering Uganda from the Sudan along the Nile is perhaps the most romantic of all ways to enter East Africa. Unfortunately this route is subject to disturbance because of the rebellion in the Southern Sudan and it should be attempted only by the intrepid with plenty of time to spare.

INTERNAL COMMUNICATIONS

Railway

This was the first form of relatively reliable and rapid communication to open up the East African interior and to allow visitors to travel in reasonable comfort. The line starts at Mombasa and after leaving the coastal strip travels through hot thorn bush country for many miles. This section traverses Tsavo Park and elephants are always seen by passengers and very occasionally hit by trains. The line then climbs steadily to Nairobi after which it goes up and over the escarpment and down into the Rift Valley to Naivasha and Nakuru. Then it goes up the other side of the Rift to Eldoret and on into Uganda at Tororo. Two lines go from Tororo, one to link up with the Nile at Pakwach and the other to go to the copper producing area at Kasese in Western Uganda. In Kenya branch lines go to Kisumu, Nanyuki, Thomson's Falls, the soda works at Magadi and the Tanzanian border at Taveta where they link with the Tanzanian system. The railway is vital for the transport of goods but its share of passenger traffic has dropped sharply with the surfacing of the roads with tarmac and the development of an extensive system of internal air travel. Nevertheless, for those with time available a journey across East Africa by rail is full of delights. The accommodation is comfortable, the food is excellent and cheap and the scenery, especially in the section from Nairobi to Tororo, is superb.

Lake Steamers

Lake traffic on Victoria was associated with the railway as an early form of transport in East Africa and a comfortable steamer, appropriately named the Victoria is still operated by the Railways. The original railway line in fact went only to Kisumu, travellers then going on to Uganda by boat. The Victoria is fitted out as a pleasant cruise ship and starting from Kisumu it makes regular five day circuits of this vast inland sea. On the way it calls at many tiny ports populated by many different peoples. Those who want an unusual form of East African holiday could not do better than this.

Road

Most people travelling around East Africa go from place to place by road. Road transport has been greatly facilitated by the rapid increase in the rate of laying tarmac surfaces since independence. The whole of the road from Mombasa to Nairobi is tarmac as is most of the stretch from Nairobi to the Uganda border, together with side branches to places like Kericho and Kisumu. The road travelling due north to Nyeri and Nanyuki is also hard and the one going south to Namanga and Tanzania is being surfaced now.

But despite this rapid progress the traveller who wants to see the country cannot avoid driving or being driven on dirt roads. All the game park and reserve roads except for the main road through Tsavo and a very short stretch in Nairobi Park are dirt. Roughly speaking, the dirt roads come into three categories, murram, sand and black cotton soil. Murram is a light brownish-grey soil which drains well, does not become excessively muddy when wet and when well laid does not easily form pot holes. It is often used to surface roads travelling across other types of soil. The main hazards of travelling on murram are the corrugations which inevitably develop on all dirt roads as a result of wheel action and the pot holes which because they are infrequent are particularly dangerous. Fortunately experienced drivers can often note the likely position of a pot hole far ahead because the colour of the road changes from grey-brown to a very pale grey or to a reddish sandy colour. These intrusions of different coloured soil are more easily eroded than the murram itself and are always likely to give trouble. The wise driver will always slow down when they are observed.

The main problems of sandy soil are that it is easily eroded to form pot holes, that water may lie in these unsuspected hollows and that loose sand may make steering difficult. But although care is always necessary, sandy soil does not present any major difficulties. The motorist's real bug bear is the soil known as black cotton. When dry it is grey and forms quite a respectable road surface. But when wet it is transformed into an unbelievably glutinous sticky mass which can bog down the toughest of vehicles. It is foolishness rather than boldness or heroism to attempt to drive over wet roads in black cotton soil country. The visitor is most likely to encounter it around Mount Kenya, in the Serengeti and on the road between Athi River and Kajiado although that is now being rapidly surfaced.

Most visitors to Kenya will be driven around and will not be responsible for the cars they use. However quite a number hire cars for one or
two day trips from Nairobi. Naivasha and Hell's Gate, Magadi and
Olorgesaillie, the Ngong Hills and Amboseli are perhaps the most
popular of these short journeys. Even on such trips it is perfectly easy to
run into trouble unless a few elementary precautions are taken. The
most important of these are:

1. Remember that petrol stations are rare or non-existent, particularly
on the Magadi Road. Ensure that you have a full tank with a spare can
if necessary.

2. Water is important as overheating can easily occur. Check personally that the radiator is full before you leave.

3. A fan belt can easily snap and cause you to be stranded. Check that
it is in good condition.

4. If possible take a small tool kit with screwdrivers and adjustable
spanners.

5. Punctures are not uncommon. Ideally carry two spares or if this is
not possible a good puncture repair outfit with tyre levers.

6. Perhaps the most important thing to remember is that if anything
does go wrong on one of the remoter roads it may be many hours before
you are rescued. It is therefore essential to carry something to drink and
some energy-giving food such as raisins, biscuits or nuts.

Those who wish to drive themselves over long distances in East
Africa must take a first-class tool kit and an extensive assortment of
spares. For such drivers the East African Automobile Association
Handbook is invaluable.

Air

Internal air travel is perhaps increasing more rapidly than any
form of transport. Daily East African Airways flights go to Malindi,
Mombasa, Dar es Salaam, Kampala, Arusha and Moshi. East African
Airways also frequently run weekend excursions to places like Seronera
in the Serengeti or Keekorok in Mara Game Reserve: you should
enquire about these from your hotel. An increasing number of first-class
private charter firms are now operating in East Africa using modern single
and twin engined light aircraft. They will take you at very reasonable rates
to any one of over five hundred small airstrips. Using this form of transport
you can rapidly see many parts of the country in maximum comfort.

24

Health for the Visitor

Nothing can mar a holiday more than ill health. This section therefore attempts to give the visitor all the information he needs to ensure that he has no health troubles in East Africa. Most tourists are concerned about health risks when travelling in a new continent and those travel organisations which say that such risks do not exist are performing a dis-service. However if you take the simple precautions outlined in this section these risks can be virtually eliminated and you will be no more likely to fall ill in East Africa than you would in your own country.

HEALTH DOCUMENTS REQUIRED

All travellers *must* have valid certificates of vaccination against smallpox and yellow fever. If your own doctor feels that for a particular reason (e.g. early pregnancy or treatment with certain drugs) you should not be vaccinated against smallpox the immigration authorities will accept an official letter from him explaining the situation. People who have recently been in a cholera-risk area are required to produce cholera vaccination certificates.

OTHER VACCINATIONS ADVISABLE

Although they are not legally required, all visitors are strongly advised to ensure that they are protected against polio and tetanus. Both diseases are obviously very serious and are common in East Africa. However modern vaccines give complete protection against them.

A vaccination which is not absolutely essential but which many doctors consider desirable is the one against typhoid, paratyphoid A and paratyphoid B, commonly known as TAB. Your own doctor will tell you whether he thinks that you personally should receive this vaccination.

TIME DISORIENTATION BECAUSE OF FLYING

Many visitors who arrive in East Africa by air have crossed rapidly many time zones, either on a journey from the Far East or on one from Europe or North America. It is now well-established that such travel may produce various symptoms including excessive tiredness and a feeling of disorientation. The arriving visitor is therefore strongly advised to spend his first few hours in Africa sleeping. A good refreshing sleep right at the beginning may make all the difference to enjoyment of the whole holiday.

ALTITUDE

Nairobi is at an altitude of 5,500 feet and many of the places which tourists visit in places like the Aberdares or Mount Kenya may be at 8,000 feet or even higher. Because the air at these heights contains less oxygen then it does at sea level you may find yourself becoming unusually breathless on mild exertion. Do not worry about this as it is perfectly normal. The altitude should however be respected and over-exertion at the beginning of the holiday avoided. This is particularly important for older people who want to climb high on Kilimanjaro or on Mount Kenya. They are strongly advised to do so only after becoming acclimatised for two or three weeks at five to eight thousand feet. The most obvious effect of altitude which almost everyone feels is a desire to go to bed early and to sleep soundly.

MALARIA

Malaria is not a problem above about 6,000 feet because the mosquitoes which carry the disease cannot complete their normal life cycle above that height. Malaria is unusual in Nairobi but it is definitely not unknown and no tourist can come to Kenya or Northern Tanzania without at some time passing through a malarial area. Since malaria is a serious disease and since it can be contracted following a single bite from an infected mosquito it is as well to take one of the modern thoroughly reliable anti-malarial preparations. These should preferably be taken for one week before coming and for at least two weeks after leaving as only then can the risk of malaria be certainly avoided. If the visitor does do this he can be categorically certain of not being troubled by the disease.

There are several types of drug but two are used particularly commonly. These are the chloroquine (Nivaquin) type which is taken weekly and the proguanil (Paludrin) type which is taken daily. Both are equally effective but some experts prefer the daily variety simply because it is less easy to forget. For pregnant women, Paludrin is preferable as it has been taken by countless pregnant women over many years with no evidence of side effects or malformations in the unborn child.

BILHARZIA

This is an unpleasant disease in which parasites can affect the bladder and intestines as well as other parts of the body. It is carried by snails which live in still or slow-running water. The parasites leave the snails and penetrate the skin of anyone foolish enough to bathe or to wash in infected water. It is therefore possible to be absolutely certain of avoiding the disease by not washing or swimming in lakes or slow-moving rivers. Not all water in East Africa is infected by any means but in the absence of specific local knowledge it is advisable for the visitor not to take any risks.

DIARRHOEA

With the possible exception of sunburn, diarrhoea is by far the commonest disease to afflict travellers in any part of the world. It is a very frequent cause of ruined holidays. Most brochures and guides which deal with East Africa say that standards of hygiene in hotels are high and the tourist need have no fears about eating any food. This is true and Europeans resident in East Africa probably have little more gut trouble than they would have in their own countries. However, for the resident a few days of diarrhoea do not present any great problem. For the visitor on safari who has paid a great deal of money for his holiday, just a few days of gut trouble can cause great misery and a ruined trip. It is therefore probably desirable for the visitor to take some preparation which will reduce the risk. Unfortunately, Enterovioform, the one which is best advertised and most often carried, is effective against only one relatively unusual organism which is a cause of diarrhoea. A much better preparation is Streptotriad which is widely employed by athletes and soldiers in situations where the avoidance of diarrhoea is vital. One tablet taken in the morning and one in the early evening has proved to be a very effective preventive treatment.

Water in Nairobi can be drunk straight from the tap. This is also true of some of the new Game Lodges which have installed their own filtering plants. In other places it is advisable to drink only the filtered water in flasks which will be brought to your room.

SUNSHINE

East Africa bestrides the Equator and the sun is much more powerful than in most of the countries from which visitors come. Furthermore, in the East African Highlands the air is thinner and lets through much more of the skin-damaging ultra-violet radiation than it does at sea level. Because of these factors sunburn here probably causes far more ruined holidays than diarrhoea. The know-all visitor who thinks he is used to the sun may find himself in hospital with severe burns. Extreme caution in exposing the skin to the sun is essential.

The hot dry atmosphere of many of the game areas also brings another problem. In order to keep the body cool, sweat is produced in large amounts but it evaporates so rapidly from the skin surface that many people do not realise that they have been sweating profusely. They unknowingly lose large quantities of water and salt in the sweat. This can cause headache and a feeling of lethargy and in severe cases heat exhaustion and prickly heat. Most visitors will feel much more comfortable if they make the effort to take rather more liquid with each meal than they feel is necessary and if salt is liberally sprinkled over food. This may make all the difference to the enjoyment of a game viewing trip.

SNAKE BITE

This is traditionally something which visitors to Africa fear greatly. In practice the risk is negligible. Although snakes are not uncommon they keep themselves to themselves and are rarely seen. Most residents probably do not see on average more than a couple of snakes a year and even those are not likely to be poisonous ones. If you look where you are walking in dry country and if you avoid putting your hand into foolish places such as holes in logs or walls the likelihood of being bitten by a snake is virtually non-existent.

Even if by some misfortune you should be bitten, the risk of serious consequences is not high. It is likely that the snake will be either non-poisonous or have venom of only a low potency. Even the deadly snakes, the mambas, cobras and puff-adders frequently fail to get a proper hold and inject negligible amounts of venom. If by some remote misfortune you should be bitten by a poisonous snake the only immediate first aid treatment of value is immobilisation of the limb, application of a *tight* tourniquet which should be released for half a minute every quarter of an hour, and local washing of the wound with clean water. Incision of the bite area, sucking the wound and insertion of potassium permanganate crystals are all completely valueless and may cause a great deal of harm and secondary infection. It goes without saying that any person with a proper snake bite should be taken to hospital as soon as possible. Fortunately this is much easier than one might expect in Africa: all the game areas are well-supplied with light airstrips and the Flying Doctor Service can be on the scene remarkably rapidly.

HEALTH SERVICES

Kenya is very well-served medically. In Nairobi there are a medical school, several good hospitals and a large number of African, Asian and European doctors. There is a well-organised Flying Doctor Service which can rapidly bring people into hospital from the remotest areas. If you are unfortunate enough to fall ill your hotel or travel organiser will quickly bring medical help.

25

Useful Information

This section of the Guide contains a whole range of facts which both local resident and visitor may find useful. Although we believe that it was correct at the time of going to press we cannot be held responsible for any errors or omissions. It would be helpful if those who use the guide could inform us about extra items of information which they would like to see in this section so that future editions can be improved.

LANGUAGES

Most educated Kenyans and Tanzanians speak three languages, their own tribal one, English, the language of the colonial power, and Swahili, the language of the coast. In Tanzania, Swahili is a true lingua franca, spoken by all classes of people in all areas of the country. This is perhaps the only good end result of the slave trade, for it was the coastal merchants who carried Swahili into the far interior. In Kenya where penetration from the coast was much less, Swahili is much less of a universal language. However, its importance is growing very quickly and the visitor will often find a little extra warmth if he makes the effort to learn just a few words.

The easiest of all Swahili words to learn is 'Jambo', the universal greeting which is roughly the equivalent of 'Hello', 'Good Morning' and 'Good Evening' all rolled into one. Someone who wants to be particularly friendly will often say 'Jambo sana' for emphasis. Sana is approximately the equivalent of 'very' or 'very much' but it cannot be precisely translated. After 'Jambo' people will often say to you 'Habari?' which means roughly 'What's your news?' or 'How are

T

you?' Your reply to 'Habari' should always be 'Mzuri' (good). Even
if you have just lost a thousand pounds your news will still be 'Mzuri'.
However, you will then follow 'Mzuri' by 'lakini' which means 'but'
and then you are free to pour out all your troubles.

In Swahili, the day starts at dawn (6.00 hours European time) and
ends at dusk (18.00 hours European time); 6 o'clock in either morning
or evening is 'Saa kumi na mbili' (12 hours). Seven o'clock is 'Saa
moja' (one hour), eight o'clock is 'Saa mbili' (two hours) and so on.

There follow some commonly used words and expressions. The
reader who would like to know just a little (but not much) more is
advised to buy a little book called *Up Country Swahili* by F. H. Le Breton
condemned by all the experts but nevertheless very useful for those
without great ambition. There are several other more advanced books,
one of the best being *Teach Yourself Swahili*.

Angalia	Look out
Asante	Thank you
Asante sana	Thank you very much
Bado	Later
Bado kidogo	A little later, in a moment
Baridi	Cold
Chai	Tea
Chakula	Food
Choo	Lavatory
Chui	Leopard
Dawa	Medicine
Dudu	Insect
Fundi	Expert, mechanic, carpenter
Gari	Vehicle, car, truck
Hapa	Here
Hapana	No
Harambee	Pull together
Hodi?	May I come in?
Kabisa	Completely
Kahawa	Coffee
Kali	Fierce, sharp
Karibu	Come in
Kazi	Work

Kesho	Tomorrow
Kiboko	Hippo
Kidogo	Small
Kifaru	Rhino
Kwa heri	Goodbye
Leo	Today
Lete	Bring
Maji	Water
Mara moja	At once
Mbaya	Bad
Mimi	I, me
Mingi	Many
Mkubwa	Big
Moto	Hot
Mtoto	Child
Mzee	Honoured old man
Mzuri	Good
Na	And
Nataka	Want
Ngapi?	How many?
Ngoja	Wait
Ngombe	Cow
Nyama	Meat
Pole pole	Slowly
Pombe	African beer
Punda mlia	Zebra
Rafiki	Friend
Saa ngapi?	When? What time is it?
Samaki	Fish
Sasa	Now
Shamba	Farm, garden
Shilingi ngapi?	How much?
Sifahamu	I do not understand
Simba	Lion
Sipendi	I do not like
Sitaki	I do not want
Tafadhali	Please
Tayari	Ready

Tembo	Elephant, beer
Twiga	Giraffe
Uhuru	Freedom
Wananchi or Watu	Ordinary people
Wapi?	Where?
Wewe	You
Ya	Of

Numbers

Moja	One
Mbili	Two
Tatu	Three
Nne	Four
Tano	Five
Sita	Six
Saba	Seven
Nane	Eight
Tisa	Nine
Kumi	Ten
Kumi na moja	Eleven
Kumi na mbili	Twelve, and so on
Ishirini	Twenty
Thalathini	Thirty
Arobaini	Forty
Hamsini	Fifty
Mia moja	One hundred
Elfu moja	One thousand

In Swahili adjectives come after the noun, e.g. 'mtoto mbaya', a bad child. 'Sana', meaning very or very much comes after the adjective, 'mtoto mbaya sana', a very bad child.

PUBLIC HOLIDAYS

Kenya	1 January	New Year's Day
	1 May	Labour Day
	1 June	Madaraka Day

20 October	Kenyatta Day
12 December	Independence Day
25 December	Christmas Day
26 December	Boxing Day

Good Friday, Easter Monday and the first Monday in August are also public holidays. Members of the Muslim and Hindu communities also have holidays on days of special religious significance.

Tanzania	12 January	Zanzibar Day
	26 April	Union Day
	1 May	Labour Day
	29 June	Mahlid
	7 July	Saba Saba Day
	9 December	Independence and Republic Day
	25 December	Christmas Day

As in Kenya, Good Friday and Easter Monday are universal public holidays, while Muslim and Hindu festival days are holidays for members of those communities.

GENERAL INFORMATION, RESTAURANTS, CINEMAS AND NIGHT LIFE

Nairobi, Mombasa, Arusha and Moshi all have excellent restaurants both inside and outside hotels. Nairobi and Mombasa in particular have several night clubs and Nairobi has an International Casino. There are cinemas in all the main towns. Because the night life picture often changes and new restaurants are appearing all the time it is pointless to attempt to list all the establishments in a guide of the sort. However, both Kenya and Tanzania are very well organised to supply this sort of information in an up-to-date form. Both produce free magazines which are available in all hotels and which are known as 'Karibu Tanzania' (monthly) and 'What's on?... an entertainment guide to Kenya' (fortnightly). Comprehensive lists of restaurants and night clubs and up-to-date information about films and plays are to be found in these invaluable publications.

There are also friendly and competent Information Bureaux in the main centres.

Nairobi   Box 2278, Telephone 23285. Between the Hilton Hotel and Government Road.

Mombasa   Box 5072, Telephone 5428. On Kilindini Road just on the harbour side of the tusks.

Moshi   Kilimanjaro Tourist Association, Box 381, Boma Road, Telephone 2330.
Tanzania Information Service, Boma Road, Box 517, Telephone 2614.

Arusha   Arusha Tourist Bureau, Box 594, Uhuru Road, Telephone 2030.
Tanzania Information Service, Box 3054, Uhuru Road, Telephone 2572.

MONEY AND EXCHANGE RATE

In both countries the basic unit of currency is the shilling which is divided into one hundred cents. Pounds do not exist officially but the term is widely used for purposes of convenience, one pound being twenty shillings.

The following are the approximate exchange rates in force at the time of going to press:

1	American dollar	Sh.	7·15
1	British pound	Sh.	17·14
1	Chinese yuan	Sh.	2·93
1	French franc	Sh.	1·33
1	German Deutsch mark	Sh.	1·94
1	Indian rupee	Sh.	0·95
100	Italian lira	Sh.	1·35
100	Japanese yen	Sh.	2·00
1	Netherlands guilder	Sh.	1·97
1	Swedish krona	Sh.	1·38
1	Swiss franc	Sh.	1·66
1	Zambian kwacha	Sh.	10·00

AIR CHARTERS

Kenya

African Safari Airways Ltd., Lugard House, Government Road, Box 6020, Nairobi

Amphibians Ltd., Box 456, Mombasa

Autair Helicopters (EA) Ltd., Box 20447, Nairobi

Boskovic Air Charters Ltd., Box 5646, Nairobi

Kenya Air Charters Ltd., Box 30603, Nairobi

Safari Air Services, Box 1951, Nairobi

Wilkenair Ltd., Box 4580, Nairobi

,,   Box 9700, Mombasa

,,   Box 133, Malindi

,,   Box 255, Nanyuki

Tanzania

Tanzanair, Box 364, Dar es Salaam

Tim-Air, Box 685, Arusha

TOUR, SAFARI AND TRAVEL SERVICES

Nairobi

Abercrombie & Kent Limited, Box 20224

Across Africa Safaris Ltd., Box 9420

African Roadways (Nairobi) Ltd., Box 6971

African Tours and Hotels Ltd., Box 30471

Akamba Travel Agencies Ltd., Box 6466

Archer's Cabs Ltd., Box 97

Brooke Bond Travel Ltd., Box 8726

Bruce Travel Ltd., Box 809

Bunson Travel Service, Box 5456

Chui Safaris Ltd., Box 8592

Dalgety Travel Service, Box 30090

Eboo's Tours and Safari Ltd., Box 898

Economic Investments Services, Box 4410

Express Travel Service, Box 433 (American Express)

Flamingo Tours Ltd., Box 4899

Fourways Travel Service Ltd., Box 3710

Funga Safari Ltd., Box 1558

Ivory Safaris Ltd., Box 5209

Kearline Tours, Box 6660

Kenatco Transport Co. Ltd., Box 6991

Ker Downy and Selby Safaris Ltd., Box 1822

Kilimanjaro Safari Club, Box 20211

Light Transport Co. Ltd., Box 18133

Lindblad Travel and Tony Irwin (EA) Ltd., Box 8559

Malaika Safaris and Travel Ltd., Box 5351

Menno Travel Service, Box 444

Nairobi Travel Services Ltd., Box 3637

Nilestar Tours Ltd., Box 2291

Northern Frontier Safaris Ltd., Box 5337

Pan African Travel Organization Ltd., Box 4209

Pollman's Tours & Safaris Ltd., Box 5895

Rent a Car and Game Tours, Box 6590

Root and Leakey's Photographic Safaris, Box 3747

Rhino Safaris, Box 8023

Safari Air Services Ltd., Box 1951

Silver Spear Tours Ltd., Box 500

Southern Cross Safaris, Box 8363

Subzali Tours and Safaris (Kenya) Ltd., Box 6595

Sungura Tours and Safaris Ltd., Box 5792

Thorn Tree Safaris Ltd., Box 2475

Travel Bureau Ltd., Box 3230

United Touring Co. Ltd., Box 2196

World Travel Bureau Ltd., Box 1178

Mombasa

African Roadways Ltd., Box 1775
Archers Tours, Box 2661
Highways, Box 9787
Kearline Tours, Box 9675
Kuldips Touring Co., Box 2662
Pollmans Tours & Safaris, Box 9198
Savannah Travel & Tours Ltd., Box 7444
United Touring Co., Box 9782

Malindi

Kingfisher Safaris, Box 29
Malindi Tours & Safaris, Box 52
Southern Cross Safaris Ltd., Box 33
United Touring Co., Box 365

Arusha and Moshi

Coopers Ltd., Box 142, Arusha
Dhillon Brothers, Box 80, Arusha
East African Wildlife Lodges, Box 3173, Arusha
Emslies Ltd., Box 29, Moshi: Box 24, Arusha
George Dove Safaris, Box 284, Arusha
Kearline Tours, Box 142, Arusha
Livingstone Tours, Box 501, Moshi
Mahendra J. Ambasna, Box 694, Arusha
Ngorongoro Crater Lodge, Box 751, Arusha
Ngorongoro Forest Lodge, Box 742, Arusha
Nilestar Tours, Box 935, Arusha
Serengeti Tours, Box 602, Arusha
Seronera Lodge, Box 3134, Arusha
Subzali Tours and Safaris, Box 3061
Tanzania Wildlife Safaris Ltd., Box 602, Arusha
United Touring Co., Box 2173, Arusha
Wildlife Tours & Safaris Ltd., Box 525, Moshi: Box 1026, Arusha

VEHICLE HIRE SERVICES

Nairobi

Archers Cabs, Box 97
Car Hire Services Ltd., Box 2304
Eboo's Tours & Safaris Ltd., Box 898
Economic Investments Services, Box 4410
Habib's Cars, Box 8095
Hertz Rent a Car, Box 2196
Ivory Safaris Ltd., Box 5209
Jambo Safaris Ltd., Box 30495
Rent a Car and Game Tours, Box 6590
Rhino Safaris Ltd., Box 8023
Subzali Tours and Safaris (Kenya) Ltd., Box 6595

Mombasa

Archers Tours, Box 2661
Avis Rent a Car Ltd., Box 9868
Avenue Motors
Hertz Rent a Car, Box 365
Highways, Box 9787
United Touring Co. Ltd., Box 9782

Malindi

Hertz Tours Ltd., Box 365
United Touring Co. Ltd., Box 365

Arusha

National Tours Ltd., Box 3040
Subzali Tours and Safaris, Box 3061
United Touring Co. Ltd., Box 3173
Wildlife Tours & Safaris Ltd., Box 1026

Moshi

Aziz Taxi Service, Box 225
Livingstone Tours, Box 501

National Tours Ltd., Box 7
Riddoch Motors (Hertz), Box 5
Wildlife Tours & Safaris Ltd., Box 525

IMMIGRATION, CUSTOMS AND HEALTH FORMALITIES

Immigration formalities to Kenya are at a minimum for those with a valid passport and a return or onward ticket. Visitors from Commonwealth Countries, Ireland, Denmark, Ethiopia, Italy, Norway, San Marino, Spain, Turkey, Uruguay, West Germany and Sweden do not require visas. Their passports will be stamped with a Visitor's Pass on arrival. Nationals of other countries should obtain visas from the nearest Kenyan Embassy. If there is no Kenyan Embassy in a country, the British High Commission, Embassy or Consulate will supply a visa.

Visitors can bring in free of duty all genuine personal effects. These must not be sold while in Kenya or Tanzania. Limited amounts of spirits, perfumes, cigars, cigarettes and tobacco are allowed in duty free. Gifts intended for friends or relatives in East Africa are dutiable. Rules about firearms are extremely strict. Guns and ammunition *must* be declared and require a police certificate: the certificate can be obtained in advance by your safari or tour organiser.

On leaving the country the major restriction applies to items made from game animals. All such items whether jewellery, skins, bags or anything else require an export permit which should be obtained when you buy the goods.

Smallpox and Yellow Fever vaccination certificates are required. Because of the recent spread of cholera a valid cholera vaccination certificate is also likely to be required.

DRIVING LICENCE

It is permissible to drive in East Africa on your own home country driving licence for 90 days. If you are going to drive a great deal or if your licence is in a language other than English it may be advisable

to have it endorsed at a Police Station. The Automobile Association
in Nairobi (Box 87, Kenyatta Avenue) will provide up-to-date advice
about this.

POSTAL RATES (at time of going to press)

Within East Africa

Surface up to 20g.		30 cents
Air up to 10g.		40 cents
Postcards:	Surface	15 cents
	Air	30 cents

Outside East Africa

Surface: Commonwealth and Ireland, up to 20g.	40 cents
Elsewhere, up to 20g.	70 cents
Postcards, Commonwealth	20 cents
Postcards, elsewhere	40 cents

Air:	Africa	Europe India	Japan America Australia
Letters up to 10g.	1/–	1/50	2/50
Postcards	50 cents	70 cents	1/30
Aerogrammes	70 cents	70 cents	70 cents

ART AND SCULPTURE GALLERIES

There are innumerable shops in Kenya and Tanzania which sell
paintings, carvings and sculptures. It is impossible to list them all but
the following are places where high class paintings and carvings
(including Makonde work) may be obtained:

Nairobi

Afrique Sculpture, Muindi Mbingu Street

Donovan Maule Gallery, Parliament Road, Box 2333

Dora Art Gallery, York Street
Gallery Africa, Government Road, Box 3335
Gallery Watatu, Standard Street, Box 21130
Inkentan Crafts, Kenyatta Avenue, Box 1356
Kenya Art Gallery, Kenyatta Avenue
Kenya Arts Society Studio, Arboretum Road, Box 392
Kumbu Kumbu, Hilton Hotel, Box 4782
Nairobi Art Gallery, Koinange Street
New Stanley Art Gallery, Kenyatta Avenue
Paa ya Paa Gallery, Sadler House, off Koinange Street, Box 9646
Studio Arts 68, Standard Street, Box 7904

Northern Tanzania

Christian Bookshop, Janesco House, Uhuru Road, Box 3182, Arusha
Christian Bookshop, KNCU Building, Old Moshi Road, Box 301, Arusha

CULTURAL AND SOCIAL ORGANISATIONS

Australian and New Zealand Society, Box 1287, Nairobi
Ballet Society, Box 744, Nairobi
Donovan Maule Theatre Club, Box 2333, Nairobi
East African Conservatoire of Music, Kenya Cultural Centre, Box 1343, Nairobi
East African Jazz Group, Box 2706, Nairobi
Film Society, Box 12148, Nairobi
History Society, Box 4474, Nairobi
Irish Society, Box 64, Nairobi
Kenya Arts Society, The Studio, Arboretum Road, Box 392, Nairobi
Kenya National Museum, Ainsworth Hill, Box 658, Nairobi
Kenya National Theatre, College Road, Box 3031, Nairobi
Lions Club: Nairobi, New Stanley Hotel, Box 7447
          Nairobi Central, Norfolk Hotel, Box 4867

Nairobi Cine Club, Box 8007, Nairobi

Nairobi Orchestra, Box 9532, Nairobi

Orient Art Circle, Kenya Cultural Centre, College Road, Nairobi

Photographic Society, Box 9879, Nairobi

Radio Society, Box 5681, Nairobi

Rotary Club, New Avenue Hotel, Kenyatta Avenue, Nairobi

Royal Scottish Country Dance Club, Box 254, Nairobi

Skal Club, Panafric Hotel, Box 14214, Nairobi

Theosophical Society, Box 5928, Nairobi

United Kenya Club, Box 2220, Nairobi.

MUSEUMS AND LIBRARIES

Alliance Francaise, (French Cultural Centre), Regal Mansion, Tom Mboya Street, Box 5475, Nairobi (Tel. 21623)

British Council Library, Kenya Cultural Centre, College Road, Box 751, Nairobi (Tel. 24805) and City House, Nyerere Avenue, Mombasa (Tel. 3076)

British Information Services Reading Room, Cotts House, Wabera St., Nairobi (Tel. 25805)

Coast Library, Sir Ali Street, Mombasa

Christian Science Reading Room, University Way, Box 30115, Nairobi (Tel. 21498)

Goethe Institute Library, Jeevan Bharati Building, Harambee Avenue, Box 9468, Nairobi (Tel. 24640)

Indian Information Services Reading Room, Jeevan Bharati Building, Harambee Avenue, Box 30074, Nairobi (Tel. 23259)

Kenya National Museum, Ainsworth Hill, Box 658, Nairobi (Tel. 20141) The Museum has a first class natural history library but permission to use it must be sought from the Museum Office

McMillan Memorial Library, Portal Street, Box 791, Nairobi (Tel. 21844). This contains a large collection of books about Africa in a reference section

Snake Park, Ainsworth Hill, Box 658, Nairobi

United States Information Services Library, Government Road (near Kenya Cinema), Box 30143, Nairobi (Tel. 20261)

University of Nairobi Library, College Road, Box 30197, Nairobi Tel 27441). Permission to use this is given only to *bona fide* scholars and must first be obtained from the Head Librarian

WILDLIFE, COUNTRYSIDE AND SPORTS ORGANISATION

Agricultural Society of Kenya, Jamhuri Park, Ngong Road, Box 30176, Nairobi

Aero Club of East Africa, Wilson Airport, Box 813, Nairobi

Cave Exploration Group of East Africa, Box 7583, Nairobi

East African Wildlife Society, Hilton Hotel, Box 20110, Nairobi

Football Association of Kenya, Box 234, Nairobi

Geographical Society of Kenya, Box 1887, Nairobi

Geological Club of Kenya, Box 4749, Nairobi

Golf Clubs: Golf Range (Tel. 24775) Nairobi
            Karen Golf Club, Box 24816, Nairobi (Karen 2405)
            Limuru Country Club, Box 10, Limuru (Tel. Tigoni 351)
            Mombasa Golf Club, Kilindini Harbour (Tel. 5832)
            Muthaiga Golf Club, Box 1651, Nairobi (Tel. 6524)
            Nyali Club, Box 117, Mombasa (Tel. 716381)
            Railway Golf Club, Box 476, Nairobi (Tel. 22116)
            Royal Nairobi Golf Club (Tel. 27333)
            Sigona Golf Club, Box 10, Kikuyu (Tel. Kikuyu 210)

In addition to those mentioned there are a number of other courses at the smaller centres in Kenya and Northern Tanzania.

Kenya Hockey Union, Box 6816, Nairobi

Kenya Lawn Tennis Association, Box 3184, Nairobi

Kenya Rifle Association, Box 70, Nairobi

Kenya Squash Rackets Association, Box 30076, Nairobi

Kenya Youth Hostels Association, Box 8661, Nairobi
Kilimanjaro Mountain Club, Box 66, Moshi
Mountain Club of Kenya, Wilson Airport, Box 5741, Nairobi

Riding, Racing and Hunting

Handley Cross Riding School, near Westwood Park Country Club, Karen, Box 24984, Nairobi (Tel. Karen 2365)

J. D. Sprague (Riding School), Lower Kabete Road, Box 568, Kabete (Tel. Kabete 286)

Jockey Club of Kenya, Ngong Road, Box 373, Nairobi (Tel. 66109)

Limuru Country Club Course, Limuru

Limuru Hunt (a drag hunt) Box 15056, Nairobi

Nairobi Polo Club, Box 1390, Nairobi (Tel. 28034, day; 66434, evening)

Nairobi Race Course, Ngong Road, Nairobi (meetings usually every other Sunday and Public Holidays)

Ngong Horse Safaris, Ololua Ridge, Karen (bookings Karen 2457, evenings, or through Ivory Safaris, Kenyatta Avenue, Box 5209, Tel. Nairobi 26623)

Pony Club, Box 24821, Nairobi (Tel. Karen 2583)

Show Jumping Association of Kenya, Box 1884, Nairobi

Sailing

Mombasa Marina, Cement Road, Nyali
Mombasa Yacht Club, Liwatoni Road, Mombasa
Naivasha Yacht Club, Lake Naivasha
Nairobi Sailing Club, Nairobi Dam, Box 9937, Nairobi (Tel. 25250)

Sports Clubs

Impala Club, Ngong Road, Box 1516, Nairobi
Mombasa Sports Club, Box 41, Mombasa (Tel. 4705)
Nairobi Club, Ngong Road, Box 30171, Nairobi (Tel. 23602)
Parklands Club, Sclaters Road, Box 116, Nairobi (Tel. 55099)

CAMPING IN KENYA AND NORTHERN TANZANIA

There are few restrictions on camping in Kenya and Northern Tanzania outside the National Parks and Game Reserves. It is usually necessary only to ask permission from the local owners of the land and this is normally readily granted. There are also many formal camp sites described below. Camping equipment can be hired from Ahamed Brothers, Kenyatta Avenue, Box 254, Nairobi or from Low and Bonar, St. John's Gate (behind the Donovan Maule Theatre), Box 2759, Nairobi.

Kenya

Aberdare National Park. There are several camp sites beautifully situated beside trout streams high on the moorland. Trout licences may be obtained at the entrance gates.

Amboseli National Park. There are several camp sites in the Ol Tukai region. They must be booked and paid for in advance at the Game Department, Box 241, Nairobi.

Bamburi (8 miles north of Mombasa). There is a camping site at Whitesands Hotel, Box 1073, Mombasa.

Kanamai (15 miles north of Mombasa). There is a camping site at the Youth Hostel on the beach. The Warden, Kanamai Youth Hostel, P.O. Kikambala, Mombasa.

Kibwezi (about half way between Nairobi and Mombasa). There is a site at the Bushwhackers. Safari Camp, P.O. Kibwezi. This is about fifteen miles north of Kibwezi itself and is reached by a clearly sign-posted track which leaves the main road.

Kitale. The site is at Greaves Farm, Box 676, Kitale, six miles from Kitale on the Eldoret Road.

Malindi. Silversands Site, Box 27, Malindi is beautifully situated right on the beach at Silversands Bay. Tents, shaded by makuti roofs, are available for hire but should be booked in advance. There is a cafeteria.

Mara Game Reserve. Camping is allowed in the undeveloped outer part of the Reserve but bookings **must** be made in advance at the

U

Game Department, Box 241, Nairobi. This is a favourite place for photographic safaris.

Meru National Park. Several camping sites are available, the most developed being at the Park Headquarters at Leopard Rock.

Mombasa. Timwani Camping Site, Box 1882, Mombasa, is three miles south of Likoni Ferry on the coast. Tents and equipment may be hired.

Mount Elgon. Camping is available at the Youth Hostel, 11,000 ft. up which is reached via Kimilili. Information may be obtained from the Warden, c/o Friends School, Kamasinga, P.O. Broderick Falls.

Mtwapa (12 miles north of Mombasa). There is a site operated by Kenya Mariners Ltd., Box 15070, Kikambala on the north side of Mtwapa Creek.

Nairobi. There are three camp sites within reasonable reach of the city centre. Booking is essential at all three.

1. City Park, Park Superintendent, Box 30075, Nairobi
2. Kabete Youth Hostel, P.O. Kabete, Lower Kabete Road, opposite Kenya Institute of Administration.
3. Westwood Park Country Club. Karen (12 miles from Nairobi), Box 1737, Nairobi.

Naivasha. There are a number of camp sites available by the lakeside. The best developed at the moment are the Marina Club, Box 85, Naivasha and M. D. Carnelley's, Box 112, Ruiru. At the time of writing the Safariland Club is closed, but it is to be re-opened.

Nakuru. There is a good site at the Agricultural Society of Kenya Showground, Box 478, Nakuru. Camping is not permitted during shows.

Namanga. There is a site at the Namanga River Hotel, P.O. Namanga. This is right on the Kenya-Tanzania border at the entrance to Amboseli Game Reserve.

Naro Moru. There is a site at the Naro Moru River Lodge, Box 18, Naro Moru. Trout fishing is available.

Nyeri. A site is available at the Asian Community Rest House on Temple Road.

Samburu-Isiolo Game Reserve. Several beautiful shaded sites are available in the Isiolo part of the Reserve. Bookings should be made in advance at the Game Dept., Box 241, Nairobi.

South Coast. Several sites are available primarily associated with hotels where meals may be obtained.

1. Jadini Hotel, P.O. Ukunda.
2. Trade Winds Hotel, P.O. Ukunda. No cooking allowed.
3. Twiga Lodge, P.O. Box 6005, Likoni. At Tiwi about 14 miles south of Mombasa.

Tsavo National Park. There are three camp sites.

1. Aruba Lodge, Tsavo East. This is exceptionally well appointed.
2. Mtito Andei Gate, Tsavo West.
3. Voi Gate, Tsavo East.

Northern Tanzania

Arusha. There are several sites available in the vicinity.

1. Arusha National Park. Several sites are available both on Meru Mountain and at the Momela Lakes. Bookings must be made through Tanzania National Parks, Box 3134, Arusha (Tel. Arusha 2335).
2. Arusha Town. Behind the Motor Mart Building, there is a site which is approached via Boma Road. Bookings are made at the Treasurer's Dept., Town Hall, but even when the Hall is closed there is a warden at the site.
3. Lake Duluti, c/o A. Czerny, Box 609, Arusha. This is eight miles from Arusha on the south side of the Moshi Road.

Lake Manyara National Park. There are several sites near the Park Entrance. Bookings should be made in advance through Tanzania National Parks, Box 3134, Arusha.

Marangu. Marangu Hotel, Box 40, Moshi.

Moshi. There is a site rather over a mile out of town at Jamhuri Playing Field.

Momela. A site is available at Momela Lodge, Box 536, Arusha just outside the Momela Gate of the Arusha National Park. Booking is essential.

Ngorongoro Crater. Simba Camp is on the Crater Rim a couple of miles from the Conservation Unit Headquarters, where bookings should be made. It is also possible to camp in the crater by special prior arrangement with the Unit Headquarters.

Serengeti National Park. There are nine camping sites at Seronera, one at Klein's Camp in the north and one at Ndakaba in the west. Bookings must be in advance through the Tanzania National Park, Box 3134, Arusha.

SELF SERVICE ACCOMMODATION

It is increasingly being recognised that the cost of staying at many of East Africa's Hotels is far beyond the reach of the local family man. In order to cater for this type of need more and more self-service units are being built both inside and outside the Game Parks and Reserves. These often take the form of 'bandas', huts with a couple of rooms equipped with basic furniture. They vary considerably in sophistication. In some nothing is provided and the visitor is expected to bring everything: this type usually costs about 5s /person/day. In others bedding, cooking equipment and crockery are available and there are bathrooms; this type usually costs 20–30s/person/day. Banda-type accommodation is very popular and advance booking is virtually essential.

Amboseli Game Reserve. Fully equipped bandas are available at Ol Tukai Lodge. Bookings must be made via the Game Department, Box 241, Nairobi.

Bamburi. There are several groups of self-service bandas at this favourite resort 8 miles north of Mombasa.
1. Coraldene Beach Cottages, Box 940, Mombasa.
2. Holiday Inn, Box 2792, Mombasa.
3. Ocean View Hotel, Box 1127, Mombasa.
4. Sandpiper Cottages, Box 2686, Mombasa.

Bushwhackers Safari Camp, P.O. Kibwezi. This is fifteen miles north of Kibwezi which is on the main Nairobi-Mombosa Road about half way along.

Kanamai, Kikambala, 15 miles north of Mombasa. Beachcomber's Cottages, Box 5060, Mombasa.

Loyengalani, Lake Rudolf. The old fishing camp was closed down during the shifta troubles but the bandas have been reopened by a group of local priests on a self-service, first come first occupied basis. Fishing boats are available for hire.

Maralal Safari Lodge. Bookings may be made through Northern Frontier Safaris Ltd., Box 5337, Nairobi.

Marsabit National Reserve. There is a small lodge which at present, is operating on a first come, first served basis. This may be changed and information should be sought from the Game Dept., Box 241, Nairobi before proceeding.

Meru National Park. Six double bandas are available at Leopard Rock. Bookings must be made in advance through the Game. Department, Box 241, Nairobi.

Naivasha, Marina Club, Box 85, Naivasha.

Naro Moru. Naro Moru River Lodge, Box 18, Naro Moru. Reservations may be made through Kearline Tours, Box 6660, Nairobi.

Olergosaillie National Park. Bookings are made through the Centre for Pre-History and Palaentology, Box 30239, Nairobi.

Samburu-Isiolo Game Reserve. Four well equipped bandas are available about four miles west of Buffalo Springs in the Isiolo part of the Reserve. Bookings must be made in advance through the Game Department, Box 241, Nairobi.

Tsavo National Park. Two self-service lodges are operating.

1. Aruba Lodge, 22 miles from Voi in Tsavo East. Bookings are made through Bunson Travel Services, New Stanley House, Box 5456, Nairobi.

2. Kitani Lodge, near Mzima Springs in Tsavo West. Again bookings are made through Bunson Travel Services.

Fishing Camps

There are a number of these in the highland areas of Kenya. They are primarily intended for trout fishermen and accommodation is extremely basic. It is advisable to consult the operating authority in advance for information about the state of the accommodation and for detailed instruction on how to get there.

Operated by Kenya Fisheries Dept., Box 241, Nairobi.
1. Thiba Camp near Embu.
2. Thego Camp near Kiganjo in Nyeri District.
3. Kimakia Camp in the Aberdares west of Thika.
4. Koiwa Camp near Kericho.

Operated by the Kapolet Fishing Association, Box 332, Kitale. This camp is near Kitale.

Operated by the Suam and Kaptega Angling Club, Box 168, Kitale. There are two huts on the Suam River about 30 miles from Kitale.

Forest Department Rest Houses

These are operated by the Forest Department, Box 30513, Nairobi. They are primarily for use by Forestry Officers on tour but can be occupied by the public when not required by the Department. The accommodation is extremely simple. Up-to-date information about the rest houses and how to reach them should be obtained from the Forest Department. There are rest houses in the Kamba Hills (1), on Mount Kenya (5), in the Aberdares (3), in the coastal forest east of Garsen (1), near Thomson's Falls (1), Kabarnet (1), Kitale (1), Kericho (1) and Elburgon in the Mau Hills (3). There is one in the Kakamega Forest 15 miles from Kakamega town which is an excellent base for bird watchers.

Northern Tanzania

Lake Duluti (8 miles from Arusha), A. Czerny, Box 609, Arusha Ngorongoro. There are two types of self-service accommodation.
1. Ngorongoro Forest Lodge (Dhillon's Lodge) Bookings Box 792, Arusha.
2. Youth Hostel Annexe. This is operated on a first come, first served basis.

Serengeti National Park.
1. Ndabaka Gate Rondavels. These are primarily for visitors who arrive too late to reach Seronera on the same day. They cannot be booked or occupied for more than one night.

2. Seronera Lodge. A few self-service rooms are available. These are strictly only for local East African residents. They must be booked in advance through East African Wildlife Lodges, Box 3123, Arusha. Bookings from travel agencies or tour operators will not be accepted.

HOTELS

This list is not meant to be comprehensive but does give most of the more important hotels in the main towns. In order to give some indication of prices, hotels have been placed in four categories based on the cost per person when two people occupy a double room. The four categories at 1971 prices are:

  A. Under £3 for full board (bed + all meals)
  B. £3–£5 for full board
  C. £5–£8 for full board
  D. Over £8 for full board

N.B. Rates and conditions can change so you are advised to check directly with your hotels. This list provides an approximate guide only.

Kenya
Aberdare National Park.
  1. Aberdare Country Club and the Ark. *D*
  2. Treetops. *D*
Amboseli Game Reserve.
  1. Amboseli New Lodge. *C*
  2. Amboseli Safari Camp. *C*
     Bookings for both the camp and the Lodge should be made through Kilimanjaro Safari Club, Box 20211, Nairobi.

Eldoret. New Lincoln Hotel, Box 47. *B*

Embu. Izaak Walton Inn, Box 1. *B*

Karatina. Three-in-One Hotel, Box 73. *A*

Kericho. Tea Hotel, Box 75. *B*

Kibwezi. Hunter's Lodge, Box 30471, Nairobi. *B*

Kilifi. Mnarani Club, Box 14. *B*

Kisii Hotel, Box 26. *A*

Kisumu.
 1. Hotel Embassy, Box 440.
 2. Kisumu Hotel, Box 9.

Kitale. Kitale Hotel, Box 41. *D*

Lamu. Peponi Hotel, Box 24. *C*

Limuru. Farm Hotel, P.O. Private Bag, Limuru. *B*

Malindi.
 1. Blue Marlin Hotel, Box 54. *A–B*
 2. Driftwood Beach Club, Box 63. *A*
 3. Eden Rock Hotel, Box 350. *A–B*
 4. Hotel Sindbad, Box 30. *B*
 5. Lawford's Hotel, Box 20. *A–B*

Mara Game Reserve. Keekorok Lodge, *C*. Bookings through Wildlife
 Lodges, Box 7557, Nairobi.

Meru. Pig and Whistle Hotel, Box 99. *B*

Molo. Highlands Hotel, Box 142. *B*

Mombasa Town.
 1. Castle Hotel, Box 9231. *A–B*
 2. Hotel Splendid, Box 7486. *A*
 3. Lotus Hotel, Box 2772. *A*
 4. Manor Hotel, Box 9851. *A–B*
 5. New Carlton Hotel, Box 9804. *B*
 6. Oceanic Hotel, Box 929. *B–C*
 7. Palm Court Hotel, Box 506. *A*

Mombasa north to Kilifi.
 1. Casuarina Hotel, Shanzu, Box 2792, Mombasa. *B*
 2. Dolphin Hotel, Shanzu, Box 1443, Mombasa. *C*
 3. Mombasa Beach Hotel, Nyali. *C*
 4. Nyali Beach Hotel, Box 581, Mombasa. *B–C*
 5. Shanzu Frigate Club, Box 2879, Mombasa. *B–C*
 6. Sun n' Sand Beach Hotel, P.O. Kikambala. *A–B*
 7. Whispering Palms Hotel, P.O. Kikambala. *B*
 8. Whitesands Hotel, Bamburi, Box 1073, Mombasa. *B*

Mombasa south to Shimoni
 1. Jadini Hotel, P.O. Ukunda. *A-B*
 2. Pemba Channel Fishing Club, P.O. Ukunda. *A-B*

3. Shelly Beach Hotel, Box 6030, Mombasa. *A-B*
4. Trade Winds, P.O. Ukunda. *B*
5. Two Fishes Hotel, P.O. Ukunda. *B*

Mtito Andei. Tsavo Inn, P.O. Mtito Andei. *B*

Nairobi.
1. Ainsworth Hotel, Ainsworth Road, Box 469. *A-B*
2. Brunners Hotel, Muindi Mbingu Street, Box 949. *B*
3. Chiromo Hotel, Salisbury Road, Box 4677. *B*
4. College Inn, University Way, Box 7470. *B*
5. Columbia Hotel, Sclaters Road, Box 10756. *A*
6. Continental Hotel, Davidson Road, Box 14301. *A*
7. Devon Hotel, Salisbury Road, Box 1123. *A-B*
8. Equator Inn, Crawford Road, Box 9279. *A-B*
9. Fairview Hotel, Bishop's Road, Box 842. *A-B*
10. Gaylord Hotel, off Ngong Road, Box 30208. *B*
11. Green View Lodge, Kirk Road, Box 2246. *A*
12. Grosvenor Hotel, Girouard Road, Box 1038. *B*
13. Hotel Ambassadeur, Government Road, Box 30399. *B-C*
14. Hotel Camay, Box 4516. *A*
15. Hotel Embassy, Bazaar Street, Box 7247. *A-B*
16. Hotel Intercontinental, Sgt. Ellis Avenue, Box 30353. *C-D*
17. Hotel Normandie, Girouard Road, Box 9985. *A*
18. Hotel Pigalle, Gulzaar Street, Box 14294. *A-B*
19. Hurlingham Hotel, Hurlingham Road, Box 3158. *A*
20. Impala Hotel, Sclaters Road, Box 14347. *A-B*
21. Mayfair Hotel, Sclaters Road, Box 2680. *A-B*
22. Motel Agip, Westlands, Box 14287. *B*
23. Nairobi Hilton, Kimathi Street, Box 30624. *C-D*
24. New Avenue Hotel, Kenyatta Avenue, Box 2362. *B*
25. New Stanley Hotel, Kenyatta Avenue, 75. *C-D*
26. Norfolk Hotel, College Road, Box 64. *B-C*
27. Panafric Hotel, Kenyatta Avenue, Box 30486. *C-D*
28. Plums Hotel, off Kikuyu Road, Box 747. *A*
29. Safariland Hotel, Salisbury Lane, Box 8119. *A*
30. Safari Park Hotel, Thika Road, Box 288. *B*
31. Sclaters House Hotel, Sclaters Road, Box 14284. *A*
32. Treeshade Family Hotel, Salisbury Lane, Box 1793. *A*

33. United Kenya Club, State House Road, Box 2220. *A*
34. Westwood Park County Club, Karen, Box 1737, Nairobi. *B*
35. Windsor Hotel, Gloucester Road, Box 20350. *A*
36. Zambezi Motel, Box 110, Kikuyu. *B*

Naivasha.
  1. Bell Inn, Box 85. *B*
  2. Lake Naivasha Hotel, Box 15. *B*

Nakuru.
  1. Midland Hotel, Box 257. *B*
  2. Stag's Head Hotel, Box 143. *B*

Namanga. Namanga Hotel, P.O. Namanga. *B*

Nanyuki.
  1. Mount Kenya Safari Club, Box 35. *D*
  2. Silverbeck Hotel, Box 20. *B*
  3. Sportsman's Arms Hotel, Box 3. *B*

Nyeri.
  1. Outspan Hotel, Box 24. *B-C*
  2. White Rhino Hotel, Box 30. *A-B*

Samburu-Isiolo Game Reserve. Samburu Lodge. *C*. Bookings through
  Wildlife Lodges, Box 7557, Nairobi.

Soy. Soy Residential Club, Box 2. *B*

Thika. Blue Posts Hotel, Box 42. *A-B*

Thomson's Falls. Thomson's Falls Lodge.

Tsavo.
  1. Kilaguni Lodge, *C*. Bookings through African Tours & Hotels,
     Box 7470, Nairobi.
  2. Ngulia Lodge, *C*. Bookings through Hallway Hotels, Box 30626,
     Nairobi.
  3. Voi Safari Lodge, *C*. Bookings through Hallway Hotels, Box
     30626, Nairobi.

Voi. Park Inn, Box 28. *B*

Watamu.
  1. Ocean Sports, Box 340, Malindi. *B*
  2. Seafarers, Box 274, Malindi. *A-B*

Northern Tanzania

Arusha.
1. Baran's Inn, Box 658. *A*
2. New Arusha Hotel, Box 88. *B*
3. Safari Hotel, Box 303. *A-B*
4. Total Inn, Box 227. *A*
5. Travelodge, Box 400. *A*

Lake Manyara Hotel. *C.* Bookings through Box 3100, Arusha.

Marangu.
1. Kibo Hotel, P.O. Private Bag Moshi. *B*
2. Marangu Hotel, Box 40, Moshi. *B*

Momela. Momela Game Lodge. *B.* Bookings through Box 3173, Arusha.

Moshi.
1. Coffee Tree Hostelry, Box 484.
2. Livingstone Hotel, Box 501.

Ngorongoro Conservation Unit.
1. Kimba Lodge, Box 284, Arusha *B.*
2. Ndutu Tented Camp. *B.* Box 284, Arusha.
3. Ngorongoro Crater Lodge. *C.* Box 751, Arusha.
4. Ngorongoro Forest Lodge, *B.* Box 792, Arusha.
5. Ngorongoro Wildlife Lodge. *C.* Box 348, Dar es Salaam.

Serengeti National Park.
1. Lobo Wildlife Lodge. *C.* Bookings through Box 348, Dar es Salaam.
2. Seronera Lodge. *B.* Bookings through Wildlife Lodges, Box 3173, Arusha.
3. Seronera Wildlife Lodge. *C.* Bookings through Box 348, Dar es Salaam.

Tarangire National Park. Tarangire Safari Camp. *C.* Bookings through Box 1182, Arusha.

Usa River.
1. Hotel Tanzanite, *B.* Box 3063, Arusha.
2. Mount Meru Game Sanctuary. *B.* Box 659, Arusha.

GUIDE TO FURTHER READING

The number of books on Africa in general and East Africa in particular is large and very rapidly growing. The following is very much a personal list of those I have found interesting, entertaining or informative. Anyone who wishes to browse through a first class African Library with many very early classical volumes, is advised to pay a visit to the reference section of the McMillan library, Portal Street, Nairobi.

General

Automobile Association Official Touring Guide to East Africa, Automobile Association, Nairobi: 1970.

Freedom and Socialism, Julius Nyerere, Oxford University Press: 1968.

Harambee Country, K. Bolton, Geoffrey Bles: 1970.

Kenya, Editorial Services, Nairobi: 1969 (a brief paperback guide).

Kilimanjaro Country, University Press of Africa: 1969 (a brief paperback guide).

Suffering without Bitterness, Jomo Kenyatta, East African Publishing House.

Tanzania Today, University Press of Africa: 1968.

Travellers' Guide to East Africa, Thornton Cox: 1970 (a paperback guide).

Prehistory of East Africa

Adam's Ancestors, L. S. B. Leakey, Methuen: 4th edition 1953.

Background to Evolution in Africa, ed. W. S. Bishop and J. D. Clark, University of Chicago Press: 1967 (a massive reference volume).

History of East Africa. The Early Period, ed. R. Oliver and G. Mathew, Oxford University Press: 1967.

Man-Apes or Ape-Men? Sir Wilfred le Gros Clark, Holt, Rinehart & Winston: 1967.

The Progress of Man in Africa, L. S. B. Leakey, Oxford University Press: 1961.

People and Landscape

A Land Full of People – Life in Kenya Today, J. S. Roberts, Eyre & Spottiswoode: 1967.

An Economic Geography of East Africa, A. N. O'Connor, G. Bell: 1966.

Dhows at Mombasa, J. H. A. Jewell, East African Publishing House: 1970.

East Africa, C. P. Kirby, Ernest Benn: 1968.

Forks and Hope, Elspeth Huxby, Chatto and Windus: 1964.

History of the Chagga People of Kilimanjaro, K. N. Stahl, Mouten: 1964.

Journey to the Jade Sea, J. Hillaby, 1964.

Nairobi: City and Region, ed. W. T. W. Morgan, Oxford University Press: 1967.

Sailing from Lamu, A. H. J. Prins, Van Gorcum: 1965.

The Africans, Basil Davidson, Longmans: 1969.

The Baluyia, J. Osogo, Oxford University Press: 1965.

The Desert's Dusty Face, C. Chenevix-Trench, Blackwood: 1964.

The Masai, S. Bleeker, Dennis Dobson: 1964.

The Masai Story, O. Koenig, Joseph: 1956.

The Peoples of Africa, C. M. Turnbull, Brockhampton Press: 1963.

The Peoples of Kenya, Joy Adamson, Collins: 1967.

The Samburu, P. Spencer, Routledge and Kegan Paul: 1965.

The Seaports of East Africa, B. S. Hoyle, East African Publishing House.

The Swahili Peoples of the Kenya Coast, 1895–1965, A. I. Salim, East African Publishing House: 1970.

History and Politics

A History of East Africa, K. Ingham, Longmans: 1962.

A History of Tanzania, ed. I. N. Kimambo and A. J. Temu, East African Publishing House.

A History of the Abaluhyia of Western Kenya, 1500–1930, G. S. Were, East African Publishing House.

Emerging Themes of African History, ed. T. O. Ranger, East African Publishing House.

Government and Politics in Kenya, ed. M. Goldschmidt, D. Rothchild and C. Gertzel, East African Publishing House.

Government and Politics in Tanzania, ed. W. Tordoff, East African Publishing House.

History of East Africa, 3 volumes, Oxford University Press.

History of the Southern Luo I, B. A. Ogot, East African Publishing House.

Imperial Frontier, James Barber, East African Publishing House.

In the Wake of Da Gama, G. Hamilton, Skeffington: 1951.

Kenyatta: A Pictorial Biography, A. Howarth, East African Publishing House.

Men and Monuments of the East African Coast, J. S. Kirkman, Butterworth: 1964.

Nation Building in Tanzania, ed. A. Rweyamamu, East African Publishing House.

Recording East Africa's Past, A. Roberts, East Africa Publishing House.

Tanganyika under German Rule, 1905–12, J. Heppe. East African Publishing House.

Tanzania before 1900, ed. A. Roberts, East African Publishing House.

The East African Coast, J. E. E. Sutton, East African Publishing House.

The East African Coast, Select Documents, ed. G. S. P. Freeman-Grenville, Oxford University Press: 1962.

The East African Slave Trade, E. A. Alpers, East African Publishing House.

The Flame Trees of Thika, Elspeth Huxley, Penguin.

The Great Siege of Fort Jesus, V. Cuthberts, East African Publishing House: 1970.

The Myth of Mau Mau, C. Rosberg and J. Nottingham, East African Publishing House.

They Built for the Future. A Chronicle of Makerere University College, M. Macpherson: 1964.

Tom Mboya: A Photographic Tribute, N. Amin, East African Publishing House.

Zamani: A survey of East African History, ed. B. A. Ogot and J. A. Kieran, East African Publishing House.

Wildlife and Sport

African Handbook of Birds. Birds of Eastern and North Eastern Africa. C. W. Mackworth, Praed and C. H. B. Grant, Longmans: 1952 and 1960.

A Field Guide to the Birds of East and Central Africa, J. E. Williams, Collins: 1963.

A Field Guide to the National Parks of East Africa, J. E. Williams, Collins: 1967.

A Guide to the Snakes of Uganda, C. R. S. Pitman, The Uganda Society: 1938.

Animals of East Africa, C. A. Spinage, Collins: 1962.

Animals of East Africa, C. T. Astley Maberley, Hodder and Stoughton: 1966.

Between the Sunlight and the Thunder: The Wild Life of Kenya, N. Simon, Collins: 1962.

Crash Strike: Game Fishing in East Africa, P. Hemphill and A. Cullen, East African Publishing House: 1970.

East African Mountains and Lakes, L. Brown, East African Publishing House: 1970.

Grasslands of East Africa, D. Vesey-Fitzgerald, East African Publishing House: 1970.

Kenya Trees and Shrubs, I. R. Dale and P. J. Greenway, Buchanan and Hatchard: 1961.

Mountains of Kenya, P. Robson, East African Publishing House: 1969.

Serengeti Shall Not Die, B. and N. Grzimek, Hamish Hamilton: 1960.

The Shell History of the East African Safari Rally, C. Disney, East African Publishing House.

The Zoology of Tropical Africa, J. L. Cloudsley-Thompson, Weidenfeld and Nicholson: 1969.

Wildlife and Safari in Kenya, ed. J. Pearson, East African Publishing House.

Window onto Wilderness, ed. A. Cullen, East African Publishing House.

Index

A

W

Printed by Eyre & Spottiswoode Limited, Portsmouth, England, and published by the East
African Publishing House, Uniafric House, Koinange Street, P.O. Box 30571, Nairobi.